CLEMATIS

Christopher Lloyd

CLEMATIS

Illustrated by

MARJORIE BLAMEY

COLLINS
St James's Place, London

William Collins Sons & Co Ltd
London · Glasgow · Sydney · Auckland
Toronto · Johannesburg

First published 1977
© Christopher Lloyd, 1977
ISBN 0 00 219588 7
Made and Printed in Great Britain by
William Collins Sons & Co Ltd Glasgow

Contents

*

Preface 9

1. The Appeal of Clematis 13
2. Background to Clematis 15
3. Making the Most of Clematis 24
4. The Choice. General Considerations 34
5. The Choice. Large-flowered Hybrids 38
   'Blue' Clematis 39
   Lavender and Mauve Clematis 44
   White and Off-white Clematis 47
   'Red' Clematis 52
   Purple Clematis 55
   Pink and Mauve-Pink Clematis 59
   Nelly Moser-type Clematis 62
6. The Choice. Species and Small-flowered Hybrids 66
   For Conservatory and Sheltered Walls 66
   The Atragenes 73
   The Montana Group 75
   The Texans 80
   The Viticellas 86
   Late-flowering Species 90
   Herbaceous Clematis and Non-climbing Shrubs 98
7. How to Grow Them 105
8. Pruning and Training 118
9. Propagation 135
10. Clematis Troubles 153
11. Descriptions of Clematis in Cultivation 168
12. Names: Their Spelling and Pronunciation 197

Glossary of Botanical Terms Used 203

Index 205

Colour Plates

*

1. Lasurstern; Lady Northcliffe; *facing page* 48
   H. F. Young; Mrs P. B. Truax; Lord Nevill;
   Mrs Cholmondeley; Elsa Späth

2. Beauty of Richmond; Lawsoniana; Prins Hen-   49
   drik; William Kennett; Mrs Hope; Will Goodwin

3. Marie Boisselot; Mrs Oud; Mrs George Jack-   64
   man; Jackmanii Rubra; Miss Bateman; Fair
   Rosamond; Henryi; Yellow Queen

4. Mme Edouard André; Ville de Lyon; Crimson   65
   King; Ernest Markham; Duchess of Suther-
   land; Mme Grangé; Mme Julia Correvon;
   Jackmanii Rubra

5. C. × *jackmanii* 'Superba'; Victoria; Perle   80
   d'Azur; Huldine; Comtesse de Bouchaud;
   Hagley Hybrid; Gipsy Queen; Ascotiensis;
   Star of India; John Warren

6. Percy Picton; Sir Garnet Wolseley; Horn of   81
   Plenty; The President; Guiding Star; Etoile de
   Paris

7. W. E. Gladstone; Mme Baron Veillard; Lady   96
   Betty Balfour; King George V; Lady Caroline
   Nevill

8. Miss Crawshay; Duchess of Edinburgh; Coun-   97
   tess of Lovelace; Daniel Deronda; Vyvyan
   Pennell; Miriam Markham; Proteus; C. *florida*
   'Sieboldii'

9. Mrs Spencer Castle; Countess of Lovelace;   112
Beauty of Worcester; Daniel Deronda; Vyvyan
Pennell; Jackmanii Rubra; Proteus

10. Barbara Dibley; Bees Jubilee; Barbara Jack-   113
man; Lincoln Star; Nelly Moser; Marcel Moser;
Mrs N. Thompson; C. W. Dowman

11. *C. napaulensis*; *C. cirrhosa* var. *balearica*; *C.*   128
afoliata; *C. armandii*; *C. paniculata*; *C.
macropetala*; *C. macropetala* 'Markham's Pink';
C. alpina 'Columbine'; *C. alpina* 'Pamela Jackman'; *C. alpina* 'Frances Rivis'; *C. alpina*
'Ruby'; *C. alpina sibirica* 'White Moth'

12. *C. montana*; *C. montana* var. *wilsonii*; *C. mon-*   129
tana var. *rubens*; *C. montana* 'Picton's Variety';
C. montana 'Elizabeth'; *C. montana* 'Tetrarose';
C. chrysocoma var. *sericea*; *C. chrysocoma*; *C.* ×
vedrariensis

13. *C. crispa*; *C. texensis*; Gravetye Beauty; Etoile   144
Rose; Sir Trevor Lawrence; Duchess of
Albany; *C. viorna*; *C. fusca*

14. *C. viticella*; *C. viticella* 'Rubra'; Purpurea Plena   145
Elegans; Minuet; Little Nell; Alba Luxurians;
Abundance; Etoile Violette; Royal Velours;
Venosa Violacea; *C. campaniflora*

15. *C. rehderiana*; *C. tangutica*; *C. tangutica* (Jack   160
Drake's form); *C. orientalis* (L & S form 13342);
C. songarica; *C. flammula*; *C. vitalba*; *C. fargesii*
var. *souliei*; *C.* × *triternata* 'Rubro-marginata';
C. serratifolia; *C. phlebantha*; *C. grata*

16. *C. integrifolia*; *C. integrifolia* 'Hendersonii';   161
C. × *eriostemon*; *C. douglasii* var. *scottii* 'Rosea';
C. integrifolia 'Olgae'; *C.* × *durandii*; *C.
jouiniana* 'Praecox'; *C. heracleifolia* var.
davidiana 'Wyevale'; *C.* × *aromatica*; *C. douglasii* var. *scottii*; *C. heracleifolia* 'Campanile'; *C.
recta*; Edward Prichard

Preface

*

HAVING finished his book the author writes his preface. There seem to be an unusually large number of people to mention in this one, making it difficult to know whom to start with, so I'll start with myself. I wrote a book 'Clematis' for Country Life which they published in 1965. When they were taken over by the great IPC Empire, soon to become part of the still larger Reed's Group, all such monographs serving small minority interests were chopped and 'Clematis' went out of print. Collins, who had handled *The Well-Tempered Garden* and *Foliage Plants*, were enthusiastic (I hope they'll let me say it, but they are astonishingly nice people to work for) about re-issuing 'Clematis' in whatever form I chose and at first I favoured dishing up the old text with a few cuts here and a few minor additions or alterations there.

'Thrift, thrift, Horatio! the funeral bak'd meats
Did coldly furnish forth the marriage tables.'

The more I thought about it the less it seemed to me that this would do. No one who is interested in his subject can remain in the same spot. Ideas, opinions and values are changing all the time. Here he discovers that he was wrong, there that a whole vein of new material is waiting to be quarried. On the technical side, advances are being made altering our entire approach to (most notably, in this case) propagation and to the control of diseases. In the end, although I used the same framework of chapter subjects, I re-wrote the entire book except for Chapter 3. I intended to re-write that and started to do so. It went stickily. The black feeling of having said it all before brooded heavily on me. I turned up the old chapter and made the disconcerting discovery that it was vastly superior to my present efforts. Chapter 6 was the one I most enjoyed. It is the longest and gave me the most trouble in its assembling but

9

the ferret leads an exciting life even though there cannot be a rabbit at the end of every passage. And the next two chapters, on planting and pruning, seemed to go well, written at high speed and with daunting illegibility.

Having devoted so much thought to this one genus I now feel that it has grabbed a disproportionate share of my gardening attention. There are so many other good plants; why specialise on one? Yet the book needed to be written, as it will, in the future, need to be frequently revised. What other clematis literature has the fanatic to turn to? In 1975 Jim Fisk brought out *his* second volume on the subject, calling it 'The Queen of Climbers.' Published privately it is available from his nursery at Westleton in Suffolk. It contains many splendid colour photographs and much good sense. Also a lot about Jim Fisk and his business. It is always delightful to write about oneself. I never tire of it. But his book is short; it does not attempt or pretend to cover the subject in detail. Stanley Whitehead's 'Garden Clematis' came out in 1959 and was reprinted; it may still be in print. It always gave me the impression that the publisher had said 'We need a book on clematis in our Gardening series, Dr Whitehead; would that be up your street?' And he had replied 'Clematis? Ah yes! Clematis. Well, I think I might be able to tackle that', and went on from there. Many of those who know most about clematis are not inclined to write about them, although Mr Rowland Jackman and Mr Walter Pennell have given useful lectures to the RHS on the subject and these have subsequently been published in the Journal. Naturally I have digested them and regurgitated parts as Lloyd's Original Pigeon-Milk. (I was immensely flattered, incidentally, to find that Mr Fisk had lifted and made his own one felicitous phrase in my 'Clematis' Mark I, on earwigs 'dangling in hordes as they revel in their midnight feasts'.) Rowland Jackman's father, A. G. Jackman, also made some historic contributions to the Journal.

I remember how thrilled I was when Ernest Markham (William Robinson's head gardener at Gravetye) brought out his little book 'Clematis' (also published by Country Life) in 1935. That reached a second edition in 1939, after his death. But it was only a little book. The subject of propagation from cuttings, for instance, was discussed in just over one page. His descriptions of cultivars were spartan: 'Lasurstern – Deep blue; very large flower.' 'Beauty of Worcester – violet-blue.' Difficult to be kindled by that.

Before Markham we had, for sustained reading, to go right back to the first book ever written on our chosen flower, 'The Clematis' by Thomas Moore and George Jackman, first edition 1872, 2nd edition 1877. A. G. Jackman made extensive notes in his copy of the latter for a revised edition some time early this century. It never came to fruition but Rowland Jackman (who, alas, is no longer with us; he died soon after completion of my script) has been most generous in lending me this copy for as long as I needed it, and as I have taken three winters over this book that must be for more than two years. It has made an invaluable link of the past with the present and I have made constant reference to Moore & Jackman in the text. Also to Bean, which means 'Trees and Shrubs Hardy in the British Isles' by W. J. Bean, who was Director of the Royal Botanic Gardens, Kew. I have used both his original 1914 edition (which my parents owned) and the 8th and latest revision of 1970 under Sir George Taylor's general editorship, Mr Desmond Clarke having shouldered the lion's share of the burden. They have kept me more or less on the straight-and-narrow insofar as they were able. In return I will point out to them that the flowers of *Clematis montana* are not solitary but in axillary clusters; and that *C.* × *durandii* and *C.* × *jouiniana* are not climbers within the generally accepted meaning of the word.

My burrowings kept me for a good many hours in the RHS Lindley library in Vincent Square but it was the late Mr Hugh Thompson who put me on to so many meaty references there, and he was a very great help in many ways as the reader will be made aware hereafter. He used to write in his small neat hand with blue ink on deep blue paper (as John Treasure does; there might be an association worth pursuing here, with a love of deep blue clematis) or else he'd cram into a postcard as much as any normal letter writer would spread over two pages. Alas, that leukemia should last year have taken him untimely, before my book was out. I've quoted from him freely because the way he expressed himself was always so good-humouredly humorous.

Preface

Everyone that I have turned to for help has been extraordinarily generous and co-operative. A visit to the House of Pennell in Lincoln not only informed me of the latest crosses coming to fruition but that Walter Pennell is a high-powered amateur astronomer with an impressive telescope occupying that key position in his garden where lesser·mortals would site the bird bath. Finally I begged to be shown more and yet more of his astral photography in preference to the nurseryman's equivalent of 'here's another of mum and the kids; she's paddling in that one' – I mean the coloured transparencies of his own clematis crosses.

I wasn't able to visit Mr Fisk but he did his best to answer my queries and he gave me a plant of his form of *C. balearica* that flowers both summer and winter.

Most of all I owe to the House of Treasure. John Treasure has been a close friend since 1952 and we learned about clematis together or separately but by interchange of ideas and information, step by step right from the outset. It was he who undertook the boring, fiddling and repetitive task of sending flower specimens for Marjorie Blamey to paint, of more than half – two thirds, perhaps – of the varieties illustrated. And never a murmur.

For Raymond Evison, who has the main responsibility of running the nursery at Treasures, clematis are almost a monomania (although I believe he is also interested in his wife and children). He probably knows more about clematis than any of us and he was as anxious that this should be a worthy book as I was. To this end he has helped me unstintingly, especially on his methods of propagation and also on the endlessly teasing questions of variety identification and naming, what different nurseries are calling the same plant, what different species and cultivars have reached his nursery and all such details. He is a highly professional and efficient person, so I am indeed lucky, here. I know he'll disagree with a number of, perhaps many, things I've written, which is my only regret. I wish he could have written the book himself. But writing is one thing I am practised in and love working on so perhaps, by mutual consultation, we have not between us done too badly.

CHAPTER I

The Appeal of Clematis

*

EVERY gardener loves clematis. I have yet to meet the man or woman that was not attracted by them. There may often be certain categories of which they disapprove – the stripy cart-wheels of Nelly Moser, for instance – but these will be out-weighed by the rest. In few florist's flowers can such popularity be taken for granted. Think of all the people who loathe chrysanthemums, dahlias, gladioli, rhododendrons, cacti and calceolarias. Mistakenly, of course, but there it is. Yet clematis are universally admired.

I must discuss why this should be at the start, because unless I can convince myself as well as you that this flower's popular-ity is based on sterling merits, there can be little excuse for writing a book on it.

Size of bloom will be the first aspect to touch us. Sheer size to make us gape. And colour; sumptuous velvety lavender, crimson and purple. And then texture. If we want to touch a flower as well as feast our eyes on it, that is a sure sign that it has us in its emotional grip. We want to enjoy it through our finger-tips. That such size should be linked with such delicacy, such fragility, is altogether irresistible.

I should like, at this point, to be able to invite the reader to bury his nose in a bloom and inhale, thus bringing yet another of our senses into satisfied play. But this sense must be kept waiting: no large-flowered clematis can assume the role of a full and deep red rose (many of which, be it noted in an aside, are sadly lacking in the scent that should be their essence). But if we look again we can revel in its shapeliness, in the generous overlap at their base of sepals that undulate and gradually taper until they expire in fine points; in the central boss of stamens wherein pale filaments are often contrasted with rich red-purple anthers. And now, since we approached our bloom with over-hasty enthusiasm (trampling on a half dozen of lowly and disregarded victims in our eager progress) we should stand back a little (trampling on another half dozen of lowly disregarded plants in our single-minded absorption) in order to admire the habit of our clematis, the way in which it has threaded its passage over a supporting shrub (assuming for the moment that it has been given the benefit of this most flattering as well as natural type of support) and has distributed its blooms in swags, ropes and garlands, as though intentionally decorating and celebrating a festive occasion.

So far we have been considering a large-flowered clematis, for it is the very size of their blooms that will make its first impact on a child (it certainly did me from the age of 10 or earlier) or the similarly unsophisticated adult on whom flowers and gardening have broken like a revelation, as often happens, for instance, when a newly married couple find themselves in possession of their own garden for the first time.

But it is not long before we come under the sway of the small-flowered clematis that make their mark by the quantities of blossom they carry instead of by their individual size. And this is where our sense of smell is brought gratifyingly into action. Vanilla, hot chocolate, almonds, lemons, primroses, cowslips, violets: all these and other essences are wafted towards us on a light and teasing current of air so that we stop in delighted perplexity and seek out the cause with exploratory eyes, looking up and down and round about us. Then light upon a clematis such as montana or flammula, and follow the first spied cluster of flowers quickly expanding into a great pool, a foaming sea of blossom, spraying in every direction and finally flinging itself into space. Small wonder we are exhilarated.

Such, then, is the burden of my song. We shall examine and revel in many more fascinating details as we pursue our subject and we shall also become painfully aware of the flies in the ointment. But I hope at the end there will be no doubt remaining that clematis are a fascinating and varied group of flowers, and that in taking it to their heart, a large public have shown their natural good taste in grateful acknowledgement.

CHAPTER 2

Background to Clematis

*

I SHALL not give a technical definition of clematis; that can easily be looked up in any flora or gardening dictionary. But there are a number of botanical features with regard to the genus that are of interest.

It belongs to the family *Ranunculaceae* (of the buttercups, *Ranunculus*) and this includes a rich selection of good garden plants, some of which cannot help but remind us, in their flowers or foliage, of clematis. A panicle of *Thalictrum dipterocarpum*, for instance, could almost be a small-flowered clematis; while single and double anemones are strongly suggestive of the larger-flowered types. A further similarity between this and some other members of the family such as *Caltha* (king-cup), *Thalictrum, Anemone, Delphinium* and *Aconitum* is that the calyx (made up of sepals) comprises the showy, colourful part of the flower while the corolla (made up of petals) is either inconspicuous or absent. In *Clematis* it is absent with the possible exception of the *Atragene* group: *C. alpina* and *C. macropetala*, in which the 'doubling' of the flower may be ascribed either to petals or to petal-like stamens or to both.

The fruits of a clematis are worthy of note since the styles which surmount them have continued to grow after the flower's fading and, with their plumed tails, often contribute a pleasing effect as the seeds ripen. In our native *C. vitalba* the styles become feathery and pale grey, and are aptly known as Old Man's Beard.

Clematis are exceptional, in their family, for being mainly (though not always) woody. And most clematis (though not all) are climbers. Their leaf stalks (petioles) are adapted for this purpose to twist round any suitable aids to support with which they come into contact. But they cannot get a grip on a flat surface, like a wall, as can the ivies and virginia creepers.

There are said to be some 230 species of clematis, of cosmopolitan distribution but concentrated primarily in the cool-temperate northern hemisphere. A large number are supremely uninteresting from a horticultural viewpoint. Most clematis are deciduous, but some of the less hardy species from warmer climates are evergreen. There is no need for an ugly rush to acquire these, as the British climate sadly batters their foliage between autumn and spring. Nine of them hail from New Zealand and an interesting point in respect of this little nucleus is that they are all dioecious (male and female organs on separate plants), whereas most clematis are hermaphrodite.

There has at times been a move among certain systematic botanists to split two sections of the genus *Clematis* off into separate genera: *Atragene* and *Viorna*. The former includes *C. alpina*, its Chinese equivalent *C. macropetala* and its North American ditto, *C. verticillaris*. It has petal-like processes (petaloid staminodes) located between the flower's real stamens and its sepals. *C. viorna* is the type of *Viornae*, characterised by a leathery, urn-shaped flower in which the four sepals are joined (connate) at the base, opening out separately at their tips. Most, if not all, of this group are North American and include the important red-flowered *C. texensis*. The European *C. integrifolia* is sometimes also included.

Atragene and *Viorna* are still included with *Clematis* in most works of reference, and are so here.

Clematis have been grown in English gardens since at least the end of the sixteenth century. Double forms of *C. viticella* were already mentioned by Gerard and Parkinson. Even so, little interest was taken in them until they began to be crossed and 'improved' in the 1850's. Thereafter, for the next twenty years, an extraordinary spate of hybridising activity was let loose throughout Western Europe. This was not peculiar to clematis alone but to all florists' flowers and was stimulated by the flood of new introductions of species and hybrids arriving at that time from all over the world. A large proportion of the clematis we grow today were created in those years.

Nowadays it is rare for a clematis to be put up for award at the Royal Horticultural Society's shows, but in the 1860's, '70's and '80's it was happening all the time and the award given was the First Class Certificate (FCC). The lower graded Award of Merit (AM) was not instituted until 1888, so it is fair to say that the awarding committees exact a higher standard for the FCC today than they did then. On the other hand the standard of cultivation was probably higher in those days than now. More care was lavished on the individual plant. Labour was cheap.

The new, large-flowered clematis derived from three Far Eastern species – *C. florida, C. patens, C. lanuginosa* – and one European, *C. viticella* (with another, the herbaceous *C. integrifolia*, peeping over its shoulder).

C. florida was a native of China but no one living has recorded seeing it in its native Hupeh (W. China). In its double-flowered cultivars it has long been grown in Japan and it was from there introduced to Europe by Thunberg in 1776. This was most likely the double greenish white cv Plena. Such, at any rate, was the opinion given in Volume 22 of Curtis's Botanical Magazine, published in 1805.

The other, even better known cv of *C. florida* is Sieboldii, also known variously as *C. sieboldii* and *C. florida bicolor*. This was introduced from Japan by Siebold and came to England from his nursery in 1836.

C. florida is closely allied to *C. patens* and some authorities consider them to be one and the same. *C. patens* was a native of both China and Japan but, again, vanished, as a wilding, into thin air like the Cheshire Cat, leaving only its grin behind. Common in cultivated form in Japanese gardens, it, too, was introduced to Europe by Siebold in 1836.

The two names we meet over and over again in accounts of 19th century hybridising work are Fortunei and Standishii. As Bean (the 1970 revision of *Trees & Shrubs Hardy in the British Isles*) remarks, whether *C. florida* is to be considered as one of the parents of the garden race of large-flowered clematis depends very much on the status of *C.* 'Fortunei'. It was a semi-double, pure white, scented variety of Japanese gardens introduced by Fortune in the 1830's or '40's and is usually ascribed to *C. florida* but is placed by Rehder under *C. patens*.

It is still common (though less so than heretofore, thank heavens) for gardeners and nurserymen to distinguish a Florida group of double, large-flowered clematis but (Bean again) 'in no sense can these be considered as varieties of *C. florida*. They are hybrids of complex origin some of which may have nothing or little of *C. florida* in their make-up. Thus the parentage of Belle of Woking is *C. (lanuginosa × patens) ×* Fortunei.' Belle of Woking has traditionally been placed in a Florida group.

If Fortunei is probably a derivative of *C. patens*, Standishii is in the same boat. Introduced by Fortune in 1861, it was a Japanese garden cultivar and was more used in hybridisation than *C. patens* itself, but some authorities confuse the issue by considering Standishii to be a cross between *C. florida* and *C. patens* rather than a selection of *C. patens* pure and simple. It seems doubtful whether we shall ever know the truth for certain.

Anyway, the hybrids typically ascribed to and taking after these chimerical *C. florida* and *C. patens* parents flower early on short shoots from the previous year's wood.

Not so *C. lanuginosa*, our third oriental, which bears its flowers successively on young shoots from spring to autumn. Of the cultivars we know and grow, Marie Boisselot and W. E. Gladstone are typical of the Lanuginosa style. Their leaves are often simple, untoothed, undivided. Their buds, stems and young leaves are woolly and the flower buds are long and pointed, not stumpy and rotund.

It was Robert Fortune's introduction of *C. lanuginosa* in 1850 that really set the ball rolling in the hybridising field. He was collecting for the RHS in the province of Chekiang, at the most eastern tip of China. In his memorandum he wrote: 'This pretty species was discovered at a place called Tein-tung, near the city of Ningpo. It is there wild on the hill-sides, and generally plants itself in light stony soil near the roots of dwarf shrubs, whose stems furnish it with support as it grows. Before the flowering season arrives it has reached the top of the brushwood, and its fine star-shaped azure blossoms are then seen from a considerable distance rearing themselves proudly above the shrubs to which it had clung for support during its growth. In this state it is most attractive, and well repays anyone who is bold enough to scramble through the brush-wood to get a nearer view.' The flowers of *C. lanuginosa* are the largest of any species though the plant, in the wild, grows only 2m high.

Turning now to the European ingredients, the species of prime importance in breeding was *C. viticella*, from Southern Europe, with purple flowers only 3 to 5cm across, composed of four obovate (broadest near the tip) sepals, hanging lantern-like and never opening flat. It flowers on its young growth from July till October. It was introduced in the late 16th century.

The first recorded clematis cross was made between this and, supposedly (the cross may well have been accidental), *C. integrifolia*, a herbaceous European species. This occurred on the Pineapple Nursery belonging to Mr Henderson at St John's Wood in 1835. *C. integrifolia* was never proved to be the other parent but, judging by results, it seems highly prob-able. *C. integrifolia*, as its name implies, has simple ovate leaves; it possesses no climbing adaptations and its offspring resembles it in this though its leaves are lobed. It is at present correct to call this hybrid *C. × eriostemon* and Henderson's particular cross *C. × eriostemon* 'Hendersonii'. At other times it has been known variously as *C. hendersonii*, *C. bergeronii*, *C. chandleri* and *C. × intermedia*. *C. integrifolia* 'Hendersonii' is another thing.

In 1858 Messrs Jackman of Woking made a (double) cross using *C. lanuginosa* as the seed parent and the pollen of both *C. × eriostemon* 'Hendersonii' and of *C. viticella* 'Atrorubens'. The famous *C. × jackmanii* was one of the two resulting seedlings, first flowered in 1862 and exhibited in 1863, when it caused a sensation. But does it have *C. integrifolia* blood in it (through *C. × eriostemon*) or is it simply the result of the *C. viticella* clone and *C. lanuginosa*? We cannot be sure but I incline to the latter possibility. If this is right then *C. integ-rifolia* has played no part in the subsequent spate of hybrids. *C. × jackmanii* founded a race and became the parent of innumerable crosses.

It is noticeable (and it was a thorn in the flesh of the early hybridists, who wanted the largest possible flowers in all their clematis) that the viticella influence, which contributes deep rich purple, is always associated, in this colour, with a smaller flower. The largest hybrids were obtained by crossing *C. patens* (together with Fortunei and Standishii) with *C. lanuginosa*, and they had paler shading. Isaac Anderson-Henry of Edinburgh made the first of these crosses in 1855 and obtained the white-flowered Henryi; also Lawsoniana, which is pale mauve. Both are still in commerce. Anderson-Henry's stock was subsequently taken over by Lawson, whose name is thus commemorated. Lawsoniana's blooms are up to 23cm across.

From now on the breeding of new clematis was a rage in Britain, France, Belgium and Germany. I shall take the opportunity to mention the raisers when discussing their cultivars individually. A. G. Jackman (founder George Jackman's son) criticised some of the Continental hybrids for having long narrow sepals, but when we consider this character in the twisted segments of a variety such as Mme Julia Correvon, those of us who enjoy informality may prefer them as garden plants to others with broad, overlapping sepals and a perfectly flat flower, though the latter would doubtless look better on the show bench.

Many clematis in those days were named either after members of the family of the nursery raising them – Mme Julia Correvon, Elsa Späth, Lucie Lemoine, Mme Grangé, Henryi, Jackmanii et al; or after titled patrons of the said nurseries. We still go on the same principles but the aristocracy, being no longer rich patrons with hordes of gardeners, have dropped out of the running. The wife of the Local Authority in command of the purse strings of Municipal Parks and Gardens is more likely to be honoured. If her name happens to be Mrs Joan Smith that's just too bad for the clematis, should it want to compete in the glamour stakes.

From 1880 or thereabouts, the excitement and the breeding died down, though a spark was engendered by the introduction rather late on, of the red-flowered *C. texensis*, which was used both here and in France for hybridising at the turn of the century.

Thereafter, hybridists seem to have run out of ideas and anyway the epidemic nature of wilt disease put a damper on clematis cultivation. Morel of Lyons gave up nursery work and handed over his collection of seedlings to William Robinson, who exhibited them at the RHS from time to time as did Ernest Markham, Robinson's head gardener, after the latter's death and when Markham died these seedlings passed to Jackman's, who named one of them Ernest Markham and another Abundance. Meantime, Jackman's themselves had continued to bring out novelties such as Crimson King, Duchess of Sutherland, King George V and Lady Betty Balfour.

From the historical account of the development of clematis cultivars as detailed above it must be agreed that it is misleading to ascribe any given cultivar to any particular group: Florida, Patens, Jackmanii or whatever. These groups are just one more thing for the amateur to learn and they lead him nowhere. The only excuse for their use is as a guide to pruning. Floridas are pruned this way, Viticellas that. It would be far more satisfactory, however, to describe the three pruning methods and then to ascribe them to the various clematis that the nurseryman is offering.

A further reason for the nurseryman breaking clematis down into groups is to facilitate their choice from the printed page. He has two alternatives. Either he can print the lot in one complete alphabetical list and indicate by a code against each variety, what the basic facts that need to be known about every clematis are: whether it is large-flowered or small, whether it flowers early or late and hence whether it falls into one pruning group or another. The advantage of the complete alphabetical treatment is that it is easy to track down any and every variety the customer wishes to find, but he may find a code tiresome.

The other alternative is to break the clematis down into groups. Thus Treasures, in their latest list, break them down into no fewer than ten groups: evergreen and early-flowering species, Alpina and Macropetala, Montana types, Early large-flowered cultivars, double and semi-double cultivars, mid-season large-flowered cultivars, Jackmanii types, late flowering species (not all species by any means), herbaceous types (some are woody, however). This makes for pleasant browsing for the potential customer who doesn't know what he wants and doesn't want to bother his poor head. But even if there is also a general index (and there is one here) it's tedious to find what you're looking for from 10 alphabetical lists. It is also inevitably misleading, as my two parentheses indicate. Also, there is little validity in Jackmanii and Viticella categories any more than there would be in Florida, Patens and Lanuginosa. Why should Ville de Lyon be classed as Jackmanii type, to take one instance? It neither looks nor behaves like Jackmanii, flowering on old wood early as well as on young wood later and its ancestral links with Jackmanii are remote and weak.

Nurserymen act for the convenience of their customers and themselves but I do think that between us we succeed in painting a pretty muddy picture.

There is little I can say about the breeding of new clematis today. There are a few Continental raisers of whom I know nothing. Their products seem to enter the country by stealth. Perhaps they don't want to be known. Rouge Cardinal, for instance. Mr Fisk tells me that he originally got it from a Dutch Nurseryman at Enfield who brought it from Holland but beyond that he knows and can find out nothing.

The breeding story in this country is a bit pathetic. Treasures, our largest clematis growers, must forgive me for saying they are doing very little of importance in the breeding line. It has really been left to Mr Walter Pennell to carry the torch. Vyvyan Pennell was his outstanding post-war introduction but I like the look of some of his most recent novelties very much, in particular Richard Pennell and Veronica's Choice. I have made a few notes on them at the end. Percy Picton, whose nursery was Ballard's (Old Court Nurseries) near Malvern, has given us and is still producing a few good 'uns, though he doesn't market clematis himself. Hagley Hybrid was his most notable contribution, just after the last war.

We still want a large-flowering yellow clematis – as bright a yellow as *C. tangutica* but having a wide, flat bloom. Is this genetically feasible? I don't know. We want more late flowering blue clematis of the Perle d'Azur style. And we want a true white Jackmanii. Jackmanii Alba, a cross between Jackmanii and Fortunei, is nothing like Jackmanii itself. The early breeders, especially Jackman's, were all striving for a white Jackmanii – something with the habit and flowers of Perle d'Azur, say, but albino, yet they never achieved it. The only white clematis with large blooms that flowers entirely on its young wood is Huldine, and this cannot be described as an all-purpose clematis by any means. Not very large, either.

Something more in the red line would be good, too, returning to the rich, pure colouring of *C. texensis*, as nearly as possible. And some more texensis hybrids in the style of Etoile Rose would be delightful. That'll be enough to be going on with. Any takers?

CHAPTER 3

Making the Most of Clematis

*

'OF course I should like a clematis, but I haven't the space; I just wouldn't know where to fit it in.' Nurserymen must have heard customers musing in this vein, time without number. Usually the old cliché: 'My garden's only the size of a pocket handkerchief' is thrown in for good measure. These remarks can mean one of two things: either that the gardener in question does not want to be tempted to buy a clematis anyway and is merely inventing reasons that endorse his disinclination, or else that he really does believe what he is saying. While there is nothing anyone can do about altering the first state of mind, the second almost certainly arises from the misapprehension that a clematis needs a special place to itself. The reverse is, in fact, the truth.

Walls

Of all plants, clematis do *not* relish isolation. (For this reason, the notion of a clematis garden, as proposed by sundry author-enthusiasts, when swept away by their missionary zeal, has always struck me as ludicrously cracked.) They are sociable, flourishing on a modicum of competition; good mixers, enjoying the company of their neighbours. (Now and again they may happen to smother and kill one of these, but 'with no offence in the world'.) Most clematis lovers, however, tend to reserve special areas of wall space for their favourites. I am certainly not going to claim that this never works out successfully, but it does tend to emphasise the worst features of the clematis – an expanse of bare and far from shapely legs and, very often, a congested lump of blossom on top. If the clematis shoots had a fairly bulky shrub like an evergreen ceanothus through which to thread their way, then their blossoms would

24

be distributed naturally and without overcrowding. In this way, too, the climber's own fundamental shapelessness would be wholly absorbed by the host shrub's structure, on which the clematis flowers would appear like jewels adorning a handsome woman's coiffure. So my own reaction to a piece of bare wall is to plant a shrub on it first and, when this has got a good lead in two years' time, say, to follow on with a clematis.

It will be worth considering, at this point, which wall shrubs make good clematis supports, bearing in mind that almost any clematis will flourish on an east, south or west aspect, and a great many on a north wall, too. Climbing roses are superlative hosts – not that they possess any structural merit with which to mitigate the clematis's lack of it. Rather is it a case of each attempting to bury its defects in the other's embraces. When flowering, of course, both overflow with the vitality of high summer, and spill their bounty with an abandon that can transform the walls of even the tritest building, for a few weeks. Clematis and rose can be chosen either to give a succession of colour or else to flower simultaneously with the maximum impact. The climbing sports of bush hybrid tea and floribunda roses start to flower in late May just at the time when the large-flowered clematis which bloom on their old wood are getting into their stride. From the pruning point of view these two types suit each other too, for in neither case is it necessary to be drastic and both can be dealt with together.

Clematis combine well with other climbing shrubs of greater vigour than their own and, in this context, wisteria is outstanding. Magnolias provide a good framework, but need several years' lead before the clematis is planted, and the same may be said of *Cotoneaster horizontalis* and *C. microphylla*. Pyracanthas, evergreen ceanothus and escallonias are robust wall plants which clematis will much improve, while for a north aspect we have *Jasminum nudiflorum, Forsythia suspensa* and *Camellia japonica* hybrids.

If you have any wall fruit trees from which you despair of ever getting a decent crop – either because the fruit turns out not to be worth eating, or because the birds refuse to allow you any without a struggle that seems not worth making – then you should certainly drape them with clematis.

Making the Most of Clematis

A gardener's natural reaction to the advice I have been giving here is: 'But won't it (the clematis) hurt my rose (forsythia, jasmine, fruit tree or whatever the supporter is going to be)? And the answer is yes, probably it will, a little, but not enough to matter. This is a danger of which we should not be too frightened. After all, a satisfying garden is not made by growing every plant in it to perfection. That, rather, is the kind of treatment which vegetables should receive. A little competition between different types of plant will enable us to gain a far more pleasing result than if we grow all our treasures in evenly spaced blocks, beds and rows.

Back to our walls. There is one type of clematis which is sometimes invaluable for filling a large space, say two storeys high by 8 or 10m across, and especially so on a rather dull, draughty north aspect. This is *C. montana* and its near relatives *C. chrysocoma* and *C.* × *vedrariensis*. They are too vigorous to be walled up with any other kind of plant, and can easily curtain the whole face, right down to the ground. But beware lest they get on to the roof and under the tiles, which they will lift recklessly. Of course, it is delightful to *see* a montana flung over a roof, someone else's roof.

Artificial support must be provided for clematis grown straight on to walls, and this will be effected either with a wooden trellis or with wires; with Weldmesh or with Netlon, both light plastic materials easy to handle by oneself and usually of decent sober colouring.

Pole, Pergola and Trellis

One of the simplest ways to grow a clematis of medium vigour effectively is on a pole. This will usually be of chestnut or larch, 4m long, the bottom metre tarred, for long-lasting underground. Some gardeners like to give their clematis support by wrapping a sleeve of wire netting round the pole, but I consider this unsightly, as parts of it are nearly always visible. I find the homely method of tying the clematis to its support with string at 15cm intervals is perfectly effective and quite invisible.

The kind of place to site a clematis on a pole will usually be as an isolated, vertical feature rising from a groundwork of lower-growing shrubs or herbaceous plants. Thus it is one of the finest adjuncts for inclusion in herbaceous, mixed or shrub borders of every kind. Sometimes it will be found that the entire weight of a clematis which is being grown over a shrub is too much for the host. A pole strategically placed can be made to take three parts of the burden, while a few strands of clematis are still allowed to wander over the shrub or other neighbouring plants.

Knowing how sensitive rose growers can be about the slightest encroachment on their darlings' territory by foreign bodies, I make my next suggestion with some diffidence, bowing to right and to left and retreating the while. Why not include a clematis or two on poles among your rose beds? The same rich soil conditions suit both shrubs ideally. I have found this practice especially successful among Hybrid Perpetual and Bourbon roses whose 2m growths are being pegged down. You can tie the odd rose shoot to the pole, for a change, while the clematis will occasionally wander away among the pegged rose shoots. An ideal blending is thus achieved.

If you object to the starkness of your poles in winter and want to spare them unnecessary weathering, it is easy and practicable to remove them in autumn and restore them at, say, the end of March (the exact time depending on whether spring is early or late). But this works only where clematis of the type that flower on the current season's young shoots are being grown.

When a row of poles has been planted by way of a feature, then I would recommend associating clematis with climbing or rambler roses, rather than have them isolated. In this context, late-flowering clematis do combine especially well with rambler-type roses. It is only necessary to be prepared to delay the ramblers' pruning until autumn, rather than do it immediately after flowering, as tidy-minded rosarians will prefer. This should be no great hardship. The flowering of each will usually overlap, but the clematis is likely to reach its peak after the rose has spent itself. We are always recommended to grow rambler roses in an open situation where there is plenty of air movement, as this discourages powdery mildew from getting a hold on them. The same argument applies to Jack-manii and a number of other summer-autumn-flowering clematis. Moreover, an anti-mildew spray or drench will be as effective on the one as on the other.

Join a row of poles with wire and you have an open fence or trellis which, when planted up with roses, clematis, honeysuckles, vines and other climbers, will make an admirable screen, taking up far less space, in terms of thickness, than the average hedge. The temptation will be, however, to space the plants along it at equal distances, whereas each clematis will be happier in every way if it can be planted with one of the other climbers, which will then automatically shade its roots. Plant them in the same hole, if you like. The same treatment applies where clematis are being worked into a pergola of, say, roses or wisteria. And always plant the clematis on the shadier side of the rose, or whatever it is.

Trees

The idea of growing a clematis over a tree is one which readily appeals, but you do want to know what you are doing, as there are a number of handy pitfalls.

If the tree is alive and flourishing, what chance has the clematis of battling with a creature so much larger and more overwhelming than itself? Any thought of planting a clematis with an oak or other forest tree should be dismissed out of hand. With crabs, ornamental cherries, any orchard tree, rowans, whitebeams and other trees of similarly moderate proportions, the prospects are brighter. But it is rather easy to forget, when planting near a deciduous tree in the dormant season, that its summer foliage will make life very trying for a plant beneath it which is struggling for light. Rowans do not cast too much shade, but cherries are especially umbrageous, while pears and whitebeams are little better. The trees' roots will also be competing for water and nutrients, so that the soil at the foot of a tree trunk is often as arid as a desert's. Here again trees vary; cherries are outstandingly greedy surface feeders while laburnum and the Judas tree *(Cercis siliquastrum)* tend to put their roots down rather than out. A sound rule of thumb is to assume that a tree's roots will spread outwards at least as far as its branches. How slight are a clematis's chances when planted at the base of a tree trunk, is easily imagined. The fact that the tree itself may be young and newly planted makes little difference. The same problem obtains but is deferred for a few years.

Growing clematis on trees. Plant the clematis on the tree's windward side, if possible, and near the tree's extremities. Lead it with string to the selected branch. Keep a large circle round the plant clear of grass and heavily manured.

The solution which is feasible whenever the tree's lower branches reach reasonably close to the ground – within 2 or 3m, let us say – is to plant the clematis underneath a branch near its extremities, and then lead it up by a string to the branch itself. Where there is any choice in the matter, it will be wise to plant on the tree's windward side so that the clematis shoots are blown in the required direction. Once in the tree's branches it can support itself from above, its stem gradually developing into a flexible rope-like liana. The original strand of string can rot at its pleasure.

Many gardeners fancy their tree adorned with the blossoms of a large-flowered clematis. Quite apart from the fact that in many situations and on many trees this would look inappropriate, the main consideration here is to choose a clematis which can cope with a tough situation. And the toughest clematis are all small flowered. But they are none the worse for that and, indeed, small trees offer a fine opportunity for growing a selection of clematis species and becoming acquainted with their great individuality and charm.

It should be added that, as trees are often grown in turf and therefore the clematis will be also, it has here yet another powerful competitor. However conscientious we are in keeping a large circle around the clematis clear of grass and heavily manured, we shall still need a robust grower.

When a clematis is required to deck a tree which is sickly, its prospects may be altogether more cheerful, with such greatly reduced competition for light, water and nutrients. I feel a bit Jeremiah-like in suggesting that here, too, a hidden danger may be lurking. Why is the tree sickly? And if the tree, why not the clematis also? Mr Basil Furneaux once asked me why an apple tree in my Long Border was dying. 'Old age,' said I, glibly. He shook his head and intimated that there was no such cause. As any fruit grower will have guessed before I say it, the tree was being killed by the parasitic honey fungus *(Armillaria mellea)*. This does not confine its attentions to fruit trees. It is practically omnivorous, and if one were to plant a clematis against an infected tree, the former might die of the same cause. And, naturally, the same argument applies to other possible causes of the tree's ill health. It might, for instance, have been starved in some way or else water-logged.

Still, there is no point in worrying oneself sick by proxy, and it will probably be best to plant the clematis anyway, giving it as generous a start as may be, and thereafter simply keep one's eyes open for trouble so that it can be nipped in the bud if possible. Dead trees should be regarded with the same wariness. They can be an excellent medium for displaying clematis and other climbers but should not be regarded as permanent fixtures. The more you cover them, the more leverage they offer to the wind. Their top-hamper of smaller branches should be considerably reduced at the start, and if the main trunk does not offer a clematis sufficient anchorage, some strands of wire can be discreetly added as they are required.

On the whole, though, my affection for dead trees, as for dead teeth, has waned with the years. Too often they become a source of later trouble; I prefer to have them out.

Shrubs

Of all the practicable and attractive ways in which clematis may be exploited, their association with shrubs offers the greatest scope. Yet to most gardeners this is still an untrodden path. It is only a matter of getting into the right frame of mind. Every mature shrub of reasonable proportions should be regarded from time to time with a questioning: 'How would you look with a clematis growing over you?' Examples of a few that I have found especially suitable hosts are: brooms (especially *Spartium*), cotoneasters, tree paeonies (species), shrub roses, viburnums, berberis, *Hibiscus syriacus*, escallonias, lilacs, *Senecio laxifolius* and spiraeas.

Shrubs of stiff habit make better supports than those which are whippy and blow about in the wind a lot. It is difficult for a clematis to make initial contact with a plant which will never keep still. One can plant quite close up to a shrub like a rose or a broom, but when it has a greedy, fibrous, surface-feeding root system, like a lilac or hibiscus, the clematis must be planted well out – perhaps as much as 2m – from the shrub's base, and then led on to its branches. Again, as for trees, plant on the windward side whenever you can.

Tree Stumps and Ground Cover

I am concerned, in this chapter, to discuss how clematis may be used in a general way and to leave consideration of the actual varieties in their special roles till later. Suffice it to say here, then, that certain clematis are good ground coverers, but with the reservation that, being deciduous, they are not properly covering the ground the whole time. The happiest solution is to grow them *among* evergreen ground coverers. Thus, an occasional clematis rambling over a groundwork of dwarf heathers (whether summer or winter flowering) is very effective indeed. Clematis that flower after midsummer on their young wood are the most useful, here, because they can be cut hard back and tidied up out of the way as soon as they have finished flowering leaving the field clear for winter ericas.

Large trees, when cut down, often leave a stump perhaps a foot high which is difficult to get rid of. A clematis will do the trick of concealment, but it is nearly always necessary to fix a piece of netting over the top of the stump first.

Ornamental Tubs, Pots and Ali Baba Jars

There is a strong demand for clematis that will enjoy being grown in tubs, pots, urns and the like. Many old country cottages, converted to a higher standard of living, have been made damp-proof only at the expense of a wide concrete footing all round their base, which precludes the planting of wall shrubs and climbers in the ground. The only possible alternative is to grow them in large tubs. Then again the patios of many a town dwelling give little or no scope for planting except in tubs and pots and, indeed, these can often be of such pleasing appearance in themselves that they lend an air to any garden.

In such circumstances, a clematis will be required to grow either up a wall, from the container, or else to flop out of and entwine the container itself – a procedure which is especially effective when the tall Ali Baba-type jar is being used. A great many clematis varieties will meet these requirements if they are given extra-specially generous and solicitous cultural treatment. It is, after all, not very pleasant to have your roots cooped up in a pot for life. The strongest (John Innes No. 3) potting compost needs to be used with additional liquid feeds during the growing season; the largest available container should be chosen so as to allow as much root room as possible, and the container must never be allowed to dry out. It must, of course have a drainage hole at the bottom. If, after four or five years, the clematis seems to be doing not so well, I should turn it out in the dormant season and completely replace all its soil with a fresh batch. Underwatering is certainly the commonest trouble with container-grown clematis, even when the owner thinks he is being a good and kindly father by administering a few well chosen daily drops and keeping the soil surface apparently damp. Think in terms of 3 or 4 litres at a daily watering throughout the growing season.

As clematis hate to be hot at the roots, they will be happier with other plants in the same container. For the same reason an east or west aspect will try them less than a south, while for those varieties which will flower freely near or against a north wall (the majority) this position will be better than any.

CHAPTER 4

The Choice. General Considerations

*

IF you feel bewildered when it comes to making a choice of a few among scores of possible varieties, at least consider how much easier it is with clematis than with roses. The turn-over among roses offered for sale is colossal. Today's novelty is constantly ousting yesterday's. One has scarcely had time to grow fond of a new rose before it is found to have been relegated.

The case with clematis, whose uses are in any case not as varied as the rose's, is far simpler. Many 19th century stalwarts are still going strong and these are as good a starting point for a collection as any. After all, a variety that has held its own for 80 or 100 years without falling out of the lists must have cardinal virtues, and so it is with such as *C.* × *jackmanii*, Nelly and Marcel Moser, Miss Bateman, William Kennett, The President and many more. With the modern varieties, you may be on to a good thing or you may not. Time will tell. You may be attracted by novelty for its own sake and I shan't be sniffy about that either. We are nearly all of us subject to this little weakness if it is one.

Most of us will strike a balance between enterprise and common sense. It is boring, as you drive through Scotland in summer, to see *C.* × *jackmanii* and nothing but *C.* × *jackmanii* being grown wherever there is a clematis to be seen, but at least it is reassuring to know that Jackmanii is a good doer and perhaps we can use it with rather more originality than the customary lump hanging out between front window and front door. I have a pole specimen in my Long Border which flowers at the same time as a neighbouring group of *Senecio doria*, this being a glorified ragwort with 2m domes of bright yellow daisies. The contrast is striking, perhaps even crude but undeniably effective and I only have to murmur 'purple and gold' to myself to feel entirely reassured.

You will find that every list including shrubs of any kind (and even some bulb catalogues do this) will include a few basic clematis that they've imported from Holland. And even if these are wrongly named, as often happens, still, you could do worse than make them your starting point. They'll be basic varieties that you must grow sooner rather than later. The only annoyance, having had your appetite and interest whetted, will be in finding, say, that the illustration of Lasurstern was yoked to an actual plant of The President and that you end up with 2 of one and none of the other.

Illustrations are a great help where you want to decide on the sort of flower form that appeals to you. Overlapping sepals promote a sense of order, fulness and well-being. Gappy, twisted sepals sound bad, defined baldly like that, but they can promote a no less welcome sense of freedom, informality and movement. You may like blossoms with an eye of stamens in a contrasting colour to form a focal point: the dark stamens in a white bloom as have Miss Bateman and Henryi, rather than the pale stamens in a pale bloom – Marie Boisselot and Mrs George Jackman. Or pale stamens in a dark bloom. I certainly prefer the pale central boss in Etoile Violette and Lady Betty Balfour to the nondescript undifferentiation of *C. × jackmanii.*

Colour in catalogue illustrations must be taken with a large pinch of salt where pink, red and blue are in question. Blues and purples are nearly always better in real life than on the printed page; pinks and reds nearly always worse. The worst deceptions regarding size of flower will be when close-ups of small blooms are illustrated and there is nothing to give scale. This happens most often with *C. tangutica* and *C. orientalis.*

A visit to a flower show can also be helpful, but fewer nurserymen are exhibiting clematis at flower shows than of old because of the great cost of bringing a large number of plants to perfection at the right moment and then of transporting them in mint condition. So it tends to boil down to exhibiting at just one show in the year, notably the Royal Horticultural Society's at Chelsea. Which means, if you get carried away, that you may accumulate a preponderance of early-flowering hybrids in your garden. Plants grown for exhibition have to be raised under cover, of course, to protect them from the vagaries of the weather, and this in itself will result in a different sort of flower – not necessarily better, by any means – from what would be obtained under garden conditions. By and large you get more intense colouring from outside blooms.

Think of the backgrounds that your clematis will have and their positions. Blue clematis will look well with every sort of rose, whether yellow, pink, red or orange. Red clematis are lost against red brick walls and if there is any pink in your brickwork, certain clematis of a magenta persuasion can look filthy against this. I have a model example of what not to do in a photograph of Barbara Dibley, fading in sunlight against such a wall. White clematis against white weather boarding or Snowcem would be considered chic in some quarters, dotty in others (hear! hear!), but on a north wall or in any shady situation, white or light shades should obviously be used in preference to purples and reds.

Indeed, it can be stated as a general precept that light colours show up best in the general setting of a garden. They will be noticed at a distance whereas the dark colours such as you find in Royal Velours, Viticella Rubra and Star of India are sumptuous and thrilling when you stand up against them with the sun behind you but on dull days they look glum and at a distance you don't see them at all whatever the light.

If you live in the south or east, as far north as Norfolk, you can expect to be successful with most clematis varieties against north or other shady walls. They will bud up without the encouragement of direct sunlight. Nevertheless, I should be chary of using *C. orientalis* L & S 13342, Huldine, Ernest Markham or Lady Betty Balfour.

In the colder parts of Britain you would have to add many clematis to this list. I cannot say exactly which, because my own experiences have all been in the south-east. Montana and alpina types would be the safest. Of the large-flowered hybrids I should experiment for a start with Comtesse de Bouchaud and Perle d'Azur. Also Nelly Moser, provided the site was sheltered from cutting winds. The larger the bloom the more vulnerable it will be to wind and draught. Remember that walls are very draughty and that the draughtiest spot in any garden is between the walls of adjacent buildings. Here you get a wind funnel. Only the smallest-flowered clematis can be expected to flourish and even then I should prefer to back some of the more cheerful ivies.

Clematis do not mind the salt-laden air of seaside gardens. They will be far too battered and bruised if placed unsheltered to face the sea but quite all right if faced inland.

CHAPTER 5

The Choice: Large-Flowered Hybrids

*

MY object now is to make a critical and comparative survey of clematis cultivars available, so that the reader has some guide lines on which to base his choices. The trouble is that I know some of my clematis far better than others, while there are also some that I have never clapped eyes on and so I cannot do them justice. Indeed, it would be foolish to bring them into this chapter at all. I must ask the reader to make the most of the half loaf I am offering. It will be quite a long half, even so, not to say tough in patches.

Starting with the large-flowered hybrids I propose to divide them into colour categories. These divisions will be arbitrary in borderline cases, as between blue and mauve, mauve and purple, purple and red, but never mind.

I must say, at the start, that it is often difficult to decide if a variety as offered in the trade is correctly named or not. Mrs Hope, for instance, will appear in one guise in one place, in another guise elsewhere. Who is to say which is correct or whether the original Mrs Hope was not yet a third variety that has gradually been replaced and has now completely disappeared? Nobody can give a final and incontrovertible opinion on these questions of identity and the best I can do is to weigh the balance of probabilities.

These large-flowered cultivars are very poorly served in their naming. And the situation appears to be as bad now as ever in the past with Tom Snooks, Dick Drab and Harry Brown being celebrated right left and centre. Mr Fisk seems to encourage the practice when he writes, apropos of raising a winner from seed of 'fame for the raiser, if he or she decides to name it after themselves.' This is an understandable piece of vanity but should be resisted. If these breeders would leave us a record of the circumstances attending the origin of their new cultivars, it would be far more to the point. But a name can tilt the balance between the successful promotion of a good plant and its relegation. Percy Lake, Percy Picton and Percy Robinson are probably all three excellent fellows (the second certainly is, I can vouch) but their names mean nothing to 99% of the clematis-buying public. Neither do they evoke any sort of mood that can be associated with a flower. Compare them with names like Moonlight, Gipsy Queen, Aurora, Blue Gem, Victoria – all of them short, easily memorised, easily spoken, in sum: attractive. If clematis namers would try to be a little less indulgent to their relations and friends, a little more imaginative, it would be a great help all round.

'BLUE' CLEMATIS

Ascotiensis	Lady Northcliffe
Beauty of Worcester	Lasurstern
Blue Gem	Lord Nevill
Countess of Lovelace	Mrs Cholmondeley
Durandii	Mrs Hope
Elsa Späth	Mrs P. B. Truax
Etoile de Paris	Perle d'Azur
H. F. Young	William Kennett

'Blue' has to stand in quotes because even the bluest clematis has a strong tinge (or taint) of mauve in it, but we shall always continue to speak of blue clematis in describing those here listed. The cynic will say that this is a nurseryman's confidence trick, as blue is the best selling colour of all. Rather is it a matter of comparison. There are so many clematis that come indisputably into the mauve-lavender-lilac bracket, that when they do verge on blue it becomes necessary to call them this.

Blue is the most exciting clematis colour. No other hardy climber carries huge blue flowers and in this it is completely differentiated from climbing roses.

The deeper blue shades are more popular than the light. Here our choice lies between four old and well tried varieties: Lasurstern, Lady Northcliffe, Lord Nevill and Beauty of Worcester. Lasurstern heads them. Blooms carried on the old wood are 15 to 18cm wide. Each has seven or eight sepals, broadly overlapping towards the axis of the flower but tapering to fine points, their margins gently undulating. The creamy-white stamens make a prominent central boss. On a healthy, carefully trained specimen I have had over 200 blooms open at a time and covering an area 1·5m high by 5m across. Really you should try and work it in with a double red climbing rose like Guinée or Etoile de Hollande, having the same flowering season.

Lady Northcliffe has much the same colouring and is as good in its way though I have seen it afflicted with mildew. The flower is quite a different shape, without fine tapering of the sepals and unwaved but the bloom as a whole has a classic purity of outline that is characteristic and always recognisable once recognised. This clematis was raised by Jackman's from a cross between Beauty of Worcester and Otto Froebel. It received the A.M. when shown by Jackman's 29 May 1906.

There is a rough readiness about Lord Nevill (introduced in 1878) that is far from aristocratic, I should have thought. The puckered surface of the sepals suggests a wind ruffled pond. The purple flower centre is even darker than the sepals. In a way I love Beauty of Worcester better than any of the foregoing, but it does not grow as strongly as one would wish. Indeed it is so free flowering that three quarters of its effort seems to be channelled in this direction leaving too little for the important business of building a strong framework. The early flowers are double, rich and intense; the later, by contrast, are so well shaped that you would never guess that doubleness could be an aspect of the plant's personality. The centre of these single flowers is very white. No wonder its marvellous qualities have been much used in hybridisation. Beauty of Worcester was raised by Messrs. R. Smith and Co. of Worcester – I should guess in the 1890's. Mr Pennell used it in the cross that produced Vyvyan Pennell.

Turning to the lighter blues, my highest award (not counting the later flowering Perle d'Azur) would go to Mrs Hope – a huge satiny bloom with a full and comfortable look that it owes to overlapping sepals. And the reddish purple eye is an excellent feature. It flowers early and late and the plant I have been describing (which is the one Marjorie Blamey has illustrated) makes a speciality of very long, acute-angled, simple leaves. But there are other Mrs Hope's around (Treasure's is not the same as mine) and their sepals are more rough in texture. Mrs Hope came out in 1875 (her maiden name is not recorded); Blue Gem in 1879 but this has suffered an even more unfortunate loss of identity and seems no longer to be a very satisfactory clematis. William Kennett is often mixed up too but should not be, as it is a distinct and easily recognised clematis. One of the old brigade but still robust and hearty. Rough-textured sepals led to Moore & Jackman's comment of its 'lacking in refinement' and we can agree, but from May till autumn William Kennett is seldom out of flower (whereas Blue Gem, as I have met it, seems seldom to be in flower).

I think I should bring in H. F. Young here. It is paler than Lady Northcliffe but has the same sort of smooth-textured refinement and a good deal more vigour. The photograph of a sumptuous specimen of H. F. Young features on the jacket of Jim Fisk's 'The Queen of Climbers'. Mrs P. B. Truax, always described in catalogues (and aptly so) as periwinkle blue, come into the same colour bracket. It is one of the earliest large-flowered hybrids in bloom and is a good doer, but has a short season with nothing in hand for later on.

Apart from its colouring this is in complete contrast to Mrs Cholmondeley, a clematis that simply can't stop flowering and yet has enough vigour to get it places. From tip to tip, the early flowers are very large but because of narrow sepals and large gaps between them towards the base, one's impression is not so much of size as of prodigality. Any massed effect in the garden should have a complementary feature to offset it and here I should like the climbing sport of an old Hybrid Tea rose, Caroline Testout or, even better, Lady Waterlow, still offered by John Mattock of Oxford. Both are pink.

By way of a light blue double-flowered clematis, full of sepals and of great depth, Countess of Lovelace. It can be breathtaking but is not necessarily an easy variety. When suited, it still (after a century in cultivation) has plenty of vigour but may take longer than most to settle down and you should give it the works as to food and drink.

We now come to two cultivars that are not quite as blue as those so far discussed. Etoile de Paris is out in my garden in mid-May and is well named Etoile as its sepals are markedly pointed. The flowers are fairly deep purple-blue on opening but fade a lot. As I have scarlet oriental poppies nearby, I always think of it in this context. My plant, in 20 years, has never given me a moment's anxiety and it flowers with a will, but all on the old wood with little or nothing to follow. Elsa Späth (often spelt Spaeth in English) is one of my greatest favourites. The colour is a strong purplish blue and the reddish-purple stamens are effective. The texture is smooth, the flowers substantial but what I specially like about this clematis is the smart cut of its sepals and the way they overlap and yet remain perfectly flat. Also it is vigorous and flowers freely both early and, even more so, late, on its young growth. Unfortunately Pennell's are calling this one Xerxes. Ever since the original Xerxes went out of cultivation (A. G. Jackman, in his revision notes for Moore and Jackman's book, made early in this century, observed that Xerxes has been superseded), nurserymen have been wanting to use the name.

Many of the blue clematis so far discussed flower well on their young wood but all are capable of flowering early on short growths from the previous season's wood; some of them do it entirely this way. We now come to two clematis – only two in this colour – that flower entirely on their young wood. Ascotiensis is the earlier of these, out from mid-June. It is a good mid-blue but the flower is a poorish shape. It was introduced in 1871 and Moore and Jackman lay particular stress on its 'large flowers of fine form'. This is strange; they are not even large, compared with other blue's. Still, it is pleasing by any standard and indispensable as the only one of its colour and kind. We do badly need some more late-flowering blue clematis, perhaps by crossing Perle d'Azur with Elsa Späth or Beauty of Worcester.

Perle d'Azur, indeed, quite eclipses Ascotiensis, such a paragon is it in so many ways. It was introduced by Morel and described in the Revue Horticole of 1885. Clearly this clematis is closely akin in habit and flower shape to *C.* × *jackmanii* and I cannot say that the individual flower starts a song in my heart, but it is well poised and presented and the aggregate of blossom never looks congested. The colour is obviously not sky blue, as often stated, but we may hope to get away with the description if the sky is overcast. It gives a blue impression, light blue, lots and lots of it. Never did a clematis have a greater will to grow and to flower – over a continuous 2-months-long season from late June to August. You should certainly grow this with your rambler roses. In fact, again and again, I find myself recommending it as the one and obvious choice for many different situations. I never tire of it as I do of the no less generous *C.* × *jackmanii*. The touch and tone are altogether lighter.

We end up with another winner but it is odd man out. Durandii has simple oval leaves and doesn't even climb. It is the unique result of an early cross between *C.* × *jackmanii* and the herbaceous south European species *C. integrifolia* and was introduced by Durand Frères of Lyons in 1870. Surely it is time that similar crosses were made again. Durandii (sometimes known as Integrifolia Durandii but this, of course, is wrong as it is a hybrid, not a variety of *C. integrifolia*) is semi-herbaceous and will put on 2m of growth in a season. You can tie it up to achieve height but against a wall it is prone to serious onslaughts by mildew. Better to let it drape itself over a metre-tall shrub in the open. I have it with the grey-leaved *Senecio laxifolius* (or *greyi*) and the yellow daisies of the latter are pretty with the deep indigo blue flowers of Durandii. These are of very moderate size; only 10cm across, deeply grooved with parallel veins like a plantain leaf and having a distinctive button-like eye of pale stamens. The flowers are not abundant but sufficient* and they cut well. They are unusual as well as beautiful and flower arrangers have taken them to their hearts. Durandii can get wilt disease but it is generally an easy clematis to grow anywhere. There is, or used

*There are exceptionally large and free flowering specimens, quite belying this statement, in the famous garden on Garnish Island in Bantry Bay, S.W. Ireland.

to be, a paler form called Pallida, which one would like to meet again.

LAVENDER AND MAUVE CLEMATIS

Beauty of Richmond	Prins Hendrik
Belle Nantaise	Ramona
Lady Caroline Nevill	Silver Moon
Lawsoniana	Vyvyan Pennell
Miriam Markham	W. E. Gladstone
Mrs Bush	Will Goodwin

I have tried to collect the bluer shades of mauve here (though some might have gone into the white group), leaving those that verge on pink till later.

Lawsoniana is of special interest because it was one of the earliest large-flowered hybrids (see Chapter 2, page 20). It was recognised as the largest flowered of all clematis with blooms 24cm (9½in) across recorded. In this it has probably not been exceeded. The blooms are rosy lavender on opening, becoming paler and bluer as they expand to their full size. Beauty of Richmond is very similar and Mrs Bush is too, being close to *C. lanuginosa*. Its anthers are buff as against the lavender-shaded ones of Lawsoniana. Mrs Bush flowers best on its old wood but Lady Caroline Nevill, although it can carry large, flattish, semi-double flowers off its old wood, often misses out on these, in the garden (especially as you get into colder climates) and concentrates on its later, new wood crop. Mr Pennell, gardening in Lincoln, recommends hard pruning so as to cater entirely for this. It is pale bluish mauve; *quite* nice.

Ramona comes in here though a thoroughly mixed up variety. Hybrida Sieboldii is synonymous with whatever we are calling Ramona (its American name) but I agree with Mr Fisk that Ramona is much to be preferred as a name and especially since *C. florida* 'Sieboldii' is the correct name for the plant more generally known as *C. florida bicolor*. I originally received Belle Nantaise from Pennell's in the dim past before the last war, as Lanuginosa. It certainly has close affinities to that species and did me proud for 25 years, carrying very large, white centred, pale lavender flowers mostly on its young wood. I have lost it and the plant now being offered as Belle Nantaise by Treasure's is different. It was a continental variety introduced by Boisselot in 1887.

Still in the general range of lavender, Lanuginosa-orientated clematis that I have been discussing, I shall include Miriam Markham. Like Lady Caroline, it is capable of flowering off the old wood but more often does it all on the young in late summer and autumn. The outstanding feature here, however, is that these blooms are double – flattened and of a charming shape. It is exceptional for large double flowers to be borne on long young current season's growth. According to Jackman's old catalogues (from the days when they used to stock it) single blooms are produced on young wood, but this is not my experience. It is a pretty clematis but never carries many blooms at a time.

Prins Hendrik (he was Queen Wilhelmina of Holland's husband) is a dramatic show clematis: it has for long been grown under glass as a cut flower on the Continent and is better known there than here. Not only are its flowers very large but so are each of the six sepals, individually. They are strongly veined in the centre and crimped at the margins but the reason for this powerful variety being so rare in British gardens is that practically no-one can make it grow! Don't ask me why.

W. E. Gladstone, on the other hand, has long been a favourite. It is typically Lanuginosa, flowering quite early if you prune it lightly and then continuing non-stop till the autumn. Never a large number of blooms at any one time but what there are, are of the largest – exceedingly well formed, smooth and silky textured (in complete contrast to Prins Hendrik) and with a telling eye of dark anthers. Like Lady Caroline Nevill and others, W. E. Gladstone is readily killed to the ground in winter; it then grows strongly from the base and flowers July onwards. Noble of the Sunningdale Nurseries introduced this clematis; it was awarded a First Class Certificate by the RHS in 1881.

Let us see what the present has to offer. Silver Moon might be roughly described as a smaller-flowered version of Belle

Nantaise – pale lavender, pale stamens and a long flowering season. It is nicely shaped and the colour of newly opened flowers is tolerable but they quickly fade to a very washed out mauve. Thumbs down.

Will Goodwin is one of Mr Walter Pennell's breeding. Incidentally, instead of the dreary tally of undistinguished and hence difficult-to-memorise names that he has saddled on many of his new clematis, why does he not, as a keen amateur astronomer, turn to the heavens for assistance? He already has a lead from any number of Etoiles, Sterns and Stars; Silver Moon, Moonlight, Twilight, Crepuscule, Aurora, Corona, Venus Victrix *et al.* Why not Orion, Hercules (a strong grower), Perseus (as a change from Percy), Andromeda (excellent ground cover when tied to a rock), Pegasus, Leo, Virgo and many more such; he will know them better than I. Anyway, Will Goodwin is not unlike Prins Hendrik in appearance with its crimped, pale bluish sepals, but smaller. It is a full looking bloom. I like it.

Vyvyan Pennell (Mrs Walter Pennell) is undoubtedly the star performer in the post-war clematis world – a cross between Beauty of Worcester and Daniel Deronda. It is a double clematis and like many doubles, has an outer frame of broad guard sepals and an inner rosette of smaller petal-like organs – they are really modified stamens. There has for many years been a dramatic specimen on a house in the High Street of Rye (my local town). It stops all who pass in gaping admiration (I won't say it actually stops the traffic also, because this is usually at a stand-still anyway). Indeed, the lady who planted it sensibly cashed in on a ravenous demand and bought in plants for re-sale at her back door. But waves of repercussion constantly reach me out here in Northiam, 8 miles away. No sooner do visitors start enquiring about a clematis they have seen than I know what's coming and can help them out of the agonies of explanation. Vyvyan Pennell has great vigour and, on its young growth, carries single blooms in autumn. But its May-June flowering is the thing.

I have transferred to the whites several clematis that I originally intended to discuss here, so will treat them next.

Belle of Woking	Lady Londesborough
Dawn	Marie Boisselot
Duchess of Edinburgh	Miss Bateman
Fair Rosamond	Mrs George Jackman
Henryi	Mrs Oud
Huldine	Wada's Primrose
Jackmanii Alba	Yellow Queen

Although far weaker than it used to be, there is still a public prejudice against white flowers. But the large white clematis have so powerful an appeal as often to override dissent. And there are and always have been a great number of them. The pity is that only one, and that not very large, comes into the late-season category by flowering entirely on its new wood.

Jackmanii Alba is nothing like *C.* × *jackmanii*, though it is said to be a cross between this and our old friend the semi-double white Fortunei. And it was made by Charles Noble at Sunningdale. So we find it, not unexpectedly, carrying double flowers early in the season from old wood but they are not a good shape and their white is impure: bluish, like skimmed milk. Later blooms with only 4, 5 or 6 sepals are more attractive (if not gashed by earwigs). It is a vigorous clematis with characteristic pale green foliage. Not in the top flight. It received a First Class Certificate in 1883. As already explained, the lower-graded Award of Merit had not then been introduced by the RHS, which is the reason for the high number of F.C.C.'s awarded to clematis between 1863 (to *C.* × *jackmanii*) and 1890, which was anyway the heyday of their development.

If you want a double white clematis, it should be Duchess of Edinburgh. When I was collecting all the available large-flowered hybrids in the early 1950's, there was an alternative in Lucie Lemoine. But the two as then offered in commerce appeared to me identical, so it was no loss when Lucie dropped out of the lists.

However, there are some interesting details worth studying, here, and I am obliged to the late Hugh Thompson for pointing them out to me. Both varieties were described in Moore and Jackman's 'The Clematis' of 1877 and their differences were marked. Lucie Lemoine was introduced by Victor Lemoine of Nancy and received the F.C.C. in 1874; Duchess of Edinburgh was a Jackman clematis and got the F.C.C. in 1876. Of Lucie Lemoine, Moore & Jackman write that the flowers consist of 75 to 90 pure white sepals 'and do not show the greenish tint which is seen in the older double white sorts.' 'the flowers are further set off . . . by a circlet of leaves, sometimes more or less coloured, which surrounds them.' Scent is not mentioned. Duchess of Edinburgh, they wrote, 'is remarkable for the depth of its flowers, which thus become almost as globular as a Guelder rose.' The width of flower was 4in. as against 5in. in Lucie Lemoine but depth was the great feature, with ten to eleven rows of sepals. Additionally, 'the flowers are very sweet-scented, so much so that a single blossom will perfume a room in which it is shut up.'

Well now, I get little or no scent from Duchess of Edinburgh, although my sense of smell is sharp. I agree that the flower has great depth but it is also exceedingly prone to greenness where it should be white. In addition there is a large area behind the flower where sepal-like leaves or leaf-like sepals abound. One wonders whether the clematis we grow as Duchess of Edinburgh may be neither that nor Lucie Lemoine but 'one of the older double white sorts' that show a greenish tint. However this may be, it is still a very popular clematis, especially with flower arrangers and the individual blooms, which are at their peak in June-July, last a long time as is the way with the doubles. My plant grows through a specimen of *Hydrangea paniculata* 'Praecox' (which flowers in early July) and causes great confusion to visitors.

Established plants seldom throw late blooms on young wood but this can happen on young plants and the blooms are always double. Belle of Woking is similar in habit and flower form but the colour 'is a delicate but decided tint of bluish-mauve or silver-gray' (Moore & Jackman). No nurseryman wanting to sell it today would dream of describing it as

1. Lasurstern
2. Lady Northcliffe
3. H. F. Young
4. Mrs P. B. Truax
5. Lord Nevill
6. Mrs Cholmondeley
7. Elsa Späth

1. Beauty of Richmond   4. William Kennett
2. Lawsoniana   5. Mrs Hope
3. Prins Hendrik   6. Will Goodwin

bluish-mauve. Silver-grey every time. The fact that Moore & Jackman felt it necessary to call the colour delicate but decided indicates, of course, that it is delicate and undecided. But it is a pretty clematis. Not as quick to settle down as Duchess of Edinburgh. I don't know how the name Belle of Woking strikes you but I always feel it would be appropriate to a gallant old steam locomotive. Not so a lady who wrote me apropos of a young plant in her garden. 'Belle of Woking has leaves no larger than a mouse's ear, but doubtless she will come flaunting down the street with ear-rings jangling.' So much for the doubles.

There are three clematis whose flowers are remarkably similar in every way except colouring. These are Miss Bateman, Lady Londesborough and Dawn. The first two were both bred and introduced by Noble of The Sunningdale Nurseries (alas, his notebooks were all destroyed in the last war) and both received First Class Certificates in May 1869. All their blooms are opened in the May-June period (except in young plants) but they are both stunners, their flowers most beautifully and symmetrically shaped, their paleness offset by the central cushion of reddish-purple (or purplish red) anthers. Lady Londesborough is coloured much like Belle of Woking, a pale lavender grey that fades to French grey. The young blooms of Miss Bateman and particularly the first of the crop, have a lot of green in them, especially down the mid-rib. As the flowers age, the green (as in parrot tulips) vanishes but it is an attractive feature in this variety.

Dawn is a modern cultivar said to result from a cross between Nelly Moser and Yellow Queen. It is blush white fading to white. I doubt if it will long stay the course as its colouring falls between two stools. It was introduced by Treasures as Aurora but when they discovered that this name had been given to a double clematis that gained the F.C.C. in 1877, they changed theirs to Dawn. Fair Rosamond is blush white too, but is more often confused with Miss Bateman than any other. Actually they are quite distinct. The stamens in Fair Rosamond are much more prominent, being nearly twice as long. The sepals are narrower and pointed – broad and blunt in Miss B. There is a definite pink flush in Fair Rosamond even in mature blooms, none in Miss B. Greenness in young blooms is common to both cultivars but Fair Rosamond is scented; 'exceedingly fragrant', say Moore & Jackman 'the scent being intermediate between that of violets and primroses.' I cannot improve on that comparison – for we can only describe scents by comparing one with another. Fair Rosamond has certainly not lost its scent as Duchess of Edinburgh seems to have done, but you shouldn't expect anything strong, as in species like *C. montana, C. rehderiana* and *C. flammula.* It needs to be sniffed out by a searching and sympathetic proboscis.

Fair Rosamond was introduced by Jackman and received a First Class Certificate in April 1873 (doubtless a pot-plant grown under glass). All the pale single clematis I have just been discussing are closely akin to *C. patens*, and if you think of them together you do get a connective feeling of similarity in foliage, habit of growth and flowers. So, too, with Yellow Queen and Wada's Primrose. They cannot be all that far from the wild *C. patens*, although that vital parent may have ceased to exist as a wilding many years ago. The 8 narrow, separated sepals, like the sails of a windmill, are common to Yellow Queen and to the illustration of *C. patens* in Moore & Jackman's book.

Yellow Queen was introduced by Treasure's in 1968 and it came to them from Holland via Denmark and Sweden, already saddled with this inappropriate name. Fisk calls the same clematis Moonlight, which is just right, for the colouring is a cream-tinted white. (The synonym is a nuisance, of course, and confusing). It has the look of a wilding and is a charming, unsophisticated flower. Wada's Primrose is very close. Large batches have been imported from Wada's nursery in Japan and they look as though they might be seedlings, in Raymond Evison's estimation. We still have no large-flowered yellow clematis! Might *C. tangutica* crossed with Huldine yield something?

But I have not reached Huldine yet, being still with the white cultivars that flower first and earliest from their old wood. Henryi was named after Anderson-Henry, who raised it all that time ago (see p. 20) and it is still one of the most popular large whites. Its pointed sepals compose a star-like flower and it has a dark 'eye'. It has many admirers but is not one of my favourites and has always refused to grow for me. But whereas I find Henryi difficult, Mrs Oud is difficult. Yet a most beautiful clematis, always described with complete aptitude as milk white. The stamens are dark and the flower form most satisfying with overlapping sepals. I wish you luck with her and please let me know when she is carrying 50 blooms or more.

The only obvious difference between Mrs George Jackman and Marie Boisselot is in their stamens. Foliage is almost identical and so is the form and size of the pure white flower but Mrs George has buff-coloured anthers whereas in Marie Boisselot they are such a pale cream as scarcely to be noticed as a feature against white sepals. Mrs George Jackman was going strong by 1873 anyway and Marie Boisselot before the end of the century. Even in those days the latter was known to be synonymous with Mme Le Coultre (A. G. Jackman notes as much in his corrections to Moore & Jackman) and this is still the case. Mme Le Coultre is the name used in Holland and it is perhaps most often adopted by nurserymen in this country who import a lot of their selling stock from Holland and don't want to have to change the tags on arrival. Certainly, whether for this reason or another, Mr Fisk used to list it as Marie Boisselot but subsequently switched. Pennell, Jackman and Treasure all use Marie Boisselot.

This is undoubtedly the finest large-flowered white clematis. Because of its broadly overlapping sepals, the flower looks very full. The fact that it has no 'eye' doesn't seem to matter. It is robust and, if it carries its old wood through the winter, starts flowering in early June. You can (and many do) prune it entirely for late flowers. But this is generally pointless as it will anyway flower abundantly on its young growth and continues right into November. It looks very pretty when associated with the Late Dutch honeysuckle, *Lonicera periclymenum* 'Serotina', both being excellent for shady places.

And so at last we reach the captious Huldine, the only fairly large-flowered clematis (its flowers are some 10cm across) that crops entirely on its young wood and therefore has a season running from July onwards – if it has a season at all. It is one of the most delightful clematis at its best. The flower and individual sepals are somewhat cupped, white above, mauve underneath but translucent. If you get the light right there is a marvellous see-through effect. Perhaps the easiest way is to grow Huldine over the top of a wall that is higher than yourself. Up a pole is very good, too. This is a rampant grower and quite often it fails to flower altogether: may flower abundantly in one position in your garden, scarcely or not at all in another. Some gardeners think they succeed with it by cutting all young growth back with shears in July, thereby obtaining a crop of blossom in September. It is advisable, both visually and culturally, to give it a sunny place.

Huldine received the A.M. when shown by Ernest Markham for William Robinson in August 1934. It was presumably of Morel's raising, some 30 years earlier. There is a strong probability of Texensis blood in it.

'RED' CLEMATIS

Crimson King	Mme Edouard André
Duchess of Sutherland	Mme Julia Correvon
Ernest Markham	Rouge Cardinal
Jackmanii Rubra	Ville de Lyon

If you are expecting a pure red large-flowered clematis you will, as with pure blue, be disappointed. More disappointed, in fact, because colour photography and printing tend to make blue clematis look less blue (or a quite impossible blue that no-one could believe) in the trade catalogues and encyclopaedias from which we make our selections, whereas the reds become pure red by cutting out all the blue in their colouring.

There are not many clematis in this class. Some of the duller shades appeared early on, viz. Mme Grangé (I've placed her among the purples) and Mme Edouard André. The brighter tones came in with Ville de Lyon and most (if not all) subsequent bright reds have Ville de Lyon in their parentage.

Ville de Lyon was introduced by Morel in 1899 and he claimed that it was bred from *C. coccinea* (now *C. texensis*) as the pollen parent and Viviand Morel as the female, seed parent.

This would explain its brilliant colouring, unique at that time in a large-flowered clematis, for *C. texensis* is the one truly red species. Viviand Morel was director of the Lyons Botanic Garden and may have procured *C. texensis* for Francisque Morel to make his cross.

Ville de Lyon is a remarkable clematis, even today. The flowers are beautifully shaped, their pure carmine red, on opening, effectively set off by cream stamens. As the flower ages, the sepal margins retain a deeper colour than the central area, which becomes a trifle muddy, like strawberries that have gone off. No clematis shows distress signals more readily when starved of food and drink, the oldest leaves dying off in a most unsightly manner. Grown well, however, the owner is amply rewarded and, by dint of light pruning, can enjoy blossom with little intermission from the last days of May till September.

Mme Julia Correvon was another of Morel's breeding, its parentage being given as *C. viticella* × Ville de Lyon (in the Revue Horticole 1900). It has narrow twisted sepals in a style that was eschewed by British breeders, but it makes a change from the full type of flower with overlapping sepals such as has always been favoured by the exhibitor. The charming informality of Mme Julia Correvon is widely recognised today. This clematis was unobtainable in commerce when I first heard of it at a lecture given by Mr Graham Thomas on National Trust gardens around 1958. He showed a slide of a plant growing at Hidcote Manor. John Treasure and I propagated it and brought it back into circulation. It is a strong grower flowering on its young wood in one protracted spate from late June and is a good bright colour.

Mme Edouard André was introduced by Baron Veillard's nursery of Orleans in 1893, having been exhibited at Tours in the previous year. It was said to be a cross between Jackmanii and Patens. Edouard André was at this time Editor of the Revue Horticole. He always signed his articles Ed. André and the clematis has invariably been known in the trade as Mme Ed. André. It is one of those clematis that seems to achieve the perfect balance between vigour and freedom of flowering: that is to say it will never worry you by growing too little but will never overwhelm you with superabundance of vegetation, because all excess energies are channelled into flowers and yet more flowers – just the one crop, but starting in mid-June and continuing for a good two months. The flowers are prettily shaped with rather pointed sepals but they are just a little too dark and matt for perfection. They are flattered in a sunny position against a light background.

Duchess of Sutherland is the handsomest red clematis with a large, well-formed bloom, its sepals broad and overlapping and of a most agreeable crimson-red colouring. It may sometimes produce a few early double blooms but most of the crop, as with other red clematis, is borne on the young wood in late summer and is single. This is, alas, not one of the easiest or quickest clematis to establish but if you are prepared to protect it against wilt disease and to manure and water it well, you should certainly grow it.

Crimson King is not of the easiest either but a good colour, again and a flatter bloom than the last with darker stamens. It was introduced by Jackman's of Woking and received an A.M. in 1917. Ernest Markham was just about the only large-flowered clematis of Markham's own raising that is going around. It was handed over to Jackman's in a batch, and simply marked Red Seedling. When Markham died not long afterwards, in 1937, Rowland Jackman named the seedling after him. Jackman calls it 'the most beautiful of all reds.' I do not agree but it is certainly an excellent clematis, of a strong bright magenta, with broad rough-textured sepals and dusty-looking stamens. It is worth pruning lightly so as to enjoy a small crop of large early blooms but most come on the young wood, which is freely produced, for this is a vigorous and easy clematis. Sometimes it is shy-flowering. Like Lady Betty Balfour, it needs plenty of sunshine but I have seen it flowering well as far north as Newby Hall in Yorkshire.

I think Jackmanii Rubra is far more beautiful but perhaps my specially soft spot for this clematis is on account of its having grown and flowered so well for me for many years.* I prune it rather lightly and get some double blooms at the start of its season in early June, this running straight into its

*It died soon after I wrote that.

main crop, which is single – a beautiful shade with quite a lot of blue in it and the flower has a nice smooth texture.

Finally I feel impelled to bring in a clematis I have only started growing of late, but which looks irresistibly good on the page even though I know it must be bluer in reality than the reproduction shows it. Mr Fisk calls Rouge Cardinal 'a new variety from France that looks like becoming the best of the red clematis.' It flowers on its young wood and its flowers are not very large but well formed with 6 blunt-ended sepals and a velvety sheen on them. The stamens are pale.

PURPLE CLEMATIS

Daniel Deronda	Mme Grangé
Edouard Desfossé	Maureen
Gipsy Queen	Percy Picton
Guiding Star	Sir Garnet Wolseley
Horn of Plenty	Serenata
C. × *jackmanii*	Star of India
C. × *jackmanii* 'Superba'	The President
Lady Betty Balfour	Victoria

Purple clematis derive their deep, rich colouring from *C. viticella.* First among the large-flowered hybrids to have a purple bloom was *C.* × *jackmanii* itself, introduced in 1863 when it received a F.C.C. It is still going strong and anyone who has got as far as reading this book will almost certainly be growing it already. Enough said. I personally grow cv Superba in my own garden. It turned up as a sport on the Jackman nurseries (I imagine in the '80's or '90's as it did not feature in Moore & Jackman's 1877 publication) and has broader sepals that are also a little darker in colour. Probably an improvement but it all depends on what you like.

The hand-drawn black-and-white illustration of *C.* × *jackmanii* in Moore & Jackman shows a perfectly symmetrical (and idealised) flower with broad, overlapping sepals that is actually far more reminiscent of Star of India.

Star of India is very close to *C.* × *jackmanii* but was actually raised by Cripps of Tunbridge Wells and was awarded a F.C.C. in 1867, so it was a very early hybrid. It is not as vigorous as *C.* × *jackmanii* or Superba but has a good constitution (except for a predisposition to mildew which is shared by *C. × jackmanii*) and its flower is far more interesting because its purple colouring is relieved and varied by a broad central band of a reddish-plum shade.

Victoria is another clematis close to *C. × jackmanii* in every way except colouring, and far to be preferred in that department for it is a light shade of purple that becomes still lighter – almost mauve – as it fades, but never mawkish. It is as vigorous as they come and associates well, in the same season, with American Pillar, if you must grow that brilliant and harsh rose (I do, twice over, and very handsome it looks in the distance against a dark yew background). Victoria was a Cripps clematis and received a F.C.C. in 1870.

Yet another Cripps product and yet another to compete (successfully, I hope) for our favours with *C. × jackmanii* is Gipsy Queen, introduced in 1877. Its dark, velvety purple colouring is very near to *C. × jackmanii* 'Superba' but the flower is a different and, I consider, a more attractive shape, with six finely tapered sepals and a conspicuous boss of dark stamens, lacking in *C. × jackmanii*. Gipsy Queen comes in about a month later, being at its best in August, in the south of England. And it is vigorous; I have seen it competing happily and takingly with the white froth of *C. flammula*, which is even more vigorous. Indeed, I photographed this pretty pair on 14th September one year, which is an interestingly late date. Gardeners always have to write their books in the depths of winter, when it is difficult to recollect details of this kind accurately, so it is reassuring to find the evidence on a slide or in a diary or notebook. Another excellent pairing that I photographed in Scotland on 3 September 1975 was Gipsy Queen with the flame nasturtium, *Tropaeolum speciosum*, this being pure red.

Mme Grangé (F.C.C. 1877) must obviously come next. It is a very distinct clematis because of the way in which its sepals remain incurved along the length of their margins, even when the flower is fully opened. And the undersides of the sepals as thus revealed are woolly, creating a dusky impression. Some blooms eventually open out flat. There is sufficient red in their colouring to qualify this as a red clematis but 'deep velvety maroon-crimson, becoming purplish with age' (Moore & Jackman) is more accurate. Vita Sackville-West was crazy about this sumptuous clematis when she saw it in my garden and acquired several plants for Sissinghurst Castle forthwith. It is almost as vigorous as *C. × jackmanii*. Mme Grangé was raised by M. Théophile Grangé, a nurseryman of Orleans, by crossing *C. lanuginosa* and *C. viticella*, the same cross as produced *C. × jackmanii* in England. Indeed, these two clematis are so similar that the likelihood of *C. integrifolia* having also played a part in the parentage of *C. × jackmanii* (see page 19) seems remote.

Lady Betty Balfour is a unique clematis and marvellous when performing as it should, for it can fill the garden with dramatic colour in September and October when few fresh contributions from bold flowers are to be expected. Chrysanthemums, yes, but the vivid blue-purple (a little reddish in the newly opened flower) of Lady Betty with its lively cream eye, is in absolute contrast. And such a grower. Its vigour is prodigious. But it must have sun and warmth, otherwise it fails to flower altogether, so this is not a clematis for gardeners in the midlands or north. I hope it will flower in Edinburgh, from where Nora King, who has recently planted it, wrote me in April 1975 that it was named after her grandmother, 'whose garden near Woking, laid out by Gertrude Jekyll, was the first to make any impression on my consciousness.' Edinburgh has a very peculiar climate and it cannot be taken for granted that because it is far north a whole range of sun-loving or half-hardy plants will not do. Evergreen ceanothus, for instance, are a great feature of the Lothians, whereas in the West Riding of Yorkshire they are a dead loss.

Lady Betty Balfour received an A.M. when shown by Messrs. Jackman of Woking in 1912 and its parentage is interesting: Gipsy Queen × Beauty of Worcester.

We now begin to move away from the influence of *C. viticella* to larger flowered clematis capable of carrying a considerable (sometimes a main) crop early in the season. The President was one of Charles Noble's raising. (He was given to using the definite article, *viz.* The Czar, The Premier, The Kelpie and The Kelpie's Bride). It does, in fact, have *C. ×*

jackmanii as one parent but carries three crops of blossom from late May onwards and is vigorous enough tó make sufficient wood to carry its flowers on. The cupped blossom enables you to admire its silvery underside even whèn the wind is not blowing. This is a good clematis on the blue side of purple, especially as the flowers age. The young foliage is characteristically bronzed and almost identical with the closely related Daniel Deronda.

And it is from the same stable. Noble must have been a George Eliot fan: he named another clematis after her ('dark lavender in colour with a distinct odour of violets') but it has dropped out of the field. The parents of Daniel Deronda are said to be *C. lanuginosa* and *C. patens* so it is a little odd that it should so closely resemble The President. The main difference is in the lighter colouring down the centre of each sepal at all ages, in Daniel Deronda, whereas this paleness only appears in old sepals in The President. Also, Daniel Deronda is capable of carrying large, flattened, semi-double blooms early in the season. These can be tremendously exciting but are usually seen on pot-grown specimens grown under glass; seldom in the garden. I don't think this clematis is anywhere near so prolific as The President but it is good all the same and has a long season.

I got Guiding Star, I forget from where, some 20 years ago and I still have it but doubt whether it was correctly named, since it should be of the Jackmanii persuasion and similar to Star of India. Mine, when it doesn't get wilt first, flowers on the old wood more than on the young. It has a lively flower with pointed sepals and bright bluish purple colouring.

Sir Garnet Wolseley is an ancient clematis of Jackman's and as good as ever it was: one of the earliest in bloom, mid-May, with moderately large, well formed, rounded flowers deep lavender or light purple in colour and dark reddish stamens. It is very free and gives a good crop on young wood. Edouard Desfossé has not stood the test of time so well. It was always esteemed as one of the largest flowered of all clematis – light purple with a conspicuous reddish purple bar. It was introduced by Desfossé, another nurseryman at Orleans, in 1880 and is still listed but has lost something in vigour, I should say.

Pink and Mauve-Pink Clematis

Turning to more modern varieties, Percy Picton celebrates its raiser and was introduced shortly after the war. It carries the largest-sized flowers, on its old wood, purple on opening but soon becoming lavender and its anthers are dark. It flowers again on the young shoots. Certainly a good clematis. Sometimes I like its shape and sometimes I don't! Really I prefer Horn of Plenty which is of much the same colouring but has a large and somewhat cupped bloom. Its stamens, as in Fair Rosamond, are a tremendous feature. I have no idea where this one came from.

Serenata, from Tag Lundell, an amateur clematis enthusiast and breeder in Sweden, and introduced by Treasure's, is a useful two-season purple clematis. The large early blooms on old wood have 6 sepals; with their pale centre they remind me of the single blooms on Beauty of Worcester but they are light purple, not blue. Later blooms on young wood are mainly 4-sepalled.

Maureen is a particularly attractive colour, described in the R.H.S. Journal at the time it received an A.M. in 1956 as violet purple. There is a good deal of red in this violet. It is not a very vigorous clematis and needs little pruning.

PINK AND MAUVE-PINK CLEMATIS

Comtesse de Bouchaud	Margot Koster
Hagley Hybrid	Miss Crawshay
John Warren	Mrs Spencer Castle
Kathleen Wheeler	Proteus
Mme Baron Veillard	Twilight
Margaret Hunt	

These all have more or less of mauve in them. Kathleen Wheeler, indeed, starts a good deal darker than mauve; that kindly warming colour known as old rose. The central veins, of a darker, pinker shade add distinction to a flower with contrasting creamy stamens. Altogether an acquisition. We owe it to Mr Walter Pennell. Another of his clematis that has lately won wide acclaim is John Warren. In the newly opened flower we not only have a pinkish mauve bar down the centre of each paler sepal but the sepal margins are dark also, and this makes for a most unusual and striking bloom, especially as the anthers are reddish. The overall colour impression is pinkish lilac and early blooms can be very large indeed. They fade none too pleasantly.

Hagley Hybrid, an immediately post-war clematis of Mr Percy Picton's, has much the same habit: compact because it flowers so freely and over such a long period (from mid-June) on its young wood that there is little time or inclination for making a lot of extension growth. This is an encouraging clematis for the beginner, causing little worry. Its six boat-shaped sepals and dark centre compose a charming flower, and the dusky mauve-pink colouring is pleasing too, in the newly opened flower, but it does fade rather too far. Twilight is a recent product of Mr Picton's and has a well shaped flower, more rounded than Hagley Hybrid and with pale stamens against pink-mauve sepals. The last three all bloom on their young wood from June-July. And so does Margaret Hunt, which I include entirely on the strength of its picture in Mr Fisk's catalogue. Once again, it is dusky pink-mauve but I like the cut of its jib. The 6 sepals are rhomboid, rather sharply angled and with uniform gaps between them that actually suit the general symmetry of the flower. How it performs in the garden and whether it fades badly, I do not know. I must in honesty record that when I saw it at the Chelsea Flower Show in 1968 I noted that it was 'a miserable thing. A poor, smaller-flowered, dimmer edition of Hagley Hybrid.' But then it must have been forced, for that show. Colour in garden-grown plants is always more intense.

Mrs Spencer Castle dates back at least to 1913 when, on 1 July, it was shown to the R.H.S. but received no award. It is pale mauve-pink but large-flowered and semi-double when it blooms on the old wood. Like Lady Caroline Nevill, however, this one often misses out on the early performance and does it all on the young wood. Miss Crawshay, on the other hand, although of much the same colouring– a little pinker, actually – flowers entirely on its old wood in early summer and is habitually semi-double, opening wide to reveal pale stamens. Very charming. Jackman's introduced it around 1873. Proteus is a more dusky shade of pinkish lilac. Introduced by Noble and awarded the R.H.S. First Class Certificate in 1876, it is still a remarkable and outstanding clematis, so full of sepals at its first flowering as to resemble a rose or, perhaps even more nearly, a double opium poppy. Single flowers borne on young shoots are meek little things. Proteus would easily find a place in the top six best double large-flowered clematis.

Comtesse de Bouchaud must be accounted the most successful pink moderately-large-flowered clematis ever raised. It is close to *C. × jackmanii* in habit and appearance but, like Perle d'Azur with which it associates so well, was raised and introduced by Francisque Morel some time between 1900 and 1906 (when Morel ceased to be interested in clematis). Ernest Markham got an A.M. for it in July 1936. There is nothing subtle about Comtesse de Bouchaud; its shape is ordinary, its light pinky-mauve colouring might be accounted crude, judged in a vacuum or against an unflattering background, though it fits in excellently with the predominant greens of the average garden setting. But this clematis has a tremendous will to live and luxuriate and carry masses of blossom with the minimum of worry on our part. The season is June-July and there is little left after early August.

Margot Koster has a moderately early season, considering that it flowers on its young wood. If you went by the diameter of its flower pinned out like a butterfly on a board, you would class this as a large bloom, large as Comtesse de Bouchaud, but its sepals are narrow (after the Continental manner) and twisted and altogether delightfully informal and of a bright rosy colouring.

Finally, Mme Baron Veillard (introduced by Baron Veillard of Orleans in 1885) which, although of a lilac-rose colouring that we have met several times already, falls into a class of its own on account of its late flowering season – from the end of August till well into October. Like Lady Betty Balfour it may therefore fail to come to the boil in colder areas. The flowers are well shaped and freely produced. For those of us who can make a go of it, a thoroughly useful and welcome clematis, and vigorous withal.

Barbara Dibley	King Edward VII
Barbara Jackman	King George V
Bees Jubilee	Lincoln Star
Bracebridge Star	Marcel Moser
Capitan Thuilleaux	Mrs N. Thompson
C. W. Dowman	Nelly Moser
Fairy Queen	Sealand Gem

Many clematis have a deeper or more brightly coloured bar running down the centre of each sepal than is present in the remaining area, but there is a group of which Nelly Moser is typical that makes a speciality of this bicolor effect. These clematis tend to have fairly large flowers and pointed sepals and they all fade notably as the bloom ages. It seems sensible to consider them together.

Because of their fading, which commonly leads to a disappointingly washed out appearance in the bloom's later stages, Nelly Moser-type clematis are frequently recommended for north walls and other shady sites. This is sensible, but they will grow as happily in sun if required to.

Nelly Moser was raised in France by Moser, the Versailles nurseryman and was introduced in 1897. Next to *C.* × *jackmanii* it is probably the most popular large-flowered hybrid to this day, for it makes a terrific show in its late May to early June season and it has a robust constitution. The sepals, although long, are rounded at their tips so that the bloom itself is wheel-like, its vivid carmine bars taking on the role of spokes. I have never been able to make out why Nelly Moser's intensity of colouring varies so much even in the newly opened flower (before fading) and on the same plant in different years and in different parts of the same season. It is a generally observed fact that the intensest colouring, when almost the entire bloom may be carmine, occurs on October or even November blooms carried terminally on the young shoots. Autumn flowers on this cultivar are a welcome extra but they amount to little in terms of display.

Marcel Moser came out a year earlier and is very similar in

colouring but has a larger bloom and more pointed sepals. Those who grow it successfully will agree that it is superior to Nelly. It doesn't grow so strongly, however*, but that is not to say it is a difficult clematis. Given good soil it is a good doer and remarkably long-lived.

Fairy Queen was introduced in 1877, 20 years earlier than the foregoing and was one of Cripps's clematis; it was one of the first I owned as a boy and was a great thrill on account of its enormous blooms, 23cm across. They are pale flesh with a pink bar and flower in June. King Edward VII seems to have undergone a sea-change. Jackman's bred it by back-crossing one of their Wokingensis hybrids (which take after their *C. texensis* parent) with a large-flowered hybrid. A. G. Jackman in a note for the revised version of Moore & Jackman that never came to fruition observes that in this cross the companulate shape completely disappeared. King Edward VII was the result of crossing Fairy Queen and Sir Trevor Lawrence and the latter is the result of a cross between *C. texensis* (then known as *C. coccinea*) and Star of India. But Jackman describes King Edward VII as pucy violet, which is hard to square with what we have now: a betwixt and between sort of colouring with a pale crimson bar but otherwise indefinite colouring, although the flower has substance.

King George V is another strange cultivar. It has always had a reputation for shy flowering but has never been dropped by the nurserymen. Blooms are more apt to be carried late in the season on young wood than in others of this class and they have a singular beauty, especially as seen on young stock on the nursery! The dusky background to the bright pink bar conveys an extraordinarily sensuous, tactile quality. I have never seen or heard of a specimen giving a good account of itself in the garden, though it is hardy enough.

A large proportion of the developments in modern clematis have been along the Nelly Moser trail. Bees Jubilee is brighter and better if it thrives for you. It does not lack vigour but is markedly prone to wilt disease. From the same house of Bees came Sealand Gem 'a mauve without the pink tints of Nelly

*This was a recorded fact even in its earliest days. See Revue Horticole 1898 p. 303.

Moser' to quote Rowland Jackman's description in a lecture to the R.H.S. A strong clematis but somewhat lacking in character.

Then the two Barbara's. Barbara Dibley has the big flower and long pointed sepals of Marcel Moser. It is a brilliant and most exciting colour in the newly opened bloom and would really qualify for the red group. Its description as pansy-violet has always appealed to the public (as periwinkle blue for Mrs P. B. Truax and milk-white for Mrs Oud). This colouring certainly is to be found in pansies but so are many other colours, and pansy-violet means nothing special to me. Still, that's a personal matter. The centre of the flower is dark, also, but the whole creation fades lamentably to a kind of wasted, raddled mauve. Actually even this can strike one as rather beautiful in an off-beat way (like 'blue' roses). If pruned hard, it flowers well on its young wood but that is not normal treatment.

Barbara Jackman is one of the best of this bunch. The background to the carmine bar is far brighter and bluer than in any of the others and it can afford to fade. Old blooms retain their charm and mix well with the young. No need, therefore, to protect this one from the sun. It grows well.

Capitan Thuilleaux is one of Jim Fisk's modern introductions from France. My French dictionary tells me that capitan means swaggerer or bully, which seems an odd epithet to attach to a clematis. Perhaps Thuilleaux started as 'capitaine' but was demoted when he crossed the Channel. The flower's bright pinky carmine bar is exceptionally broad; the pale margins are correspondingly narrow. The flower form is as in Nelly Moser and the dark anthers likewise. A striking clematis but one gets the feeling, after a time, that there are too many in this category with a close family resemblance.

Pennell's have introduced those that follow and Lincoln Star (someone said it sounds like a race-horse) impresses me as the best of their bunch. As with Nelly Moser, the flower colouring can vary a great deal but in the garden, in early summer, it is a vivid raspberry pink that suffuses nine-tenths of the sepal area. The blooms are of only moderate size and truly star-like, with sharp points. It is not an over-vigorous clematis but happy

3

1. Marie Boisselot
2. Mrs Oud
3. Mrs George Jackman
4. Jackmanii Rubra
5. Miss Bateman
6. Fair Rosamond
7. Henryi
8. Yellow Queen

1. Mme Edouard André
2. Ville de Lyon
3. Crimson King
4. Ernest Markham
5. Duchess of Sutherland
6. Mme Grangé
7. Mme Julia Correvon
8. Jackmanii Rubra

once it has settled down. Bracebridge Star has a similar flower form and is elegant. I don't hold gaps between the sepals against it, but the lavender colouring is not very special.

C. W. Dowman is the pinkest clematis in this group that we have seen yet. If only it would hold the colouring of the newly opened flower, it would be wonderful, but it quickly fades to non-description. Mrs N. Thompson is (unlike its namesake, I hope) a real eye-catcher that sells on sight. The carmine bar is set dramatically against a deep violet base. The flowers are all sorts of shapes and not at all well formed when, as often happens, there are only 4 sepals. Although this clematis can grow strongly when established it is a slow starter.

CHAPTER 6

The Choice: Species and Small-Flowered Hybrids

*

(1) FOR CONSERVATORY AND SHELTERED WALLS

C. *afoliata*	C. *napaulensis*
C. *armandii*	C. *paniculata* 'Lobata'
C. *cirrhosa* var. *balearica*	C. *phlebantha*
C. *florida* cv's	

It is mid-February as I write. Only in the dead season is there time for this sort of major operation. I am surrounded by books, notes made over the past 10 years, trade catalogues, dogs in various attitudes of abandon before the fire – but many's the time when I should like to be able to nip out into the garden and verify some point or other that I am wanting to describe. To no avail. But there is one co-operative member of the genus that is now at the top of its form, *Clematis cirrhosa* var. *balearica*, better known as *C. calycina.* I picked a trail from the garden yesterday afternoon, boiled its stem for 40 seconds, immersed in water for an hour and it stands radiantly before me. There are 24 buds-and-flowers on it. They hang like green-mouthed bells but when you look into one you see the reddish brown freckles (against a pale green background) that are typical of the clone of this plant commonly grown in Britain. They look like mottled eggs, my gardener remarked, and two days ago a visitor (only keen visitors come near us at this season) likened these flowers to a hellebore's, as well he might, for they are close cousins.

It isn't just the flowers, in their axillary clusters of 1, 2 and 3, that one admires but the boldly toothed evergreen foliage, lightly bronzed at this winter season. Many evergreens take

66

on bronzed or purplish tints in the cold weather. It's the vegetable equivalent of a bottle nose.

And then there is its scent. Seldom is it warm enough in the garden for this to make an impact (whereas *Mahonia japonica* knocks you backwards in the current mild weather), but as soon as you bring the flowers into a living room they release their citrous fragrance, which is both astringent and sweet. Or they will fill a conservatory with their scent, provided they do not have to compete with *Jasminum polyanthum*.

My *C. cirrhosa* var. *balearica* grows on an 8ft wall and is planted on its north side, but most of its growth is on the wall top, where there is most light and if we get a hard frost its blossom will all be ruined. I should do better to grow it on a really high wall from whose protection it could not escape, or in some other sheltered corner, perhaps under an overhanging eave, where frost is a rare visitor. The plant is hardy through most of Britain – a point that was discussed by the R.H.S. Committee which gave this clematis an A.M. in January 1974 when Graham Thomas showed it. (Odd that such an old favourite should be thus honoured so late in the day, but the putting up of plants for award is a hit-and-miss affair and probably makes little difference to the popularity of a stalwart of this kind, one way or the other, since it is already widely acclaimed.)

Where conservatory space is available it will be well deserved and *C. cirrhosa* var. *balearica* will give you the greatest pleasure. It will then, at a minimum temperature of, say, 6 degrees C. start flowering in late autumn. As soon as flowering has ended, the plant should be pruned hard back to a metre or so from its roots, for this is a vigorous species and will otherwise occupy far too much space. The same treatment applies to several other clematis deserving of conservatory space and benefiting from it either because of their hardiness problems, their frailty or simply because they can acquit themselves so much better if not harassed by our stormy climate.

C. napaulensis is closely related to *C. cirrhosa*, is rather less hardy and would similarly benefit from greenhouse protection. My knowledge of it is confined to one large specimen on a high garden wall at Malahide Castle, Co. Dublin, in full flower at the time of my visit one February, though often blooming in January even in the open and in the late autumn under glass. It was absolutely smoothered in blossom and quite a spectacle, notwithstanding its modest colouring. The notable features of this species, in its season, are the crowded axillary flower clusters and the purple colouring of the long and conspicuously extruded stamens. There is no scent and the evergreen foliage, at its best, is moderately unattractive. This species received an A.M. as a cool greenhouse plant when exhibited by the Director of Kew on 22 October 1957.

C. phlebantha also comes from Nepal but was discovered by Polunin, Sykes and Williams as recently as 1952. It grows in the west of that country on hot dry cliffs at 2500 to 3500 metres and is sometimes of a trailing habit, at others makes an upright bush, only 0·6m high. Even as a trailer its branches, in the wild, are only 1·5m long. It is non-climbing but needs, in this country, a warm wall for protection and support. At first it was grown at Wisley under glass but it seems to be pretty hardy. Well worth growing, as much for its leaves as for its flowers. The leaves are pinnate and hairy, so much so on their undersides as to make them silvery here. There are usually 7 pinnae and these are boldly lobed. The leaf surface is heavily grooved with veins and the conspicuousness of the flowers' veining suggested the specific epithet. *Phlebantha* means grooved flower. These flowers usually have 6 sepals and are white, of an excellent shape (reminding me of *C. fargesii*), 3 to 4cm across and therefore bold enough to be effective.

The specimen I saw at Wakehurst, in Sussex, was 4 or 5 years old and clearly showed how differently a species can be expected to behave when it comes into the flesh-pots of English garden life. This specimen was 2·5m high on a wall of that height and 5m across. Its freedom of flowering doubtless depends on how much ripening its old wood has received and how much of this it has brought through the winter. By early August, only a few blooms remained but the main flowering season is in June-July.

C. phlebantha received the A.M. on 6 August 1968.

I now come to a clematis that has suffered a most unfortunate, because confusing, name change. For years, right back

into the last century it has been grown and greatly esteemed as
C. indivisa lobata. But the latest edition of Bean tells us
inexorably that we must call it *C. paniculata* 'Lobata' whereas
the clematis we knew as *C. paniculata* is correctly *C. maximowicziana*. What a bore.

Anyway, this clematis is one of the finest New Zealanders
and like all of that group it is dioecious. Its evergreen foliage is
pleasantly unobtrusive and the blossom is magically pure. I
grew it on a warm wall for several years and it flowered in
April. Then came a hard winter . . . But under glass we could
enjoy it without meteorological palpitations, in March at the
latest. In a cultivar named Stead's Variety, *C. indivisa lobata*
won a F.C.C. when shown to the R.H.S. by Lord Aberconway
on 1 May 1934. It was described as tender, then, but must
have been grown outside to be flowering so late.

And so we come to the famous *C. armandii*, always in great
demand, always in short supply. Its popularity is founded
partly on solid virtues, partly on sentiment – genuine but
unjustified.

C. armandii was introduced at the comparatively late date of
1900 by E. H. Wilson and is a native of central and western
China. It is hardier than is even now generally supposed and
can thrive, on a warm wall, in such an inhospitable spot as the
City of Birmingham. A sunny wall is advisable, in general, but
if there is a large shrub, as it might be a myrtle or a ceanothus,
projecting from the wall over which the clematis can fling
some of its vines, it will look all the better.

The main reason for armandii's popularity is because it is
evergreen, and gardening journalists are always cracking up its
splendid, bold, handsome evergreen foliage. *C. cirrhosa* is
popular for the same reason and more justly, I think, but then
C. armandii does have the edge over the latter in the department of flower power. The flowers are up to 5cm across and
fairly packed into each axil of the previous season's long trails.
They can make a most impressive display. On the other hand
they can fail to make any display. The reasons for this are not
always clear. That the swelling buds can be damaged by early
spring frosts is an undeniably frequent cause of failure. And,
although one so often reads that only the large-flowered

clematis hybrids are afflicted by wilt disease, *C. armandii* is actually one of the commonest victims. It is not so often that the whole plant is cut off near ground level (though this does happen) but that parts of the plant, branches and vines, are hit and die in a most unsightly manner on any part of the plant. *C. armandii* is also, incidentally, the one and only clematis I have known to be attacked by sap-sucking scale insects.

But there is another ticklish question. Some armandii stock going around carries miserably small flowers as a matter of genetical inevitability. Why don't the nurserymen propagate from stocks that are known to flower well, you may wonder? Well, some of the best flowerers are the most difficult to propagate. Jackman's used to have a magnificent clone called Snowdrift (the fact that you may come across Snowdrift in a trade catalogue does not necessarily mean – probably won't mean – that it is the same clone as the one I am writing about). But I have always found it quite swinish to propagate from cuttings. Whether for this reason or for another (the firm has dropped one third of the clematis varieties offered since it changed hands), Snowdrift is no longer stocked by Jackman's. As I said at the start, *C. armandii* is always in excess demand and nurserymen are continually obliged to buy stock in, so it is difficult, often impossible to know whether they are trading in a good strain or not. The plants will have been retailed long before they have flowered. I sometimes wonder if imported plants are not often mere seedlings, so mixed are they in appearance. It is well known that some of the earlier types from Wilson's seed produced handsome foliage but small, greenish white flowers. I should be wrong to paint too black a picture, though, because there is a lot of good stock in this country, too, and much of it is propagated here from parents known to be good performers.

The most popular clone of *C. armandii* is Apple Blossom. It is a wonderful selling name. Snowdrift is good but definitely shuddery. Apple Blossom spells April, the lilt of spring, balm in the air, bees, butterflies, bird song . . . tra! la! la! and tirralirra! I hate to disappoint, but the glow on Apple Blossom's cheek is of the ruddy, chapped variety, most noticeable on the opening buds, disappearing (mercifully) on the fully expanded bloom but a blush may return shortly before sepal-fall as is so often the way with aging white flowers. Apple Blossom received an A.M. on 9 March 1926 and a F.C.C. on 7 April 1936. These exhibits will have been from plants grown under glass and they point the moral. Apple Blossom grown under protection really does deserve its name. A pink blush is retained in the expanded bloom, the flowers are soft and lovable, unbuffeted by harsh spring weather and the *scent* . . . I haven't mentioned armandii's scent up to now but it is very strongly of vanilla, even in the garden. In the conservatory it is overwhelming.

The leaves of *C. armandii* are very large, smooth, hard to the touch. They rattle in the wind, disconsolately. You may say that they prattle in the wind, companionably, but I know better. All that noise means that the foliage is being bruised and it does become exceedingly dowdy long before winter's end. The more reason for choosing a sheltered site. But the young leaves are a marvel, I do admit, when very young and a beautiful light bronze colour.

The revised Bean recommends pruning *C. armandii* as little as possible but I think this is wrong. It is extremely vigorous, will make 4 or 5m of growth in a season and is not in the least reluctant to break from older wood. I knew a specimen grown on a cottage wall where space was limited and its owner pruned severely every year after flowering. The results were spectacular. Unpruned specimens tend to accumulate a lot of unsightly debris.

An early spring-flowering species that will appeal to the specialist is the curious and fascinating Rush-stemmed clematis, *C. afoliata*, from New Zealand. Its green stems perform the function of leaves and the latter are reduced to a mere tendril. There was a photograph of a vast specimen in Ernest Markham's book (published 1935) and he wrote that it had long since reached the top of an 8ft.-high wall. I have never seen one like that. It is worth risking in a sheltered place outside but would be safer under glass. And perhaps there, one might catch a whiff of the 'most pleasant Daphne odour' Markham describes. My clone has yielded my eager olfactories no scent at all. This clematis received an A.M. when exhibited by Miss Willmott of Great Warley, Essex on 11 May 1916. It was described as 'a hardy species suitable for walls'.

Because I don't know where else to fit them in I shall discuss the two extant cultivars of *C. florida* here. They are not early flowerers, like the foregoing, but they are good conservatory plants. Generally, however, they are grown on warm walls in the garden. They have a frail and ancient look that does not bely them. They seem to have stepped out of an old hand-painted illustration and it is a compliment to have them with us still, in the flesh.

C. florida 'Sieboldii', more often met with as *C. florida bicolor*, but also as *C. sieboldii*, was introduced in 1836 having originally been a variety cultivated in Japanese gardens. It is a wispy plant but may often surprise its anxious owner by growing and flowering with a will and apparently uninhibited by its ancient lineage. On other occasions it gives up the ghost without a struggle. Often likened to and mistaken for a Passion Flower, its structure is really far less intricate but it is a far more effective flower in the garden. Its six regular and well-formed white sepals frame the central feature, which is a boss of crowded staminodes or petal-like stamens; bright purple with paler flecks. As with so many double flowers, they are long-lasting; indeed, the centre of the flower lasts for quite a time after the sepals have been shed. The plant makes a good deal of young growth before starting to flower on it, in late June or early July, its season extending well into August. If you want something unusual and beautiful, here's your challenge, but don't ask for my shoulder to cry on if you fail.

Its team-mate is *C. florida* 'Plena' (syn. *C. florida* 'Alba Plena'). It was illustrated in Curtis's Bot. Mag. in 1805 and is exactly the same today. It was unobtainable in this country at the time I wrote my first clematis book but has returned to one or two nursery lists in the interval. Its habit is identical with *C. florida* 'Sieboldii's' but the central rosette of petal-like stamens is considerably enlarged and the overall colouring is greenish white. I hope that gardeners and nurserymen alike will keep it going for its extinction would be lamentable as the the dodo's, and there would be less excuse: it wouldn't make a meal.

(2) THE ATRAGENES

C. alpina	*C. alpina sibirica*
C. alpina 'Columbine'	*C. alpina sibirica* 'White Moth'
C. alpina 'Frances Rivis'	*C. macropetala*
C. alpina 'Pamela Jackman'	*C. macropetala* 'Maidwell Hall'
C. alpina 'Ruby'	*C. macropetala* 'Markham's Pink'

In April there starts the season of the atragenes. These are clematis that always feature petal-like staminodes in the centre of the flower, not because of an aberration or mutation selected by man, but because this is their nature. Some botanists would hive this group off into a separate genus, *Atragene*. I am glad that most of them have so far refrained. However, it is easily recognisable as a natural group and it comprises the species *C. alpina* and *C. macropetala* from Europe and Asia; *C. verticillaris* from North America. The last can be quickly dismissed; it sometimes makes its appearance in a nurseryman's list but never seems to establish well in this country. My own plant of it was unthrifty, while it lived.

In this group the flowers nod; they hang over the plant like crowds of fairy lanterns – rather a hackneyed simile but so apt that I cannot think of any improvement. A few blooms are commonly produced at the ends of the current season's shoots in summer and autumn, but the vast majority are borne, singly, in the axils of the previous season's vines, in April and May. I first saw *C. alpina* growing wild in the Engadine in Switzerland, where it scrambled over rocks in open woodland. That was in July, but then spring arrives late, above 2000 metres.

The typical colouring is blue. As you would expect, a number of improved selections have been made. That with the longest sepals is called Frances Rivis (though it first, mistakenly, received its A.M. in 1965 as Blue Giant) and was cultivated by the eponymous lady in her garden at Rosehill, Saxmundham, Suffolk. But the original seedling was raised by Sir Cedric Morris, increased by cuttings by Hilda Davenport-

Jones and subsequently introduced and named by her. The sepals are up to 5cm long.

Columbine is a delightful light blue of Ernest Markham's raising and Ruby I take to be the plant he exhibited at the same time in 1937 as *C. macropetala* 'Ruby', though it is clearly an alpina. The colouring is a dusky reddish-mauve, not entirely satisfactory. Pamela Jackman, named after Rowland Jackman's daughter, is a fine deep blue. I have it clambering over a *Pieris*, whose shrimp-red young foliage is at its brightest just when the clematis is flowering. They contrast well.

C. alpina sibirica has white or off-white flowers and its foliage is a paler green. A correspondent in Norway tells me that a small colony of it grows there, near Lillehammer, in quite severe conditions (minus 30 degrees C.), that it is not found at all in Sweden but recurs in Finland, again in a very restricted locality. Of course it has a wide Asiatic distribution. The cultivar to grow, of this, is White Moth. I think it is really my favourite of the whole atragene group. In *C. alpina* itself, the staminodes are short and scarcely show, but White Moth is more like *C. macropetala* in having long, conspicuous staminodes that fill the bloom out in a plump and pleasing fashion. Its white flowers go very appropriately with its pale green foliage and it flowers in mid and late May after the main alpina season is past. It is less vigorous than its team mates but no less healthy.

C. macropetala was introduced from China by Purdom and later by Farrer (around 1914) and received the A.M. on 24 April 1923. It is more showy than *C. alpina* because of its full flower and the extruded staminodes. Its colouring can be indifferent but most nurseries trade in good colour forms only, whether they call them by special cv names like Lagoon or Maidwell Hall or not. I got *C. macropetala* without frills, from one source and Maidwell Hall from another and they seemed to me identical.

C. macropetala 'Markham's Pink' (sometimes incorrectly listed as Markhamii) was of Ernest Markham's raising and gained an Award of Merit on 5 March 1935 – probably a forced plant. It is rosy mauve and purple (not pink, of course), and contrasts well with a blue form of macropetala. Vita Sackville-West had the idea of growing the two together in an

Ali-Baba jar, from which they were allowed to cascade at their will. The idea was a good one and has been much repeated.

As a group, then, these atragenes are remarkable for their gaiety and freshness. They will thrive as well in a sunless position as elsewhere and they are excellent mixers with shrubs of moderate vigour to match their own. If they fail to flower it is probably because the birds have pecked out and eaten their developing buds though late frost on an exposed plant could also be lethal.

(3) THE MONTANA GROUP

C. chrysocoma	C. montana wilsonii
C. chrysocoma sericea	C. montana rubens cv's
C. montana	Elizabeth,
C. montana 'Grandiflora'	Picton's Variety,
C. montana rubens	Pink Perfection,
	Tetrarose etc.

The montana group of clematis is easily recognised. It stands apart from the rest in appearance and its members are all so vigorous that they may be set the popular task of climbing into and draping quite large trees. If you have a number of trees you want pepped up in this way, you will soon discover that the variations on the montana theme are all pretty much alike. All are either pinky-mauve or white, all flower in May or only slightly later, all have 4 sepals as a general rule. At flowering they are exceedingly prolific but the display lasts little longer than a fortnight. I don't hold this against them. After all you can grow them in places where the alternative would most probably be to grow nothing, so everything they give can be regarded as a bonus.

Let us start with *C. montana* itself and its natural 'pink' variety, *C. montana rubens*. The former was introduced by Lady Amherst from the Himalaya in 1831, the latter by E. H. Wilson from China in 1900. Bean optimistically describes the latter as 'a beautiful rosy red'. It is rosy mauve, at best but often of so washed out a colouring that you wish it were white. The reason for these poor forms (I have several in my garden) is that *C. montana* seeds itself so readily and one is loath to get rid of a self-grown seedling if it has placed itself well. There are many named clones and these will predictably give more satisfaction than the self-sown product, but you cannot rely on these clones being true to name, even so. Pink Perfection, as I once had it, was indistinguishable from Elizabeth, but Fisk makes clear distinctions between the two.

Clematis montana is white. You don't have to call it montana alba or anything of that sort: it is white by definition. The gardening public is often unaware of this and think that, if they order a montana, it will be pink, which is, of course (but why, all the same?) the more popular colour. If they want a pink montana they must say so.

Another misconception arises over the question of scent. Because the pale pink clone of *C. montana rubens* called Elizabeth is sold mainly on its strong vanilla scent, there is a widespread notion that *C. montana* is not generally scented. But, on the contrary, it often is, both in the white species and in many clones of *C. montana rubens*. I have a far more strongly coloured *C. montana rubens* than Elizabeth but its scent is terrific; so is that of the old white *C. montana* in my rose garden, and its blooms are 7 or 8cm across – but the sepals are narrow.

This is another point to watch out for: width of sepal. I don't mind them fairly narrow, myself: they look like the sails of a windmill, but you may prefer a less lean and hungry flower, something more prosperous and full. *C. montana* 'Grandiflora' is that; so are the pink clones Elizabeth and Tetrarose; also *C. chrysocoma* and *C. c. sericea* and *C. × vedrariensis*.

Despite its pale colouring, I do think Elizabeth is a good clone with a very sizeable flower. Remember, though, that if you plant it in a shady position (as I have, with an enormous mulberry tree on one side of it and an enormous apple on the other) the flowers will come practically white. You may not mind this and I do not, but these words may prevent you from telling the nurseryman that he supplied you with the wrong variety.

Picton's Variety is as deep a colour as I have seen (but not so deep if grown in shade, funnily enough – you might think that absence of bleaching sunlight would give rise to stronger colouring, but this is not so) and I have a high regard for this cultivar, which often has 5 or even 6 sepals in its flower instead of the normal four. It is not quite as vigorous (though just as healthy) as the general run of *C. montana rubens* and this can be an advantage if you want a pink montana but don't want to be smothered by it. Not much scent, here. Incidentally the pigmentation of these pink montanas shows very clearly in their young stems, leaf stalks and foliage: the deeper the flower colouring, the deeper the dye throughout the plant.

A popular clone at the moment is Tetrarose. It was produced artificially in Holland, the plant's chromosome number being doubled by treatment with colchicine. Its flowers and foliage are hence larger and coarser than have heretofore been seen. I have also noticed a marked tendency to die-back in young shoots during the winter. You can have it (probably you already have and I shall receive a stream of angry letters).

Two more points about *C. montana* and *C. montana rubens* are worth noting. There are some clones that, from young rooted cuttings, take several years of growing and settling down before they start flowering. In general, montanas flower abundantly from the first year and never look back, so the other condition can be a worry. The perplexed owner wonders if it needs pruning. On the contrary, he should leave well alone. In due course, his plant will flower as freely as any other and once it has started it won't have second thoughts. This was the case with the plant of *C. montana* 'Grandiflora' that I used to own – but I'm sure there are many clones around under this name and that some of them are precocious flowerers. It was also the predicament of a pink montana that I bought from the late Hilda Davenport-Jones – a great plantswoman, and I did not regret my purchase but it was a slow starter.

It grew into a Blenheim Orange apple tree. This was not a clever association and brings me to my second point. Montanas flower in May at much the same season as apples. If you fling a pink montana into a pink apple tree and there is pink apple blossom all around, no-one will look at it once, let alone twice.

Now we come to *C. montana wilsonii*, which is another natural variety introduced by the eponymous Wilson. It is immensely popular as a follow-on to montana itself because, as you will read in every textbook except mine, its flowers, to quote Bean, 'appear in July and August.' He also states that it has larger white flowers, 3in. in diameter. The Nursery firm of J. Veitch & Sons called it 'the autumn flowering C. montana'! ! In Curtis's Botanical Magazine (t.8365, 1911) its flowering season is given as 2 months later than *C. montana*, and it is said to flower from the nodes of the previous season's wood. How it could do this as late as July, when the whole plant would be a mass of young growth, is hard to imagine.

There are at least two, completely different, clones purporting to be this clematis, going around. There is a breath-taking example of the one I feel confident to be the genuine article growing on Keillour Castle (home of my cousin, Mary Knox Finlay) in Perthshire. I have seen this plant on many occasions in early summer and it normally starts flowering in mid-June. It is slow to get going and if you see it at the start of its flowering period you will think what a miserable thing: greenish white and spidery. But the whole plant, from roof to ground – a matter of 12m (40ft.) is one sheet of white and giving off great wafts of hot chocolate aroma. It is most impressive. The flowers are actually 9cm (3½in.) in diameter but the sepals look narrow because, in the mature flower, their margins roll back. The stamens make a prominent brush. Now, this is habitually at its peak around 24 June, which is certainly a month later than most montanas. Not the two or more months some authorities would lead us to expect, but still very well worth cultivating as a sequel to *C. montana* and without overlap.

The plant I originally bought from Jackman's may well have been this but I was so disappointed in the miserable, greenish white flowers of the young plant that I discarded it (and so have Jackman's) before I had given it a real chance and allowed it to develop to maturity.

Meantime Percy Picton had got hold of a clone that he believed to be the true *C. montana wilsonii* and it is the clone till recently offered by Treasures of Tenbury and myself. It is as handsome a white montana as I have seen, with broad sepals and hence an exceptionally well-formed flower. But it blooms only a few days later than others of its kind and it is without scent. A. G. Jackman, in revision notes for Moore & Jackman (circa 1910), mentions fragrance. Raymond Evison tells me that this is the same plant as Hillier and Fisk offer as *C. chrysocoma sericea* and *C. spooneri*, respectively.

Questions of identity still plague us when we turn to *C. chrysocoma*, which was discovered in Yunnan, W. China, by Delavay in 1884 and presented to Kew by Monsieur de Vilmorin in 1910. It cannot have been long there when Bean wrote of it (Trees & Shrubs Hardy in the British Isles, 1st edition 1914) as a 'semi-woody shrub 6 to 8ft., perhaps more, high'; he also writes of its 'short, erect habit' and of being 'rather tender at Kew.' These entries remain unaltered in the latest, revised edition of Bean of 1970. They bear no relevance to the plant as we know and grow it, which climbs with a will to 6 or 9 metres and appears – at any rate in maturity – (I have had winter casualities among young plants) to be as hardy as *C. montana*. If a shrubby form is still extant, I should like to meet it. Fully hardy or not, it would be an acquisition. It figured in Curtis's Bot. Mag. (t.8395) in 1911 and was said to have died to the ground at Kew in its first winter (1910–11). Its illustration has an unreal and stylised appearance but gives a distinctly chunky impression. I think the plant was written up before its appearance and capabilities were properly known.

C. chrysocoma is a very beautiful clematis with more quality (that indefinable something) than *C. montana*. Young leaves, stems and flower buds are all covered with soft down (*chrysocoma* means with golden hair). The leaves are very handsome, with their bold lobing. The flowers are borne on extra long stalks and they hence present themselves importantly. They are a soft but definite rosy mauve, of an excellent shape with 4 broad sepals, but no scent.

It is a habit in this species, especially when growing actively in youth or because it has been pruned, to carry a second, spasmodic crop of extra-fine blossoms on its young trails. This explains how it managed to get an Award of Merit on 7 July (when exhibited by Ernest Markham in 1936).

C. spooneri was recognised by Rehder and Wilson who

described it under this name, as being a close relation of
C. chrysocoma. It is now generally accepted (i.e. Lloyd now ac-
cepts it) as being a variety of the latter and should be known
as *C. chrysocoma* var. *sericea*. This seems sensible. The leaves
are similarly broad for their length, downy on both surfaces.
The flowers are bold, 8cm across, odourless. In the clone I
acquired from Captain Collingwood Ingram there is a slight
pinkish flush along the central veins of each sepal, which
seems appropriate to the species, but as mentioned above the
clone offered by Hillier *et al.* is pure white. There is no scent in
either case but plenty of vigour.

The cross between *C. chrysocoma* and *C. montana rubens* is
called *C. × vedrariensis*. In trade catalogues you often meet it
as Spooneri Rosea. The original cross was made by Messrs.
Vilmorin, the famous Versailles nursery firm, and they first
exhibited it in 1914. Similar crosses have been made on a
number of occasions since, sometimes using *C. chrysocoma
sericea* as one parent with *C. montana rubens* as the other.
Various clones such as Highdown and Hidcote have been
named, though the latter appears to be a good form of
C. montana rubens pure and simple.

C. × vedrariensis received an A.M. when exhibited by
Ernest Markham on 9 June 1936. It is always an excellent
clematis – just about the best going for size and quantity of
blossoms of a good pink colour on an ultra-vigorous plant. I
find it roots and gets going from cuttings much more slowly
than the montanas themselves.

(4) THE TEXANS

C. addisonii	Duchess of Albany
C. crispa	Etoile Rose
C. pitcheri	Gravetye Beauty
C. texensis	Sir Trevor Lawrence
C. viorna	

Clematis texensis is potentially one of the most exciting
species within the genus. Its colouring (and, incidentally, the
size of its flowers) varies greatly and may be pinkish or purplish but at its best is pure, bright red. The flower form is

5

1. *C.* × *jackmanii* 'Superba'
2. Victoria
3. Perle d'Azur
4. Huldine
5. Comtesse de Bouchaud

6. Hagley Hybrid
7. Gipsy Queen
8. Ascotiensis
9. Star of India
10. John Warren

1. Percy Picton
2. Sir Garnet Wolseley
3. Horn of Plenty

4. The President
5. Guiding Star
6. Etoile de Paris

intriguing, too, so it is no wonder that hybridists both here and on the Continent were busying themselves at the turn of the century on breeding texensis features into the modern garden hybrids. Their efforts met with considerable success but came to an abrupt halt in the early 1900's. The clematis was suffering a temporary eclipse at this time, mainly on account of wilt disease and its serious effect on the clematis market which, in its turn, put a damper on developments in clematis breeding from which the plant has never fully recovered. We know more about wilt disease and how to live with it, at last, and it is to be hoped that the charm and appeal of cultivars like Etoile Rose and Duchess of Albany will encourage a few enterprising clematis fans to probe further in the texensis field. There is obviously scope for development, here.

Clematis viorna is usually taken as the type for a group of clematis from the South Eastern United States having urn- or pitcher-shaped flowers consisting of 4 thick, leathery sepals with connate (i.e. joined) margins, opening out only at the tips. This section is sometimes called *Viornae* sometimes *Urnigerae*. The plants are climbers but often herbaceous or sub-shrubby; that is, dying back a good deal if not right to the base, in winter.

Of *C. viorna* Bean writes 'Although interesting and curious, this species is not particularly attractive.' If our interest and curiosity are aroused, are we not attracted? However, Bean is clearly using the word attractive in its popular sense and one must admit that small flowers of subfusc colouring are not calculated to make the onlooker put on his dark glasses, gasp, jump back in horror or upwards for joy. I'm fond of this species and have grown it for many years, but the conspicuous seed heads are its main feature. I have likened them to tropical spiders (though they have far more than the quota of 8 legs to which even the largest and most tropical spider must, presumably, be limited).

In another species of this group that I have seen *C. crispa* to wit, the colouring was pale bluish, rather like Davidiana, and the sepals more spreading than usual among *Viornae*, and twisted. I have also clapped eyes on *C. addisonii*, which is rosy purple outside, cream within and along the outer margins.

Most of these clematis come readily from seed (*C. viorna* certainly does) and one can sometimes locate this in the lists sent out by Botanic Gardens.

C. pitcheri was supposed to have been used as well as *C. texensis* in the late 19th century hybridising work done on the Continent, but there was some confusion of identity, here, and it seems probable that *C. texensis* was, in fact, being used all the time.

Let us get back to this species and see what it has done for us and we for it. It is not supposed to be fully hardy but seems to be pretty nearly so in Britain and is, as I have seen it at Malahide Castle, beautiful as well as curious and interesting. But it rarely comes on the market and when it does, you're usually offered a seedling which is more than likely to give disappointing results. The fact is that *C. texensis* is a bit of a pig to propagate from cuttings. The little seed of it that has come my way has failed to germinate.

C. texensis is said to have been introduced into Europe in 1868. It was taken up and improved by Max Leichtlin (I owe the ferreting out of this information to Hugh Thompson) who had his own private botanic garden at Baden Baden. In those days the species was known as *C. coccinea*. In William Robinson's publication 'The Garden' 8 August 1903, Leichtlin wrote the following note: 'Of *Clematis coccinea* I have by constant selection and constant sowings now produced a fine seedling, the flowers of which are three times the size of the wild plant.' This would seem to be a different plant from the *C. coccinea major* referred to by Bean, of which a plant once grew at Abbotswood. The flowers of this were only half as large again as in the normal species. Both the one and the other have disappeared, in any case.

But Max Leichtlin was also the first person, around 1885, to cross *C. coccinea* with large-flowered hybrids. He passed on the handsome deep reddish purple variety so obtained to Louis Späth, after which we hear no more of it. (This cross is recorded in 'Les Clematites' by Boucher and Mottet 1898). Leichtlin was also responsible for the introduction of *C. coccinea* to England in 1880.

In his notes for the revision of Moore & Jackman, A. G.

Jackman pencilled in: 'In the summer of 1890 another interesting new type was raised at the Woking Nurseries by crossing C. Star of India with pollen from the American species *C. coccinea,* which resulted in the introduction of the pretty campanulate hybrids, C. Countess of Onslow, C. Duchess of Albany, C. Duchess of York, Grace Darling, Sir Trevor Lawrence and Admiration, showing great variety in shades of colours not previously obtained in Clematis, intermediate in sizes between the two parents, of more open campanulate form than *C. coccinea,* but partaking very closely to it in the substance of the sepals and foliage and also in the character of the growth, being of a sub-shrubby habit.'

These clematis became known as the Wokingensis hybrids. Only Duchess of Albany and Sir Trevor Lawrence remain certainly with us. A variety is marketed as Grace Darling in New Zealand but the coloured transparencies I have seen of this exactly resemble Duchess of Albany. A. G. Jackman describes Duchess of Albany as we know it today: 'bright pink, deeper down the centre, softening down to a lilac pink round the margin . . . .' Grace Darling he describes without differentiation as 'bright rosy carmine'. Countess of Onslow is a puzzle. I once owned what was supposed to be this variety (I had it from Jackman's). It had bell-shaped flowers with 4 sepals, pale pink at the margins deepening to cerise at the centre on both surfaces, but the colour transition was more marked on the outside. A. G. Jackman, however, describes the flower as 'bright violet purple with a broad band of scarlet down the centre of each sepal'. A very different matter. Anyway, I lost my plant of whatever it was in the '63 winter. Jackman's still list Countess of Onslow but no one has been able to buy a plant from them for many years, so it rather looks as though we have lost both the Countess and the pseudo-Countess.

Of the two Wokingensis hybrids left, Duchess of Albany is a highly satisfactory clematis. Its bells are rather elongated and it is as near pink as you will find in a clematis. It dies back but not all the way back in the winter and can make 3 or 4 metres of growth in a season. Its bells are held upright (like the blooms of a lily-flowered tulip) in an open situation and it associates particularly prettily, as I have seen it in John Treasure's garden, with the powder-blue panicles of *Ceanothus* 'Gloire de Versailles'.

I was responsible for rescuing Sir Trevor Lawrence from oblivion. It grows at Sissinghurst Place, Kent, in the garden belonging till recently to Mrs Lindsay Drummond, was planted by her mother-in-law years ago and was fortunately labelled with one of those embossed metal efforts that usually outlast the plants they are identifying. Mrs Drummond allowed me to take cuttings, which root easily. The plant grows for me over a *Cotoneaster horizontalis* and is a real eye-catcher; shaped like Duchess of Albany and with 4, 5 or 6 sepals but of a luminous cherry red colouring. A. G. Jackman's 'bright crimson' will do. Sir Trevor Lawrence, the man, was for long President of the RHS.

Now we come to what is undoubtedly the pick of the bunch, though always in short supply (for no valid reason, that I can see). Unlike the last two, the flowers of Etoile Rose are nodding; they are open-bell shaped and rather short. The plant dies right to the ground or within 0·4 metres of it each winter but is immensely vigorous (3 or 4m in a season), starts flowering early or mid-June and continues for 2 or 3 months with remarkable freedom and reliability. Like other texensis hybrids, it is subject to mutilation by mildew, so I would recommend an open site unless you are prepared to take protective measures. The flower has 4 sepals which are silvery pink at the margins, deep cherry purple in the centre.

Nearly all the plants now being grown originated at Abbotswood, Stow-on-the-Wold, where it was introduced by the then owner, Mr Mark Fenwick in 1929 or '30, from a Monsieur Chenault in France. Fenwick showed it to the RHS on 4 July 1939 as *C. viticella* 'Etoile Rose' and it was sent for trial to Wisley. War intervened. The Sunningdale Nurseries, through Mr Graham Thomas, subsequently obtained stock from the Abbotswood plant and got an Award of Merit for it on 7 July 1959. Hugh Thompson has traced the early history of this cultivar (Journal RHS No. 95, p. 189–190). It was described in the List No. 158 (1903) of V. Lemoine et Fils, and Lemoine was the raiser. He gave the parentage as *C.* × *globulosa* and a variety (unspecified) of *C. viticella*. The parentage of *C.* × *globulosa,* also raised by Lemoine, was *C. douglasii var. scottii* and *C. texensis.* If you consider the open bells and the way they are presented, it is not so surprising to find that *C. viticella* played a part in the making of Etoile Rose. *C. douglasii* var. *scottii*, the purely herbaceous, outlying species from the west side of the United States, is a surprise, however.

Finally, Gravetye Beauty. We know that nearly all the clematis raised and exhibited from Gravetye by William Robinson and Ernest Markham came to them originally as seedlings from Morel, and this one was no exception as was expressly stated when exhibited to the RHS (it received an A.M.) by Ernest Markham in September 1935. It was raised by Morel of Lyons and introduced to England by William Robinson in 1914. Morel had been using *C. texensis (C. coccinea)* for hybridisation but what the other parent was is hard to guess. The blooms start the typical elongated-bell shape of the Wokingensis hybrids, but then open wide into a narrow-limbed star of 4, 5 or 6 sepals with inrolled margins. The shape at this stage is not particularly good but all in all this is an excellent clematis, of a rich crimson colouring. Often it dies back to the ground in winter but when it keeps any old wood, it starts flowering in June; otherwise not till August. It is a thoroughly good doer but does not make an inconvenient length of growth and is hence suitable for association with shrubs of moderate vigour such as *Paeonia delavayi*.

In the Revue Horticole of 1904 (p. 308) there is a delightful plate of 3 of Morel's texensis hybrids, the 3 other parents used in these crosses being Gipsy Queen, Comtesse de Bouchaud and Ville de Lyon. Unfortunately these hybrids have disappeared.

In a letter to me from John Treasure written in 1971, he remarks that texensis hybrids seldom set seed on their own but that when he pollinated his Etoile Rose with *C. viticella,* the 3 blooms thus treated set good seed. 'I am determined one day to produce more of these lovely clematis (I'm so fed up with the Large flowered ones!!!).' This can happen!!!

C. *campaniflora*	Minuet
C. *viticella*	Pourpre Mat
Abundance	Purpurea Plena
Alba Luxurians	Purpurea Plena Elegans
Etoile Violette	Royal Velours
Kermesina	Rubra
Little Nell	Venosa Violacea

And so we move easily forward to C. *viticella* and its satellites. C. *viticella* has a place in the parentage of so many hybrids that I am reluctant to use its title for a group that is bound to be arbitrary. Why is Huldine not here?, you may ask, why not Margot Koster? If they are being excluded, why not Etoile Violette also? My only answer is that I have grouped them as I have for my own convenience. Full Stop.

John Gerard wrote of C. *viticella* 'it climbeth aloft and taketh hold with his crooked claspers upon everything that standeth nere unto it.' As you would expect of a species that has been cultivated in this country both for itself and as a stock for grafted varieties, since the 16th century; that is, moreover, easily rasied from seed and that grows wild almost on our doorstep in South Europe, C. *viticella* is very variable even before you start crossing it with this and with that. It has far greater elegance in the manner its flowers are presented than any of the cultivars we shall consider. Flower size varies a lot: in a good strain flowers may be 8 or 9cm across, but they look less, for there are only 4 sepals and they are narrow or look narrow, their margins being often rolled back. The beauty of this species, to my way of thinking, is that the flowers all nod and that they are held well out from the plant on extra-long stalks. Stalks and flowers are purple, the colouring being more intense on the upper side of the bloom, so it is a pleasure to look down on it.

In none of the viticella hybrids (and I feel sure they are all hybrids rather than selections or mutations) is the same elegance retained; none have the long stalk and the flowers, if they nod at all, do not do so consistently. They look out at you boldly rather than down, demurely.

Perhaps Alba Luxurians comes nearest to its parent in charm and elegance. We have already remarked on the narrow boundary between leaves and sepals in *Clematis*. The earliest blooms of Alba Luxurians are entirely green, some of their segments broadened and lobed and closely resembling leaflets. The normal condition in the main crop of blossom is a white sepal with green tips and dark anthers. Sometimes the flower is white throughout. There is a tendency in the foliar flowers for the sepals not to be shed, when dying, but to remain in a brown condition on the plant. This doesn't matter too much. It received the A.G.M. in 1931.

Bean opines that this clematis was probably raised at Veitch's Coombe Wood nursery. Its name was pencilled into Moore & Jackman by A. G. Jackman for his proposed revision, so it has been in existence for at least 70 years. There were whitish cultivars of *C. viticella* style around before this.

From the time it was first brought into cultivation, *C. viticella* has been curiously ready to produce double sports (as one imagines the early examples must have been) and hybrids. Gerard cultivated both *C. viticella* and the double flowered Plena: 'they grow in my garden at Holborn and flourish exceedingly.' (Why couldn't he have made some less banal observations?) Bean says of the double-flowered variety that it is one of the least attractive 'owing to an excessive multiplication of the sepals, which gives the flower a heavy, lumpy aspect.' He was wrong in writing of only one double variety and one wonders which of the many that were current in his day he was thus anathematising. Graham Thomas is as fastidious a gardener as we have among us today, and writes of the one he called *C.v. elegans plena*: 'As a rule, double clematises do not appeal to me but this has such a neat rosette of flattened petals, about 2½ inches across, and its colour is of such a soft lilac purple, reminiscent of some of the old roses, that it seems too good to be lost' (Journal RHS 90 – 1965 – p. 402). The lilac-purple, old-rose flowers that he describes are, indeed, almost brown, and very intriguing at close range. The plant is vigorous and gives no trouble in cultivation. It grew in Mark

Fenwick's garden at Abbotswood and, like Etoile Rose, was put into circulation again by the Sunningdale Nurseries through Mr. Thomas's connection with that firm. They listed it as *C. viticella elegans plena* but Treasures of Tenbury have subsequently re-named it Purpurea Plena Elegans. This needs further explanation and a new paragraph.

At the turn of the last century and this, Lemoine of Nancy and Morel of Lyons were bringing out a number of double viticellas. Two of the latter's were described by Edouard André in the Revue Horticole of 1899. These were Viticella purpurea plena and Viticella purpurea plena elegans. Treasure's have decided on the latter as the possible/probable original of the Abbotswood Elegans Plena. The other name, Purpurea plena, they gave to a double viticella of which they received blooms and propagating material from a garden in Dorset (or Devon; they forget which). I never saw this and they subsequently lost their stock of it, but I am given to understand that its flowers are (or were) of a bluer shade of purple than the other. André doesn't help much, because in describing the flower colour of Purpurea Plena and Purpurea Plena Elegans, he in both cases gives it as 'violet-pourpre foncé' – deep violet-purple. All in all I think it may fairly be said that you pay your money and you make your choice. We could be growing Morel's clematis or we could be growing others – of his or of someone else's.

A similar muddle with Kermesina and Viticella Rubra. No doubt they were distinct at one time, but Kermesina as seen today is identical with Rubra and Percy Picton told me that the latter was the correct name. At Sissinghurst Castle they have several red viticella hybrids that are similar but not quite the same. They are unnamed and no-one can say just what they are. The original Kermesina was raised by Lemoine.

Under whichever name you get it, this clematis is first class: of a bright colouring, effective and prolific. Also very vigorous, easily making 4m of growth in a season. Abundance comes nearest to this in colouring and is very similar in size and habit. The colour is a bluer shade of red and lighter. G. S. Thomas calls it 'warm claret-crimson', but I should be deeply suspicious of any claret with so much blue in it. Generally speaking this is a most satisfying clematis but I must in honesty record that with me it flowers shyly, although its vigour is terrific. I have it in heavy soil – which it obviously likes – and it does not receive much sunlight until after noon. If it can behave like this in one garden it may in another.

Abundance was one of the seedlings given by Ernest Markham to Jackman's and was named by them. There is therefore a strong probability that it was one of Morel's raising and was among those obtained by William Robinson before the First World War at the time when Morel turned from nursery work to garden design. The same provenance is likely to apply to Minuet and Little Nell, both named and introduced by Markham, whose wife's name was Nell.

Neither of these varieties has received an award and I can quite understand this as they are essentially garden plants, effective in a garden setting but not when divorced from it. Both have typical small viticella flowers and are pale in colouring – basically white, in fact, but Minuet is margined in light purple and Little Nell in a paler mauve. You may suspect that they will look pasty and anaemic but this is not actually the case.

Royal Velours is the darkest of the dark. It has a similar history to the above with a strong suspicion of Morel as raiser. William Robinson exhibited it to the RHS in August 1934, but whereas he got an award for Huldine on that day, Royal Velours was passed over. But it got the A.M. when shown by Walter Bentley of Quarry Wood on 20 July 1948. There is a famous specimen at Hidcote. Graham Thomas wrote (Journal RHS 1965) of its being of intense dark wine-purple, velvety texture and of annually causing much comment in association with the orange-red fruits of the Japanese wine-berry *(Rubus phoenicolaseus)*. Very dark clematis do need careful placing to be effective.

Pourpre Mat is probably another such, though I have not seen it and it is no longer offered but may still exist on Jackman's nursery. This was definitely one of Robinson's introductions from France (Morel) as was stated when it received an A.M. on 10 September 1935. Mr Rowland Jackman tells me, however, that it is disappointing and that A.M.'s were more freely granted in those days! Its blooms were (are)

5in. across, so it was one of the larger hybrids ascribed to
C. viticella.

So are Etoile Violette and Venosa Violacea. Etoile Violette
is of much the same purple colouring as *C.* × *jackmanii,* but,
although it can have only 4 or 5 sepals, most of the time it has 6
and the flower is of a far more pleasing outline. Furthermore,
its eye of creamy stamens gives a focus to every bloom. Etoile
Violette has an earlier season than many clematis flowering
on their young wood: it is commonly at its best in the first
half of July. It was raised and introduced by Morel around
1885.

Venosa Violacea (which is distinct from the earlier Viticella
Venosa) was raised by Lemoine and might be compared with
an enlarged Minuet. The ground is white overlaid with reddish
purple veins in the centre, but uniformly purple at the margins. The flower is quite differently shaped from Minuet,
however, with its 5 or 6 boat-shaped sepals. An intriguing
clematis.

Finally we can return to an untrammelled, unimproved
species, *C. campaniflora.* It comes from Portugal and is very
close to *C. viticella* but the flowers are almost white with a faint
suggestion of violet. Rowland Jackman well described it as 'a
dear little flower, like little nodding, delicate mauve bells.'
They are, in fact, quite open bells, only 2 or 3cm across.

(6) LATE-FLOWERING SPECIES

C. brachiata	*C. serratifolia*
C. fargesii var. *souliei*	*C. tangutica*
C. flammula	*C.* × *triternata*
C. maximowicziana	'Rubro-marginata'
C. orientalis	*C. vitalba*
C. rehderiana	

My next group is homogeneous only in that it consists
almost entirely of species and that they are all late flowering,
on their young wood. So, although mainly rampant, they can
be shortened back as hard as you please each winter. On the
other hand, if you don't prune them they will get along quite
nicely as they would in nature. Untidily, maybe, but over a

small tree or large bush they will not appear untidy, except in the dormant season. And they will start flowering a good deal earlier.

If you want a yellow clematis, this is where you should seek. The brightest, lemon (or even buttercup) colouring is found in *C. orientalis* and *C. tangutica*. Since the latter is often considered as a mere variety of the former (and I find myself, in many instances, hard put to it to say which is which), I will take *C. orientalis* first. It was originally introduced in 1731 and its synonym, *C. graveolens,* is often met with in literature. *C. orientalis* has such a wide distribution, from the Caucasus to N. China and Manchuria, that its variability is not to be wondered at. In modern times, gardeners took little notice of it (preferring the forms referred to *C. tangutica*) until Ludlow and Sherriff made their remarkable introduction, under the number L & S 13342, from their Himalayan expedition of 1947.

C. orientalis L & S 13342 has delicate, finely cut foliage that makes a misty fretwork of green, and globular flower buds that open into 4 thick sepals having the colouring and thickness (or an impression of the thickness) of lemon peel. Unfortunately the name Orange Peel is sometimes applied to this clematis or to seedlings from it, but the colouring is only ever orange on fading blooms in a sunny position. It is not typical.

I find it difficult to advise on whether you should prefer this clematis (it received the A.M. when shown by Messrs. Ingwersen on 10 October 1950) to a good form of *C. tangutica* or not. The foliage is certainly superior. The plant itself has similar vigour but its hardiness record is not unstained. I have known a number of cases from the north where plants have died in the winter though whether from cold or from another cause I cannot say. Although it may flower excellently in a sunless position in the south, it is very apt to run to leaf, under these circumstances. If there is any tendency in this direction, let up on the pruning. Indeed, light pruning gives a very long season, from June onwards. I may say that on a sunny wall in north-west Scotland (Dundonnell House, in Wester Ross) *C. orientalis* L & S 13342 gives a splendid account of itself.

It should always be raised from cuttings, which root easily and quickly but also rot quickly, having rooted, unless potted and hardened off promptly. It has, however, often been propagated from seed, which gives a variable and generally inferior product. If you buy *Clematis* 'Orange Peel' or The Orange Peel Clematis, you have no guarantee of its pedigree. If you buy L & S 13342 you should, from a conscientious nursery, be safe.

Treasure's market the progeny of a self-sown clematis in John Treasure's garden that is probably a hybrid between *C. orientalis* and *C. tangutica,* calling it *C. orientalis* 'Burford Variety'. This is showy and vigorous. John Treasure doesn't like it. As the price of flower power one must always expect a certain coarseness in such hybrids.

While comparing the two species, a drawback to *C. orientalis* that should be mentioned is that its seed heads are not striking in the manner of *C. tangutica.* It has been said of both species that their flowers are sweetly scented. I have tried umpteen samples without the faintest response, but the allegation cannot be safely refuted, since the closely allied *C. serratifolia* is strongly scented. Somewhere there may be scented clones of the two species under consideration but perhaps they were so inferior in other respects as to have dropped out of cultivation.

C. tangutica first reached this country from the Imperial Gardens of St. Petersburg (now Leningrad) as recently as 1898, though its home is central Asia and it has frequently been re-introduced since then. It reached France earlier. Writing in 1902 in the Revue Horticole, Francisque Morel says he received his first plant some 15 years earlier. He says that (unlike *C. orientalis*) it would not flower at all if hard pruned: only off the old wood. The illustration shows an open-flowered form up to 8cm across at the mouth and very like a specimen on Jack Drake's nursery near Aviemore in Inverness-shire, from which he has distributed seedlings from time to time. The sepals are some 5cm long.

However, *C. tangutica* var. *obtusiuscula* was introduced by Wilson in 1908 and Purdom in 1910 from Szechwan and Kansu in W. China, and this has smaller more bell-like flowers. Not so showy but displayed well on long stalks. From seed collected in 1911 and sown at Goring-by-Sea in Sussex in 1912, Frederick C. Stern won an Award of Merit in July 1913 at his plants' first flowering. All these yellow-flowered clematis are very quick and easy from seed. I have raised *C. tangutica* from seed to flower between spring and autumn in the same year.

In the report of his expedition to Kansu in 1914–15, Reginald Farrer wrote of *C. tangutica obtusiuscula* that it 'unfurls a coil almost as long as its name over the river-shingles of all the streams above Jo-ni, ascending to about 10,000ft on the fringes of the alpine coppice. In August it is all a dancing carillon of big, yellow bells like gay golden Fritillarias, succeeded in November by the most voluminous fluffs of soft silver that I know among these Clematids.' (RHS Proceedings 1921).

Most of the plants you see in gardens are undistinguished seedlings but good even at their worst. Lightly pruned, they start flowering in June and the succession produced over the next four months is soon joined by the seed heads that are such a distinctive feature in this species – grey and yellow, youth and old age, together.

You can reckon on 4 or 5 metres for this clematis and *C. orientalis,* so they cannot compete with big-bully cherries like the double white gean, but can with a large shrub or small tree, like the morello cherry.

In a way, *C. serratifolia* must be reckoned a collector's piece. Though similar to the two foregoing it is rarely as showy, but it has its points. The flowers appear in August-September and would politely be described as soft yellow, less sympathetically as wan yellow. They all come in a rush together, which makes for a good display, but this season is correspondingly short, say 3 weeks. One of their points of distinction is the boss of purple stamens, which are conspicuous. The other is their scent, which is strongly of lemon. The feathery styles on the ripened seeds are also charming and come in swags. If you want them to last you must pick them promptly for the house, as they soon disintegrate, unlike Old Man's Beard.

C. rehderiana is a very pale yellow, paler than primrose, but what a clematis. Time and again, journalists enthuse about it and an attractive photograph points their praises but the trade is quite unable to meet the resulting deluge of orders. Like *C. orientalis* it is quickly rooted from cuttings but these as quickly rot if kept close for a few days too long. If hardened off and potted as soon as rooted, there are no problems.

This is a slightly more vigorous clematis than those just described and will grow 8m into a tree. On the other hand it can be cut hard back every winter and will always flower abundantly from August to October. The pinnate leaves are conspicuously hairy; you cannot miss this feature. The flowers are numerous in their panicles and the sepals touch at their margins to form a genuine bell-shape, the sepal tips being recurved so that there are no points. And then there is that tremendous scent of cowslips. Really delicious.

Seed was first sent from W. China (Szechwan) by Père Aubert to L. Henry of Paris in 1898 and this was flowered in 1899 but wrongly identified as *C. buchananiana*. Henry wrote it up in the Revue Horticole 1905 and likened the flowers' scent to orange blossom. He was a nurseryman and had perhaps never met any flower as humble as the cowslip. Wilson re-introduced the species in 1908. He and Rehder subsequently described it as *C. nutans* var. *thyrsoidea* but in 1914 Kew raised it to specific rank as *C. rehderiana*. *C. veitchiana* is very close but I have not met it. *C. rehderiana* received the A.M. in 1936 and has recently been granted a well deserved Award of Garden Merit.

I have now finished with the yellow-flowered species and turn to some that are white. Of these, *C. fargesii* var. *souliei* was another of Wilson's introductions from China, in 1911. Its leaves are bold, pinnate and somewhat hairy. The flowers on a lightly pruned or unpruned specimen open from early June onwards through the summer and autumn; never many at a time, so this is no great display, but enough to be pleasing. They are sizeable, as small-flowered species go, 5 or 6cm across and, being composed of 6 broad, rounded sepals, they are well shaped and not at all unlike a white anemone. A nice clematis. *C. fargesii* itself is not in cultivation.

C. vitalba is our one native species, popularly called Old Man's Beard. Its little off-white flowers are moderately attractive, in quantity, but the grey seed heads are a great deal better than that. The way you see them draping rough hedges and small trees like hawthorns in the wild (generally in chalk or limestone country) should give the gardener ideas. The gardener, that is, with a largeish piece of land in a rural setting; certainly not the urban or suburban gardener, for *C. vitalba* is a rough, untamed creature and its habit of self-sowing can be a nuisance in an intensively cultivated garden. But if you had an old, unpruned yew tree, for instance, you could hardly do better than encourage curtains of old man's beard to swing through it. Another circumstance in which I have seen this clematis looking particularly arresting was in the branches of a larch, in November, when the larch's own deciduous foliage had changed to yellow and was caught by low sunlight. Larches are large trees with greedy roots. Not many climbers could cope, but *C. vitalba* is tough and can climb to 12 metres. Moreover its seed heads remain in condition throughout the autumn and for a large part of the winter.

Still, there's no getting away from the coarseness of the growing plant in summer, particularly of its foliage. This is where the South European *C. flammula* (one of my favourite species) is so vastly superior. The leaves are dark green but neat and gleamingly polished. The flowers are tiny cruciform little things again but pure white and strongly scented of meadow sweet or hawthorn – a sickly kind of fragrance that yet meets you very pleasantly on the air. Even when lightly pruned, *C. flammula* seldom reaches its peak until mid-August and continues throughout September – a useful season. It is not as vigorous as vitalba and can be used to enliven large shrubs like escallonias or lilacs. The seed heads are nothing to boast of and anyway develop so late that in most seasons the seeds cannot ripen, in this country, before cold weather cuts short their development. Flammula builds up a thick trunk that becomes hollow after ten years or so and at this age your plant is liable to die suddenly and unexpectedly. It is not, in my experience, a very long-lived species. Cuttings are rather tricky to root but imported seed gives excellent results; so does your own after a hot summer and an open autumn.

I have already described the effect of *C. flammula* mixed

with Gipsy Queen. *C. viticella* would also make an excellent purple associate of the same flowering period and pruning requirements. Flammula with *C. tangutica* would also look nice. I rather like Moore & Jackman's recommendation for siting it 'on some rocky eminence, where, being allowed to assume a decumbent habit, its myriads of pure white blossoms seem to pour down the declivities like masses of drifting snow, at the same time embalming the air with their fragrance.' Few of us have rocky eminences to play with, but obviously the author must have seen it growing in this way (perhaps in the wild) to be able to communicate such a vivid pen picture.

The plant called Rubro-marginata (F.C.C. 1863) was at first known as *C. flammula roseo-purpurea*. It was a product of Jackman's. Moore & Jackman write of it as being 'believed to be a natural hybrid between *C. flammula* and *C. viticella,* the seeds of the former from which it was raised having been grown in contiguity to some of the varieties of the latter species. In its vigorous growth, its profusion of flowers, its strongly-marked hawthorn scent, and its late summer and autumn-flowering habit, it partakes strongly of its mother-parent.' The flowers are, indeed, cruciform like flammula's but rather larger, 4 to 5cm across, and each sepal is purple round the margin shading to white in the centre. I was unkind to this clematis in my last book, dismissing it as 'grubby and ineffective' but I have to eat my words after seeing a well grown and mature specimen in a Berkshire garden. When I tried to grow it on a scruffy piece of yew hedging, it liked the position no better than the yew did. Crosses between *C. flammula* and *C. viticella* should be known as *C. × triternata,* so this clone becomes *C. × triternata* 'Rubro-marginata'.

It is unfortunate that *C. maximowicziana* is the correct name of the species more widely known and grown as *C. paniculata*. It comes from Japan (introduced 1796) and has long been popular in American gardens. Even in France it gives a good account of itself, flowering from late August to October, but it needs greater summer heat than we can generally stoke up. In most years, flowering in England starts too late and is beaten by the weather. The flowers, like flammula's, are carried in 'axillary panicles through most of the length of every trail, thus

1. W. E. Gladstone
2. Mme Baron Veillard
3. Lady Betty Balfour
4. King George V
5. Lady Caroline Nevill

8

1. Miss Crawshay
2. Duchess of Edinburgh
3. Countess of Lovelace
4. Daniel Deronda
5. Vyvyan Pennell
6. Miriam Markham
7. Proteus
8. *C. florida* 'Sieboldii'

making up long flowering garlands' (Revue Horticole 1902). There is the same flammula hawthorn scent. It would be worth having a stab at this species against a hot south wall in the south-east of England.

C. brachiata is similarly late flowering. I unfortunately made no record and have no recollection of how it came to me or when I planted it but I did at least label my plant and I should think it had been in position for 2 years when Romke van de Kaa, who is gardening with me here at Dixter, drew my attention one October's day in 1975 to the fact that it was in full flower. As my eyes are usually cast modestly down upon the ground or else, at this season, focused on the sky in search of a few reassuring late swallows or martins, I had missed it. Summer and autumn had both been excellent and the blossom was in mint condition but could, I suppose, easily fail in a normal year.

This is a South African species, perhaps the only one such cultivated in Britain. Its leaves, at flowering time, are tatty but one in unaware of them because of the profuse garlands of cruciform flowers, each 4cm across, green-tinted white with prominent stamens. There is a faint but pleasing scent. Others declare that the scent is quite strong but I see no reason to believe that their sense of smell is more acute than mine; they must be showing off.

Romke thought that I should take it up to the next RHS Show on 28 October and we duly set about preparing out material on the previous afternoon. We could not have laid a corpse out with greater solicitude. The clematis grows on an old espalier pear in an open and exposed part of the garden. We used all the flowering material and carefully detached each trail from its support; then re-attached them with clips on to stiff red branches of dogwood. *Cornus alba,* whose leaves had just been shed. First I had taken the precaution of boiling the cut clematis stems for 50 seconds. The reconstituted plant was next plunged in a deep florist's bucket, for the night, in my porch. We stood back to admire. 'Fantastic' was Romke's reaction and I must say it did look good but not showy. I doubted whether the committee would be impressed. But they were and it got an A.M. the next day as 'a tender flowering climber.' I rather resent that word 'tender', seeing that I could not have given my plant a colder position, but I suppose they have to play safe and it is true we haven't experienced a hard winter for more years than I've had the clematis.

(7) HERBACEOUS CLEMATIS AND NON-CLIMBING SHRUBS

C. × *aromatica*
C. *douglasii* var. *scottii* and cv Rosea
Edward Prichard
C. × *eriostemon*
C. *heracleifolia* and cv's Campanile, Crépuscule, Côte d'Azur
C. *heracleifolia* var. *davidiana* and cv Wyevale
C. *integrifolia* and cv's Hendersonii, Olgae
C. × *jouiniana* and cv Praecox
Mrs Robert Brydon
C. *recta* and cv Purpurea
C. *songarica*
C. *stans*

We can progress easily from the last group to this by way of C. × *aromatica,* whose parents are credibly presumed to be C. *flammula* (whence the scent) and C. *integrifolia* (whence the flower and habit). It has often been known as C. *coerulea odorata* and was described in the Revue Horticole of 1877, so probably originated in France about that date. Moore & Jackman wrote of it with enthusiasm as a continuous and abundant bloomer, from early July till autumn, so floriferous 'that the plants have the appearance of huge bouquets.' The flowers have 'a strong and delicious fragrance, resembling that of hawthorn.' It is semi-herbaceous and non-climbing, dying back to a woody base in winter and as it grows 4 to 6ft high it should, they say, be fastened to some kind of support. The flowers are about 4cm across with 4 violet-coloured sepals that look narrow as their margins roll back. The button-like eye of stamens is in contrasting white.

If the reader feels that this is something he must have, that's how I felt and I eventually got a piece from John Treasure's plant (it is not all that easily propagated). Alas, it seems to have lost a great deal in stamina during the century since its birth (well, don't we all?). My plant is a wee, frail little old thing. The scent is still there in the few flowers it opens but the plant, now 8 or 10 years old, has a distressing not-long-for-this-world look. Incidentally, Boucher et Mottet in Les Clématites (a disappointing little book on the whole) write of the flowers of *C.* × *aromatica* that they 'exhalent un agréeable parfum d'Héliotrope très suave', a description with a caress.

C. integrifolia had better be considered next. It is a herbaceous species from S.E. Europe and is sometimes classified as a member of the otherwise American section *Viornae*. But its sepals are not connate, as theirs are, and its foliage, devoid of any climbing properties and undivided, is utterly different. As a garden plant it still has its place. Growing 1m tall, each clumpy plant makes a forest of young stems from the crown in spring, and each stem terminates in one nodding indigo-blue flower of a somewhat leathery substance. If there are plants around it that will support its stems in their lower regions, that is ideal; otherwise you must give it discreet and sympathetic support yourself. Don't truss it to a stake.

The cultivar called Olgae is about the same colour and size but the sepals are even more attractively twisted and the flowers have some scent. Another cultivar, Hendersonii, received an A.M. when shown at the Chelsea Flower Show on 25 May 1965. It is easily brought on to flower for this show although it naturally has a midsummer season. The plant is usually less than 1m tall and the flowers are larger, bolder, more effective than in the unimproved species. They hang with wide-spreading sepals so that their total spread is 7cm and they are dusky indigo-blue, paler at the margins which undulate slightly. Although there is only one bloom to each stem, it stands well above (15 to 20cm) the foliage.

C. integrifolia 'Hendersonii', just described, must not be confused with *C.* × *eriostemon*, among whose several synonyms *C. hendersonii* is one. *C.* × *eriostemon*, as already mentioned, was the earliest hybrid, the cross arising in 1835, probably between *C. integrifolia* and *C. viticella*. It is a non-climbing plant, its weak though woody stems up to 3m tall. The flowers take after *C. integrifolia* but are not really sufficiently numerous or impressive for the size of the plant. After growing it in my mixed border for a number of years,

I decided that it made too much fuss with too little result.

In all the early literature, *C. heracleifolia* was referred to as *C. tubulosa*. There is a clematis group still referred to as Section *Tubulosae,* of which this is horticulturally the most important species with *C. stans* as also-ran. Their sepals are joined at the base in a tube and the flower form, colouring and size is very much that of a hyacinth's.

C. heracleifolia is a common sub-shrubby clematis and variable too. There are a number of clones derived directly from it; others from crosses with *C. stans.* Lemoine of Nancy was particularly keen on improving these small-flowered herbaceous or sub-shrubby species and the greatest number of crosses were made by that nursery. Campanile is one such that is still with us (by name anyway and the early descriptions more or less fit). It received an A.M. in 1917 when shown by Messrs Paul of Cheshunt. They described it as herbaceous but today's plant makes thick woody stems in course of time. 'Lilac blue flowers with white centres', as described in 'Le Jardin' at that time fits well. Côte d'Azur is said to have deep azure blue flowers, but was, as I acquired it, identical with Campanile. Once again there has been a mix-up.

C. heracleifolia is a coarse clematis on account of its voluminous leaves which tend to be out of all proportion to the size and quantity of blossom. However, a well-flowered specimen is worth looking at.

This species comes from central and north China and was introduced in 1837. *C. heracleifolia* var. *davidiana* was collected by Père David near Peking and was sent by him to Paris in 1863. Botanically, the most obvious features distinguishing this from the type are (1) that *C. heracleifolia* is monoecious (male and female organs on different flowers but on the same plant) while var. *davidiana* is dioecious (the sexes on different plants); (2) that the sepals roll back at the tips in *C. heracleifolia* but merely spread outwards without rolling back in the variety. I go along with the first distinction; the second is less marked. Davidiana rolls back quite a lot, especially in the *newly* opened flower, funnily enough. Writing as a gardener and not as a botanist, the main distinctions as I see them in the plants we have in cultivation are that *C. heracleifolia,* the type, is sub-shrubby, the annual growths dying back to a noticeably woody and permanent framework; while David's variety is truly herbaceous. The latter spreads, moreover, like many herbaceous plants, by means of underground rhizomatous shoots into a clump that is readily divisible; not so *C. heracleifolia*. Furthermore, var. *davidiana* is strongly scented – a somewhat disconcerting hair oil scent– whereas the type plant hasn't a vestige of scent.

The flowers in this species are carried in dense axillary clusters and are larger in var. *davidiana* than in the type, but largest in *C.h. davidiana* 'Wyevale', an excellent clone in which the colouring is a strong blue throughout the flower, which also has attractively crimped sepal margins. If only there weren't all that suffocating foliage.

Among Lemoine's many *heracleifolia × stans* crosses, Crépuscule is one that has survived, but I cannot remember seeing it. Mrs Robert Brydon, raised in the USA may be pure *C. heracleifolia* or it may be a *C. × jouiniana* cultivar: a strong grower to 2m (it needs good support) with sprays of pale off-white blossom faintly blue-tinged. The flowers open wide, curling back at the tips and have no tube (which suggests vitalba blood). The white stamens are prominent. This is mildly agreeable but of a too dirty colouring. If I haven't sufficiently damned with faint praise let me add, unequivocally that it is a poor thing.

So is *C. stans*. This is a floppy 1 to 1·3m herbaceous species carrying flowers of a spitefully non-contributory off-white, skimmed-milk colouring. 'Of little importance', wrote Moore & Jackman. Hear! Hear!

Now for an interesting and worth-while clematis, the hybrid *C. × jouiniana,* widely and erroneously distributed, in former times, as *C. grata,* which, however, is a genuine (if undistinguished) species in its own right related to *C. vitalba*. Jouiniana itself is a cross between *C. heracleifolia* var. *davidiana* and *C. vitalba*: the only cross, as far as I know, in which our native clematis has been used as one parent. It was made (or should I say the hybrid occurred?) about the end of the last century and was named after E. Jouin, manager of the Simon-Louis nurseries at Metz.

Seeing that both its parents wear coarse, obtrusive leaves, for which I have duly castigated them, you might think that the hybrid would be similarly burdened. Indeed, its large pinnate foliage is no asset but the flowers are so numerous that, once in full spate, the leaves practically disappear. These flowers make wide open, off-white stars, having a bluish tinge that is strongest on the sepals' underside. There is no perceptible scent but the blossom is popular with butterflies, as is Davidiana's.

The habit of the plant is to make a basic, permanent woody frame up to 1m high and then long annual growths to 3m that flower as a compound panicle along almost their entire length. Given wire supports, *C. × jouiniana* can hoist itself up the walls of a two-storey building, although it has no climbing devices. I use it as a border feature and give it height by tying the old stems to a post; from this the young growths spray outwards and downwards in all directions. But *C. × jouiniana* is also one of the best clematis to use as ground cover in an open situation or even in thin woodland, and it can mask old tree stumps.

The original type-plant of this hybrid does not start flowering till September. Usefully late, you might think, but in fact this very late start does unnecessarily curtail its season. The cultivar called Praecox should be chosen in preference almost every time, because its season starts in July and thereafter continues without abatement to the end of September or further.

Edward Prichard is the interesting result of a unique cross between *C. heracleifolia* var. *davidiana* and *C. recta*. It was made by Mr Russell V. Prichard in Australia and the firm of Maurice Prichard (lately of Christchurch, Hants. but now defunct, alas) gained an A.M. for it on 29 August 1950. Its herbaceous growth is thin and weak to 1m and it carries sprays of pale mauve, strongly scented cruciform flowers (the sepals narrow for their length) in late summer and autumn. It never does much in my mixed border. I think capsids eat out its young shoot tips and buds. But it can be a really charming clematis. Perhaps it is not quite robust enough to cope with the hurly burly of mixed border life.

And so to *C. recta,* at one time called *C. erecta,* which means the same thing and seems to me the silliest name that could have been chosen for a clematis that is so floppy by nature that this aspect of its habit is the most difficult to cope with in the garden. You can embattle its young growth with 2m-long pea-sticks at an early age, but this is expensive and tedious and looks as though you'd planted a witch's broom. Or you can let it flop, but that's not much fun for the neighbours on whom it collapses. There are strains of this clematis that grow only 1m high and are more manageable but it is generally twice as tall. As it self-sows extremely readily, there are innumerable clones in circulation.

I shouldn't bother about *C. recta* straight. You might just as well go for Purpurea, which flowers similarly for 3 weeks at midsummer with a delightful foam of small white cruciform blossom (excellent for flower arrangements if you boil the stems first), but additionally is sumptuous in spring when the young shoots are coloured rich purple. This really does take the eye, but the colouring fades to dark green as the foliage expands. Even Purpurea is not a fixed clone as it has often been propagated from seed. Hilda Davenport Jones told me that she treated it this way, for sale, discarding the green seedlings and selling the purple. That's too hit-and-miss a method for my liking. You can divide old clumps or you can take cuttings of young shoots in early spring when only 5cm long, detaching them right at the base where they arise from the crown.

As a garden plant I must admit to finding *C. recta* tiresome, by and large. Lemoine brought out a double form, Plena or Flore Pleno, which won a F.C.C. when shown by Messrs Paul to the RHS in July 1890. It is mouth-wateringly described by Moore & Jackman as having 'pure white flowers which differ from those of the type in being fully double, like the silvery, button-like blossoms of *Ranunculus aconitifolius plenus*', to which, of course, it is related. I bought a plant under this name from Thompson & Morgan years ago, but it was just the ordinary single-flowered species, in the event. A sad loss.

C. songarica is an interesting autumn-flowering species from Siberia (introduced 1880), of a sub-shrubby habit reaching to 2m against a wall. The smooth green leaves are entire; the flowers, in terminal clusters of about 30 are pure white and starry about 3·5cm across having 5 sepals usually. They are hawthorn- or meadow-sweet-scented. There is a specimen in the car park (an old walled garden) at the National Pinetum, Bedgbury, Kent, which they had from Kew: near the entrance to the pinetum itself. Most of the clematis on these walls are Vitalbas!

Finally Scottii, a variety of the herbaceous loner *C. douglasii,* discovered by Douglas himself in the Rocky Mountains of the USA. When suited, this variety makes a handsome clump to 1m tall at flowering, in early summer, with somewhat glaucous pinnate foliage and solitary, nodding bell-shaped flowers, 4cm long, opened at the mouth, blue, darker within than without. Scottii Rosea is a good shade of pink, not muddy.

This clematis is easily raised from seed but seems reluctant to make a good plant thereafter – with me, at any rate. It grows well in John Treasure's garden at Burford (Shropshire).

CHAPTER 7

How to Grow Them

*

CLEMATIS have a reputation for being difficult. I was recently sent for review a 'Handbook of Easy Garden Plants' intended to recommend to beginners a range of trouble-free plants that will allow the housewife to lounge in a deck chair rather than take up a gardening tool. Naturally I looked up clematis first. The only two allowed by the author were *C. montana* and *C. tangutica*. After describing them she goes on to say: 'The large-flowered hybrids are less easy to establish than the above species, and are decidedly fussy, so have regretfully been excluded from this book.' End of clematis.

I admit I'm no deck chair gardener. The pleasure you get out of gardening is in proportion to the mental and physical effort you put into it. That's the way it works with me, anyway, but if you're a reluctant gardener and have been pushed into gardening against your inclinations, then what about the large-flowered clematis for you? Are they really so fussy that you can never be recommended to plant one? Quite frankly, I find you such a bore that I don't care whether you do or you don't. I can say that here without giving offence, because you certainly won't be reading this book. Only the converted clematis fan will be doing that. However, I must point out that from the north of Scotland down to the south-west of Cornwall any motorist with his eye off the road will see thousands upon thousands of purple Jackmanii clematis flowering on innumerable house walls and porches every July and August. Don't tell me that they thrive only by the sweat of each owner's brow. On the contrary, ninetynine out of a hundred of them were planted with no more thought than is given to drinking a glass of water.

In a specialist book on the clematis, I am naturally going to give a good many details and instructions to help the reader get the best from his plants but this wealth of detail should never be allowed to obscure the fact that if you simply dig a small hole, place the clematis in it, fill in the hole, turn your back on it and make for the nearest deck chair, that clematis stands an excellent chance not merely of survival but of flourishing in a manner that does you credit such as you most certainly do not deserve.

I have in the past weeks during a fantastically mild January, planted about two dozen clematis against old, unproductive espalier pears (they'll be even less productive now). I am sure I didn't average ten minutes of my time on each of them; five would be nearer the mark. But I should add that the soil has long been cultivated and is, on the whole, in good heart, as the saying goes. Only here and there was I battling with yellow, cheesy clay that had to be replaced with soil-lightening grit.

When to Plant

The question that a nurseryman is asked more frequently than any other is 'When is the right time to plant a clematis?'. It is usually asked by someone who wishes to defer the issue and doesn't feel ready to cope. He does not wish to be told that now is the moment, and yet, as clematis are nearly always pot-grown, they can, without disturbance or damage to their roots, be planted at any season. Obviously not if the ground is frozen solid, but you can keep the plant by you in a cold shed until the frost relents. Obviously not if the ground is flooded, but in that case the situation is unsuitable anyway and steps must first be taken to drain it adequately. If the ground is bone dry, you can, unless there are water restrictions in force, water it until it reaches saturation point; wait for it to dry a little and then plant your clematis. But the point to make here is that there is no close season for clematis planting and plants will be available from garden centres throughout the year.

Mail orders will be despatched between late September and the end of March, generally speaking, though they may continue through the spring as late as early June. Clematis are seldom despatched to customers during the summer (a) because, being in full growth they are more liable to damage by rough handling or delays in transit; they may dry out or get too hot in their parcel during a heat wave; (b) because a nurseryman has many other calls on his time in the summer and wants to use his labour force then on other tasks than packing and despatching.

A clematis that is being committed to public transport will travel best when temperatures are low (they are seldom too low) and the plant is dormant so that it is carrying no soft and easily damaged growth.

Some gardeners have definite preferences as between autumn and spring planting, having discovered from experience that one or the other has been followed by losses. More often than not this is *post hoc* and not *propter hoc*. Most clematis being fully hardy in Britain, winter losses can seldom be ascribed to the cold killing a not yet established plant. Spring planting may often be followed by drought and if you or your mind are not on the spot, an unestablished plant could easily fold up; but forewarned is forearmed.

In sum, my recommendation is to buy any common clematis when you are ready for them and plant them forthwith and to snap up the uncommon kinds that are frequently out of stock, whenever you can lay hands on them. They can easily be heeled in, in a spare bit of ground, till you have made their permanent quarters ready, even though that may be months later. Desirable clematis that are often in short supply include *C. armandii*, Beauty of Worcester, Countess of Lovelace, Duchess of Albany, Durandii, Etoile Rose, *C. florida* 'Sieboldii', Gravetye Beauty, *C. rehderiana*, Royal Velours, Sir Trevor Lawrence and *C. texensis*.

Soil and Moisture

To the question 'what do clematis like?' the short answer is 'everything you can give them.' And I find it helpful to add that if clematis are fed as most gardeners feed their roses, they will be well content. Roses, in fact, are often overfed but this is unlikely to happen with clematis provided ample moisture is there.

But first to consider what soils clematis like and to what

extent you can or should try to modify your soil as you find it.

The commonest misconception is that clematis need providing with lime if none is already present in the soil. Let me assure you straightaway that this is quite unnecessary (unless your soil is so acid that it needs extra lime for everything you grow, and this is rare in British gardens). There is no need to go scrounging with your bucket for mortar rubble out of old buildings. All the same, you will still read in many books and articles on clematis that lime is a prerequisite. I have no doubt this notion arose from the fact that our one native clematis, *C. vitalba,* is most often found wild on chalk or limestone. One swallow doesn't make a summer. *C. vitalba* has sired only one hybrid grown in gardens. And anyway itself will grow perfectly well in acid soil if you ask it to. So will all the rest. I remember Miles Hadfield telling of the large collection of clematis in his parents' garden in Birmingham (and indeed I remember an ancient *C. armandii* on a wall of their house) where the soil was excessively acid on account of being impregnated by sulphurous industrial fumes. But the clematis flourished exceedingly. This may also, I suspect, be linked with the fact that they got less wilt disease, because the sulphur dioxide in the air acts as a fungicide. It is well known that potatoes do not get blight nor roses black spot – both fungal diseases – in areas of industrial pollution and smog. I am not a town gardener myself but my London friends seem to do clematis very well and with the minimum of trouble from wilt.

Walter Pennell thinks differently from me on this matter. He wished to go on record as believing that chalk or lime in the soil where clematis grow materially reduces the incidence of wilt. His own garden is on limy soil and he gets little or no trouble from this disease. If he is right, we have yet to be given a clue as to the reason. It used to be the practice to whitewash the trunks and branches of fruit trees with lime, in the interests of orchard hygiene. No one does it now. I presume that the whiteness of the lime gave the grower a notion of cleanliness and hence of protection against disease.

The disadvantages of adding lime to the soil where you grow a mixed collection of plants are clear. It won't hurt the clematis but it will make rhododendrons, camellias and most heathers difficult or impossible to grow, all of them excellent host plants for clematis to clamber over and there are many more that are similarly calcifuge.

The most difficult soil on which to make a success of any but the toughest clematis is a hungry sand. Such are the Folke-stone and Bagshot sands: poor soils that dry out. Gertrude Jekyll gardened on this kind of soil at Godalming, in Surrey and she commented on the long years that it took to establish a *C. × jackmanii*. 'In my garden it is difficult to get the Clematis to grow at all', she wrote. 'But good gardening means patience and dogged determination. There must be many failures and losses, but by always pushing on there will also be the reward of success. Those who do not know are apt to think that hardy flower gardening of the best kind is easy. It is not easy at all. It has taken me half a life-time merely to find out what is best worth doing, and a good slice out of another half to puzzle out the ways of doing it.'

It is the lack of moisture that makes a sandy soil difficult. Thin soils overlying chalk can be tricky for the same reason. But some limy soils are surprisingly moist even in times of drought. Provided their drainage is adequate, soils overlying clay are among the best for clematis, but even these can dry out at times and this must be guarded against.

Remember that clematis are frequently planted near walls. The wall itself laps up a large share of any moisture that's going and its physical presence also prevents a good deal of the rain that falls from reaching the soil at its feet. So clematis near walls need extra special consideration, on the water front.

There are two ways in which the gardener should, concur-rently, approach this problem. The first is by adding water to the soil himself, the second is by facilitating retention of water in the soil once it is there.

The best kind of soil from every point of view is that which is rich in humus: decayed vegetable matter like leaf mould, peat, farmyard manure, garden compost, straw, spent hops, sewage sludge, road sweepings, ground bark as a forestry biproduct, deep litter chicken manure based on sawdust or wood shavings. When I am asked what I recommend as a soil conditioner for clematis, I think of all these things, but which to recommend depends so much on the individual's locality and what he can acquire or make most conveniently at the lowest cost.

Some in the list I've just given have feed value, others (like peat) are purely or mainly soil conditioners in the form of humus, which will hold moisture, aerate the soil physically and also encourage the soil fauna of which earthworms are the most noteworthy. So you want to add humus to the soil before you plant your clematis and you subsequently want to add it as a surface dressing or mulch, topping it up for as long as the clematis lives. Mulches must be applied when the soil is well saturated, which usually means in winter, and they will then, if thick enough, keep the soil beneath cool and damp even through quite prolonged droughts.

If you are obliged to plant a clematis in a quite small aperture surrounded by paving, there is little opportunity for adding humus and mulching. As long as the paving slabs are not cemented together, however, they do keep the soil underneath them remarkably cool and moist so the clematis may be better off than you'd think. Scope for feeding will be restricted and if the soil is poor anyway you may have to settle for strong clematis like montanas, macropetalas, alpinas and viticellas that are not too fussy.

Now as to actually watering your clematis yourself. When you have decided to do this, the great thing is to give them enough so that it penetrates deep into the soil and reaches all the plant's roots. If there is a surface mulch you won't have to water so often but when you do you'll have to be even more thorough than usual, because the water has to saturate the mulch before it can reach the soil underneath. A noticeable benefit from the mulch is that it will prevent water from running off and away, as it is so liable to do when it falls on a hard, impermeable soil surface. That, of course, is useless and must at all costs be avoided. A slow application in fine droplets will ensure that the water is absorbed where you want it.

As to quantities, think of them in this way. The growing plant (not only clematis) needs 25mm (i.e. an inch) of rain or other water every ten days. Your watering needs to make good the deficiency in natural rainfall in each ten-day period.

Twenty-five mm of water is equivalent to 25 litres to the square metre (or 4½ gallons to the square yard). This is a great deal more than most people imagine a plant needs at a watering, especially if they are putting it on from a watering can.

Many gardeners (indulging in the lazy streak that lurks in them) object to watering on the alleged grounds that once you start you have got to go on. I cannot myself see that this is an objection, except for the bother of it. Of course you should go on, for as long as the need is there. Even so, one thorough watering in a dry spell is better than none even if you don't keep it up just as one good day's rain in the middle of a dry spell would be better than none.

If you live in a district where restrictions on water use are frequently imposed during times of drought, then it is the more important to be liberal with the humus and to keep your mulches thick at all seasons. If mulches build up too high around the stems of some shrubs, they can induce neck rot, a horrid complaint, as you can quickly appreciate simply by murmuring those two words over and over again to yourself: neck rot, neck rot, neck rot. Terminal neck rot, indeed. But you can heave a sigh: it luckily works the opposite way with clematis. They positively enjoy having the goodies piled around their necks and react by rooting into them. Also, in many cases, by throwing up strong shoots from below mulch level.

Before continuing with details of planting preparations and procedures, I might as well finish off the general subject of feeding, as we have already been teetering on the brink of it for some time.

Although I said at the start of the chapter that clematis are greedy, that does not mean they need better treatment than the plants which I hope you are growing all around them. Under garden conditions, nearly all plants need and deserve generous treatment.

Some of the forms of humus that I have been reviewing also have considerable feed value: farmyard manure, for instance, especially if it has been stacked under cover so that most of its nutrients have been retained, not washed away by rain. Deep litter chicken manure is exceedingly rich because chicken droppings are anyway strong and also because practically nothing is lost in the making, which is automatically under cover. When you empty the deep litter house you must keep the litter in a dry place and it may want turning once or twice before it loses its strong ammoniacal smell. Until then it will not be sufficiently rotted to be applied safely to growing plants. I use a lot of deep litter manure myself, as our hens make it, but a little goes a long way. It only needs thin spreading.

Grass mowings, on the other hand, can be spread thickly – say 10cm deep. They won't heat at that depth but they will, in the course of rotting, take nitrogen *from* the soil rather than contribute nitrogen *to* the soil. And that goes for any undecomposed vegetable material that you may apply as a mulch. Straw, for instance, or farmyard manure in which the straw has not yet broken into short pieces and the animal smell is still obvious.

Such materials can be applied safely as a surface mulch to woody plants like clematis, especially in the dormant season, but as soon as growth recommences in the spring, you should add a surface dressing of nitrogenous fertiliser to make good what is being lost from the soil to the mulch in the course of decomposition. Your mulch will also break down much more quickly and become valuable as a manure itself, if you add nitrogen. Sulphate of ammonia or nitro-chalk will do very well.

Planting Preparations

Planting preparations on a good soil will take two minutes. You will simply fork in some humus to a fork's depth. Earthworms will carry it down as much lower as it needs to go. If the humus you add is peat or some other non-nutritive material, then you should also include a couple of handfuls of John Innes Base Fertiliser, which contains nitrogen, phosphorus and potassium, and will release these nutrients over a longish period, not all at once. But I don't add this where my soil is really good.

On nasty soil, adequate preparations may take half an hour for each plant. And that is in addition to the adequate drainage

9

1
2
3
4
5
6
7

1. Mrs Spencer Castle
2. Countess of Lovelace
3. Beauty of Worcester
4. Daniel Deronda

5. Vyvyan Pennell
6. Jackmanii Rubra
7. Proteus

10

1. Barbara Dibley
2. Bees Jubilee
3. Barbara Jackman
4. Lincoln Star

5. Nelly Moser
6. Marcel Moser
7. Mrs N. Thompson
8. C. W. Dowman

provisions which are a *sine qua non* for all gardening except in bog and pond. If you dig out a large hole the sides of which are neat clay, the fact that you fill in with delicious John Innes No. 3 Potting Compost will not prevent your hole from becoming a sump, unless tile drains have been laid near at hand.

Assuming that you are on clay but have solved the drainage problem, I recommend (and this is what I do myself in the grottier parts of my garden) setting the reasonably good top soil on one side of an area $0 \cdot 7$ m (2ft) square. Then, down to a depth of $0 \cdot 5$ m, extract and remove the yellow cheese. Replace the top soil (which will now be at a lower level) and add a similar bulk of horticultural grit. Also some humus and organic manure as already discussed. Mix these together with a long-tined garden fork. Top up with more top-soil filched from elsewhere or, better still if you can get it, with the aforementioned John Innes No. 3 compost.

Horticultural grit is available all over the country but you may have to show initiative to locate a source. In my part of the south-east, in Kent, Sussex and Surrey, it is available from M. P. Harris, the builders' merchants. If you order a load (currently measured as 5 cubic yards) at a time, they will deliver. This sounds like a lot of grit but it has many uses in the garden: to mix as 'sand' in John Innes composts, to bond paving stones, to spread on much trodden dirt paths, to lighten the ground where you intend planting a lavender hedge, to use as a surface dressing to keep down weeds or to make them easy to pull out. If you only want a small quantity you can take your bag or sack to the nearest depot.

The grit around here is ground up shingle or 'beach' as we know it locally. What you see in heaps by the roadside 'Grit for Icy Roads' is very similar. In other parts of the country, what you want may be sold by different merchants and come from a different source. A correspondent on the north side of Newcastle-on-Tyne wrote to me asking where she was to get any. Fortunately I have a friend up there and he discovered that excellent grit, granite of just the right coarseness, was obtainable from Robson's garden centre at Hexham in the South Tyne valley.

Back to our planting site. Similar preparations to those described will be worth making in any unpleasant soil, whether sandy, gravelly, rocky, chalky or whatever. The lighter the sub-soil the greater the bulk of humus that should be added. This is where peat is so valuable and it is marvellously easy to handle, but has become fearfully expensive latterly.

Planting

Although the actual planting of a clematis takes a matter of seconds, there is quite a lot of jabber apropos. First, as to the type of plant you have bought and the season at which you're planting it.

Most young clematis will be pot grown but some will be acquired in plastic bags and be quite devoid of soil. No harm in that, especially if they are dormant. Dig a hole large enough to accommodate the roots spread out – not a small hole into which the roots have to be bunched up.

Pot-grown clematis have the advantage of needing very little root disturbance in the process of planting. Clematis root systems vary a lot in appearance: that is, in their thickness and strength. The majority of the hybrids have thick, tough roots distinctly reminiscent of leather bootlaces. Parkinson, in 1629, wrote of them in his Paradisus as 'a bundell of brownish yellow strong strings'. If they were cramped in their pot it is a good idea, before planting, to unwind and release them a little one from another, working from the bottom of the root ball. In this way you help them to make quick contact with the new soil into which you are about to plant them. So tough are these roots, that your handling of them will do practically no damage. But I shouldn't mess around in this way if the plant is green and growing strongly at the time you are planting it. In that case (say it's spring or summer), turn it out of its container (even if it's a perishable paper pot) as gently as possible; place it in its hole and then pour in a gallon – sorry, I mean pour in 4·546 litres of water, quickly. As this is draining away, quickly fill in with top soil.

Some clematis have very fine, easily damaged roots and you

should not manhandle these at all at any season. The alpinas and macropetalas come to mind as examples but worst of all is *C. orientalis.* If you are a bit careless, the ball of soil and roots can break clean away from the stem while you're handling them, and the plant will certainly die. Don't thereupon write an irate and self-righteous letter to the nurseryman telling him that his clematis had no roots. It did have roots, but quite unlike those on the hybrids that you possibly bought at the same time. And you bungled. Of course if it was a mail order, the accident may have happened through inadequate packing and rough handling in transit.

If you receive your clematis in autumn or winter, they may be hung with dead leaves and look completely dead. The trouble with the majority of large-flowered hybrids is that they cling to their old leaves at the end of the growing season, since they have not the knack (as has *C. montana*, for instance) of shedding them. This certainly looks terrible but it means nothing. I do think, though, that it is wise of the nurseryman to pick off these dead leaves before despatching plants, because a naked plant looks so much better than a scarecrow. Also, some of the dead leaves might be carrying fungus spores and act as a source of infection by wilt disease at a later stage.

Another trap for the unwary. Young clematis are generally tied to canes. If the cane was not placed fairly centrally in the pot or if it was rather too heavy for the strength of the roots in their ball of soil, then, when you turn the clematis upside down so as to knock or jerk it out of its pot, the cane may take on a life of its own in a most disconcerting fashion. It may twist sideways and kink or even break the clematis stem near the base. That is not necessarily fatal by any means but it may, with the fine-rooted kinds I've just been describing, bring about a severing of roots from stem, which is the end.

If you receive the clematis in a paper pot or in a polybag (a black polythene bag in which it was grown), you can cut and peel the containing material away from the ball of roots while the latter are sitting in their hole, ready for planting and there'll be no need to turn anything upside down. But if the plant is being turned out of a rigid pot, hold it vertically upside down (not obliquely) before you tap the pot rim to extract its contents, and stretch the fingers of your left hand (the hand that's going to support the ball of soil) round both sides of the cane (two on one side, two on the other), so that they cover the whole top surface of the ball and grip the cane at the same time. It is just at the moment of extraction that nasty things are liable to happen. Righting the plant is not nearly so tricky. After ruining a dozen or two you'll find you've got the knack and wonder what all the fuss was about.

Two other pre-planting points are perhaps worth making. If the ball of soil is dry on arrival, as it may well be after a journey under the aegis of national transport, drop it, container and all, into a bucket of water. Half-an-hour will be long enough if the plant was grown in a soil compost like the John Innes formula. Nowadays it is more likely to have been grown in a peat and sand compost without soil, and it should then be soaked overnight, as dry peat is very reluctant to take up moisture.

Second point: if the plant was grown in one of these soilless composts and you are not ready to plant it on arrival, remember that it will soon run out of nutrients and should be given liquid feeds, say once a week in the growing season, if the delay in planting is going to be protracted.

When planting, firm the plant in so that the soil round and below it isn't too soft and spongy and get it placed so that the lowest 2cm of the clematis stem is below the soil surface. Water in well if there is the slightest hint of the soil being dry.

The special problems of planting clematis in turf or in the proximity of tree, shrub or hedge roots have already been discussed in Chapter 3. If you must plant in turf, keep the grass back from the clematis stem by at least 0·7m. Water and feed extra-generously. If birds scratch your mulches on to the grass you'll have to net them in.

After Care

The pruning of young stock is described in the next chapter.

The main point to remember with a young clematis, even more than with an established one, is that it shall not go short of water. An old gardening friend who has long been a clematis addict, recommended to me (years ago) knocking the bottom out of used claret bottles and then sinking them in the ground, bottom up, beside the newly planted clematis so that, by watering through the bottle you made sure of getting down to their roots. In order to make things easy, he gave me a case of excellent claret which I drank with great pleasure but entirely forgot to use the bottles afterwards. I'm not sure that Burgundy would come to the same thing. A snag we're running into today is that fewer bottles are being made with a kick-up, which is a perfect funnel when you're watering. It also facilitates knocking a hole in the bottom without breaking the entire bottle.

It is a fact that puppies are very much given to cutting their second teeth on clematis stems. With a dreamy, far-away look in their eyes, they chomp and chew right through even quite thick trunks. Humans themselves have been known to tear through young clematis stems when they intended to be doing something quite different. You can resort to a circle of wire netting. I don't like the look of the stuff myself and would rather risk disaster, but then I've always got young clematis coming on that I want to find places for.

Once a clematis is established you must resist any temptation to dig round it as the roots reach right to the surface and spread far and wide beyond the trunk. The best way to ensure being good is to keep that surface mulch going. Wherever there's a mulch in the garden you won't want to dig – another point in its favour.

CHAPTER 8

Pruning and Training

*

AN unpruned clematis looks like a disembowelled mattress –
a painful sight. From year to year its owner grows more
despairing; his only comfort is that the birds are nesting in the
tangle and perhaps not all of them are sparrows. Every time he
bumps into this dropsical lump, his face, neck, clothes get
sprayed with water. He loves clematis but he abhors this
loathsome abortion. What is he to do?

The trouble with clematis is that they cannot all be pruned
in the same way. For the busy man who has not the time to go
into why's and wherefores, my kindest policy to save him
reading further, will be to lay down three basic pruning
methods, one of which can be applied to almost any clematis
he may grow.

Group A Prune only if space is limited. In that case cut out
all shoots that have flowered immediately after flowering.
This method applies to the earliest, spring-flowering species,
hybrids and cultivars, notably *C. alpina, C. macropetala,
C. armandii, C. montana* and *C. chrysocoma*.

Group B Cut out dead growth. Shorten all remaining vines to
the first pair of strong buds. Time of pruning: February-
March, when the buds referred to will already be plump and
green. To this group belong all the large-flowered hybrids
(including the doubles) that are expected to start their main
flush of blossoming before mid-June. Examples: Nelly Moser,
Lasurstern, Miss Bateman, Duchess of Edinburgh, Vyvyan
Pennell, Mrs Cholmondeley.

Group C Cut all growth hard back to one metre or considerably less above ground level. Time: February-March. This will
entail the removal of many healthy-looking green shoots but
don't let that worry or deter you. The method applies to all

later flowering clematis that are required to make their main contribution after mid-June (perhaps as late as September, in some cases). Examples: *C. viticella, C. rehderiana, C. flammula, C. tangutica, C.* × *jackmanii*, Perle d'Azur, Royal Velours, Lady Betty Balfour, Duchess of Albany.

In the alphabetical descriptive section at the end of this book, an A, B or C will be found against every clematis that can be attached to one of these groups. A few will obligingly slot into either Group B or C, allowing considerable latitude and indulgence for carelessness. Anyone wishing to work to a quick rule of thumb should thus be satisfied.

*

Now let us start at the beginning again and take an intelligent interest in how the different kinds of clematis are behaving and how our pruning is best calculated to take account of their behaviour.

The earliest clematis (Group A), including *C. cirrhosa* var. *balearica* (syn. *C. calycina*) have flowers that are 'borne directly on the last season's wood' (to borrow Mr Pennell's wording). The cluster of from 1 to 6 flowers and leaves that you get in the axil of each main leaf are really condensed shoots: so condensed, indeed, that they are stemless. In clematis flowering a little later, however (Group B), these axillary shoots do make a little extension growth and at least one pair of young leaves before you reach the terminal flower bud. 'Flowers borne on short growth from last season's wood' is the way Pennell's succinctly phrase it. Nelly Moser and Marcel Moser are typical here.

We next come to certain clematis that refuse to conform to one pattern. First they produce a flower at the end of each fairly short growth from last season's wood; then they make masses of extension growth on long, vigorous young shoots and proceed to flower along the last metre or so of this, carrying one or more blooms in the axil of each leaf. Typical here are Ville de Lyon, Ernest Markham, Hagley Hybrid, Marie Boisselot, Mrs Cholmondeley and Duchess of Sutherland.

Finally we reach the late, Group C, flowerers which do it all on the last metre or two of long current season's shoots. Even here one may get the occasional early bloom off the old wood on an unpruned specimen. I have known Gipsy Queen do this in June, although its main flowering is in August. The most prolific and long-flowering within this group carry many blooms in the axils of each node, not just one (as in Ville de Lyon). The main axillary bloom will be supported by further flower buds which will open later and extend the flowering season, albeit with smaller blooms. Such are Comtesse de Bouchaud and Perle d'Azur.

I hope you get the overall picture. No new growth has to be made to enable the earliest flowering clematis to perform, but the later you get in the season, the more growth has to be put on before any flower buds are formed until we reach Lady Betty Balfour, in September, flowering at the ends of 3 or 4 metre-long shoots of the current season.

The main point about pruning is to help each clematis to carry the maximum of flowers. To this end, of course, pruning must go hand in hand with watering and feeding.

Back to the early flowerers again. Group A includes some very vigorous clematis, and *C. montana* is far and away the most vigorous of the lot. They are set the task of masking eyesores like new garages quickly but, having done so, are then required to lay off it. But you can't explain that sort of rule or requirement to a plant and, not unexpectedly, they just keep on growing. This exposes them to the most damaging line in butchery. The irate owner, finding that he can no longer see out of his windows nor drive into his car port, gets cracking with his secateurs in the autumn, which is the gardener's natural tidying up season. I am not saying that drastic action may not be necessary then, at the end of the growing season, but I do think that if the owner, given a reasonably phlegmatic temperament, realised that with every trail of new montana or macropetala growth that he was removing in the autumn or winter he was depriving himself of 50 or more blooms the next spring, he might well find that 'operation haircut' could be deferred until after the flowers had been enjoyed. Sometime in May or early June in nearly all cases.

If pruning after flowering, in May, you can cut a clematis back to a framework of branches, leaving not a stitch of foliage on the whole plant. No harm will come. With the whole summer before it, your plant will start into growth again very shortly after its massacre and will be amply covered with strong young vines by the autumn. On these it will flower in the following spring.

On these early flowerers, then, we practise a kind of delayed pruning and it is worth observing that many others of the earliest flowering shrubs are treated in like manner, e.g. *Prunus triloba* and *P. tenella, Spiraea thunbergii* and *S. × arguta, Forsythia suspensa* and *Jasminum nudiflorum.* You can shorten the branches on all these after flowering because they have the summer before them in which to make next year's flowering wood.

Treated thus, these early clematis will also carry the largest blossoms although their overall growth is restricted. I have a *C. montana* that I cut back hard each late May, otherwise it gets under the tiles of the roof above, but the result of my efforts is that each bloom carried is 8 or 9cm across instead of the more normal 5 or 6cm on an unpruned specimen.

I think *C. armandii* is all the better for regular pruning. You can train it to cover an allotted wall space and subsequently cut all its flowered trails back to this framework immediately after flowering, in mid-May. You may be grieved to find you cannot avoid cutting its young shoots at the same time but you shouldn't let this worry you. More will come, in next to no time and the whole plant will wear a rejuvenated appearance. After all, the old leaves on this evergreen species do look pretty tatty at winter's end.

Since writing the above I have had an interesting correspondence apropos, so I shall quote it fairly fully. Mrs Davies lives at Haddenham, near Aylesbury, Bucks. and wrote on 24 April. 'Dear Mr Lloyd, The autumn before last I bought a clematis armandii. It is the success story to end all success stories but I'm now writing to ask for help. It made about 15ft of growth last season and this year has been a mass of blossom. It now looks all set to repeat its growth pattern and I am beginning (while enchanted and proud) to feel slightly hounded, as I spend a good many of my waking hours tying in and generally striving to control this abundance. I live in a bungalow and I read that this clematis should not be pruned; it is now beginning to riot over the roof! Where I should be very grateful for your help is in advising me a) whether and b) when I can prune it a little? I enclose s.a.e. for your reply.' I wish everyone would think of that.

I told her to prune all flowered trails hard immediately, as I have just been telling you, and asked her to let me know the result in the autumn, as the information would be useful for my book. She wrote on 25 September.

'Early in May you advised me on pruning clematis armandii and asked for a progress report in the autumn. I cut it back very hard then as you suggested. It has responded well, putting out plenty of new growth. It then produced a second flush of growth in August, which showed signs of being healthy, plentiful and vigorous. At this point the saga takes a sad turn. What I take to have been grey squirrels have systematically stripped *all* this new growth – they have done the same to C. calycina . . . They don't take the early flush of growth, only the later. Even so, armandii has made about 6ft in every direction (it is trained round a bay window) and looks splendid.'

I replied that earwigs, not squirrels, were certainly the culprits, that they never damage early growth because their numbers have not built up when this is made but that they are particularly troublesome on young shoots late in the season, and had been particularly numerous and tiresome everywhere in the year in question. However, I was able to reassure her that the first flush of growth would be quite sufficient to provide a handsome display in the spring.

After that *histoire* let me return you to base. There are many circumstances where you'll never want to prune even a montana (though never is an absolute word that I hesitate to leave unqualified). If it is to romp through a tree you will just let it romp. Even so, after 20 years or more (here comes the qualification) a time may yet arrive when an old montana is no longer giving you the pleasure it once did. New growth piles up on an ever-increasing substrate of old, dead debris. At this stage the only sort of pruning that may seem at all on the cards is the complete removal of everything within sight except for 2 or 3 metres of old trunks at the base. My advice is: go ahead and do it. There is a risk of killing the plant. There is a risk of greatly weakening it so that the response in terms of young growth from very old wood is half-hearted and slow. In that case finish the job and replant with a youngster. You may, on the other hand, get satisfactory rejuvenation of the old plant and the risk is worth taking because you'll never be happy again with an old monster once you have noticed just how monstrous it has become.

The same applies to *C. macropetala* and *C. alpina*. They don't enjoy being cut back into 10-year-old wood but it may still be the wisest course. I recently cut an old, really thick-stemmed *C. alpina* 'Columbine' back to 0·5m. It has responded but weakly, with thin spindly shoots from the old stumps. Had I made a practice of clipping it over every year after flowering, all would have been plain sailing, though tiresome for me at a busy season. As it is, the plant may or may not pull itself together. I applied the same treatment to an old *C. macropetala* (in the interests of this book, actually). From the cuts I made into 1cm.-thick wood, it immediately made new green buds, but when the young shoots were about 5cm. long it changed its mind and the plant died.

In sum, clematis are pretty good about breaking from old wood if they have been made accustomed from their youth to an annual massacre. But if they are left to their own devices for many years and then massacred, their response is in greater doubt. Another example: I have a friend to whom I gave a Lasurstern layer many years ago and for many years it grew and flowered well against his house without more than a little pruning and trimming. But its legs became bare and stemmy. Because of a hedge growing in front of it, it was rather dark in its nether regions and this was the probable cause of its legginess. Lasurstern generally breaks well and frequently from low down, right through its life. Anyway, I recommended him to cut this old chap hard back to a foot or so (we weren't metric then), and he did. And it did break, but weakly. It was never the same again and gradually faded away. He never reproached me, either: a true sign of friendship.

With Lasurstern as guide, we move on to Group B and take note of the fact that Mr Fisk, in his handsome catalogue, tells us that none of this group need pruning. In fact, doubtless appreciating that customers like to be told that a quiet life is good for them and the best way of living, he has reduced all his pruning recommendations to one of two succinct words: either 'Hard' or 'None'. Makes me wonder if this chapter is just a lot of padding.

So, according to him, it's None for Nelly Moser and all her May-June-flowering companions. 'I want a large-flowered clematis that doesn't need pruning' is a request that often comes my way. In vain for me to protest that the clematis which absolutely demand hard and regular pruning are much the easiest to deal with. They won't believe me.

OK, sell them a Nelly Moser, tell them it wants no pruning and let them get on with it. As she flowers on the previous season's wood, she'll flower all right but in a very few years we shall be back among the birds' nests and the old mattress. Then we shall be forced into drastic action; we shall at best lose most of one year's blossom and at worst be unlucky as in the case of the Lasurstern on my friend's house.

It is far preferable to do some pruning every year. If you are really conscientious about the way you do it, this is a fiddling task, so be sure to choose mild weather (the season being February or early March) and for preference a nice bit of sunshine warming your back through your winter woollies.

Remove all dead shoots or pieces of shoots. Clematis make far more growth in one year than they will ever carry forward into the next, so there is always plenty of dead to remove. Especially where they have flowered. The 'short growths from last season's wood' on which the flowers were borne will generally die at the end of the season. Long, new young vines will have taken their place and are what need to be cherished for the next season's blossom.

All the healthy young wood that is to be saved will be clinging together in a tangled skein. Snip carefully between the interlocking vines so that they can be separated and trained in various directions so as to cover the maximum possible area. This is a nerve-racking job as, from time to time, you'll find you've accidentally snipped through a live and healthy shoot. But you must develop the quality of phlegm. Surgeons, after all, do far worse things to their patients and it really matters, sometimes, with them, but the surgeon remains a very jolly sort of person with a schoolboy sense of humour. Surgeons make excellent growers of clematis.

The point of all this separating and training is that it enables the clematis to present its blossoms in the most flattering manner: not all bunched up and overlapping but so that they can *all* be enjoyed.

Now, I realise that one doesn't necessarily have time for this caper. In that case, having cut out all dead wood and shortened the rest to a pair of strong buds, as I instructed at the beginning of the chapter, plaster what remains against its support as best you can without further disentanglement. That'll do well enough. The main thing is that you'll have done enough to prevent the clematis from accumulating a mass of its own dead debris and thus developing into the dreaded dropsical lump.

What would happen if you made a practice of pruning Group B clematis hard back as though they belonged to Group C? That is a very interesting question, as the politicians say, playing for time in the face of an awkward poser.

In some cases this treatment will provoke another perennial question: 'why does my clematis not flower?' If it is one that insists on flowering on its old wood or not at all, it'll never have any old wood to flower on and hence won't flower. Q.E.D.

But the fascinating thing about clematis is that so many of them won't obey rules; they make their own as they go along. Some of our Group B lot can flower on young wood as well as off those short growths from the old (and when we say old, we merely mean shoots that were young in the previous year: year-old wood, in fact). Nelly and Marcel Moser, for instance. Even if they've flowered freely in May-June, healthy specimens can be expected to carry at least one bloom (sometimes several) at the ends of the current season's new vines any time from August to November. A hard pruning of all the previous year's growth, in February, will pre-empt the entire May-June crop but will tend to swell the numbers carried in late summer and autumn on the superabundance of young shoots. This is quite logical. The May-June flowering is admittedly what we are generally aiming for in Group B, but the production of a mass of blossom then has a very inhibiting effect on the subsequent production of young shoots. I know of a Miss Bateman, growing in a rather tight, starved corner, that flowers so heavily in some years as to be incapable of producing any young shoots for the remainder of that year. Consequently it hardly flowers at all in the next year.

So this coin has two sides. If the Miss Bateman I write of were sufficiently well nourished and watered, it would be able to flower and shoot well all in the same season and hence every season, and that would be ideal in most cases.

However, supposing you were taking your holiday in the South of France in May-June. What use would it be to you to be told that your Nelly Moser had never flowered so well as in your absence? To rub salt into the wound, 'they' might take a coloured photograph of it to show you what you had missed and to impress on you the folly of being out of England in May-June and especially when, crowning insult, the weather on the Riviera turned out to be far worse than it was at home. Well then, you could put a stop to at least one opportunity for *Schadenfreude* by pruning your Nelly Moser hard back in February. There'd be no flowers in your absence and perhaps an increased bonus crop in the autumn. Lasurstern is even more strongly predisposed to flowering well on its young wood in August-September if pruned hard in late winter. I know of 2 instances near me (ones I drive past) where this is its regular treatment. They grow next to the front door and I expect their owners dislike their winter appearance and cut them back in self defence. They're missing a lot but their method undeniably works: the late summer display is good.

And so we edge towards those varieties which the pundits will instruct you to cut hard back as a regular routine but which I should be inclined to give a double chance. A keen clematis-growing friend in Dorset wrote me one February: 'Have you read what Tony Venison says about pruning Clematis in today's Country Life? I never knew that Mrs Cholmondeley was Jackmanii group and it is always the first of the large ones to flower with me. I shall most certainly *never* cut it, or rather

her, down.' If your Mrs Cholmondeley is well fed and watered, she will flower abundantly both early and late, given the Group B treatment, but there may be circumstances when it is preferable to treat her as Group C, thus limiting yourself to the one crop.

The same with Ville de Lyon, a variety that puts out distress signals sooner than any other if at all deprived of food and drink. All the lower stem leaves die prematurely (and remain on the plant, of course) which can look most unsightly if it is grown on a wall. If you cannot avoid this condition (but you can), then do as the pundits tell you. Cut Ville de Lyon hard back annually and let it concentrate its efforts on just the one, late crop. But if it is growing in a well manured border and luxuriating with an abundance of growth, a light pruning will enable you to enjoy early blooms and these are much the largest and handsomest of the whole season. Neither will there be any shortage of late blossom. It will continue through most of the summer and early autumn.

I draw attention to this potential in other varieties where I deal with them individually. There is one further point to emphasise here. Nearly all the large-flowered double clematis carry their double flowers on short growth off the previous season's wood. If you prune them hard you'll get no double flowers, only singles (Duchess of Edinburgh and Miriam Markham are the only exceptions I can think of, and the small-flowered doubles of viticella affinity, do come double on young wood). This would be disastrous in varieties like Vyvyan Pennell and Proteus, where the main charm or excitement, rather, of the flower is in its doubleness. It would matter less in Daniel Deronda, Jackmanii Rubra or Jackmanii Alba, where the early double flowers are a bonus and the main crop is single, however lightly you prune.

We can now, at a stately pace, move forward to the late flowerers, those which flower wholeheartedly on the last few metres of the young growth they have made in the current season. By pruning them hard annually you not merely clean the plant up but you encourage it to put on masses of productive young growth. Many amateur gardeners object to this pruning. In the first place, they don't realise how easy and quick it is. You simply make a series of vicious cuts at a low level, then grab the severed stems in both hands, pull downwards and outwards and away they all come from their support, leaving only a few random leaves behind to tell the tale. Even if their support is a climbing rose or an evergreen ceanothus, say, the clematis will break away from it cleanly and sweetly.

The amateur's second objection is that, as he has expressly planted the clematis to cover a piece of blank wall, he doesn't want to have to expose it again, which is what this type of pruning entails. What he fails to realise and what the nurseryman/salesman can hardly be expected to explain, is that, at the time pruning should be done and for months afterwards, the wall will look better without a shabby clematis on it than with. If the clematis belongs to Groups A or B, he'll have to endure its prolonged dishevelled appearance in the winter half of the year willy nilly but if it is a Group C clematis he can give himself a blessed rest from it.

But he doesn't like his bare wall? Then he shouldn't grow a clematis on it – not in isolated squalor, which is what I've been trying to say all along. First cover the wall with suitable clothing, for goodness sake: cotoneasters, ceanothus, chaenomeles, climbing roses, figs, wisterias, magnolias, myrtles; their name is legion – and then grow your clematis over them.

The clematis in Group C lend themselves particularly well to the pole treatment: as vertical features, a column of blossom rising above lower surroundings. The clematis is cut annually to within 0·3m of the ground. As it makes its young growth in spring and early summer you tie this in to the pole (you'll need a step ladder for the top ties because the pole can rise to 3m above ground level). Use a heavy grade of tarred string for these ties. If the string is soft and fluffy (as is fillis) sparrows will tear it off and use it as nesting material.

If the clematis is to be grown into a small tree, you may not want to prune it so low, as extra height is required of it. Always prune low in its first year, but in subsequent years you can ease up a bit and leave a greater length of old stem each time. But there are few occasions when this is necessary.

11

1. *C. napaulensis*
2. *C. cirrhosa* var. *balearica*
3. *C. afoliata*
4. *C. armandii*
5. *C. paniculata*
6. *C. macropetala*
7. *C. macropetala* 'Markham's Pink'
8. *C. alpina* 'Columbine'
9. *C. alpina* 'Pamela Jackman'
10. *C. alpina* 'Frances Rivis'
11. *C. alpina* 'Ruby'
12. *C. alpina sibirica* 'White Moth'

12

1. *C. montana*
2. *C. montana* var. *wilsonii*
3. *C. montana* var. *rubens*
4. *C. montana* 'Picton's Variety'
5. *C. montana* 'Elizabeth'
6. *C. montana* 'Tetrarose'
7. *C. chrysocoma* var. *sericea*
8. *C. chrysocoma*
9. *C.* × *vedrariensis*

Pruning and Training

Although *C. orientalis* and *C. tangutica* belong to Group C there is quite a lot to be said for pruning them fairly lightly, back to a permanent framework that may reach up to 2m. This is because of their non-stop habit of flowering, once they have started. Light pruning enables them to start before June is out, and they will then continue right into October or even later.

Most of this group have one long but limited flowering season. It is longer than the comparable season of *C. montana* (Group A) or the first flowering of Nelly Moser (Group B) because in those the buds all form at one and the same time and all open more or less together, whereas in Group C we have panicles of blossom in which the centre ones of each cluster open first and are followed at a distance by subtending buds and these, in some cases, by buds subtending the subtenders. But when all these have flowered there is nothing more to follow and the revels are at an end even though autumn may scarcely have arrived.

If you are growing a Group C clematis against a wall, you can greatly increase the area it will cover by intelligent pruning. If you cut all the vines back to the same point, the young growths will all rush up together in one vertical skein – just what you want when a pole is the support but seldom what is required on a wall, unless there are windows on either side. The way to prune in this case is to cut the shoots back by different amounts: some hard, some less hard and some so as to leave as much as 2m of old stem. Then they are trained fan-wise to right and to left leaving the shortest in the centre and keeping all as low as you conveniently can. The young shoots will, as always, develop from the extreme pair of buds above which each pruning cut was made and will run up the wall like the prongs of a fork, covering a large area.

*

I am often asked what can be done to prevent a clematis from rushing up a wall and flowering out of sight at the top. This habit is usually most noticeable on dark, sunless walls. The clematis is rushing upwards in search of light. Group C clematis are the most likely to frustrate you by this disappointing performance. There is little you can do to control their growth while they are actually growing, and they flower at the height that pleases them while they are still growing. Group B clematis can be more easily persuaded to flower where you want them to. Even if their new growth has run up too high for your sight lines, you can re-distribute and train it against the lower wall face at pruning time. The flowers will be borne on short growths from this re-distributed old wood and you'll have them where you want them.

There are refinements worth discussing on the season of pruning. Apart from Group A, whose pruning is delayed until after flowering, all clematis are normally pruned in February or March. By then you can see what's live and what's dead because the live shoots will be on the move. Most clematis are very precocious in this respect. It is particularly important to know what's living and what isn't in the pruning and training of Group B, so there is little scope for choice of other pruning months between autumn and spring in their case. You could do it in January but . . . . I am writing these words in January – a very mild one – and the Group B clematis are already amazingly forward. But if I sorted them over now I should inevitably expose their young buds to a greater extent than they are exposed before pruning, when the tangle of old, dead shoots does afford them some protection against frost. Every one of these green Group B leaf clusters that are now plain to see contains a flower bud: not yet visible but there just the same. If I lose it through frost damage in February or March, the loss is total and without redress, so I shall walk delicately and delay my pruning yet awhile.

Not so with Group C clematis. These are the most hideous of all in their off season, a tangle of dark shoots and blackened foliage that they refuse to shed. To endure this spectacle throughout the winter is asking a lot and I seldom do. I cut them hard back – give them the full pruning treatment, in fact – at any time that suits me from when they become dormant, in November, onwards. This will do no harm to a strongly established specimen. In fact it is much like pruning your roses early as is nowadays widely practised instead of leaving them to the traditional March season.

It is true that, having been pruned early, Group C will sprout new young shoots dangerously early from just below where you made your cuts. I have just, late January, checked on this in my rose garden where I pruned the clematis at the same time as the roses a month ago. Perle d'Azur and Star of India both have young shoots on them from 15 to 30cm long. Mme Julia Correvon only 13cm long and less still – 3cm – on Viticella Rubra. The most forward are sure to get frosted or battered by wind before we're out of the wood but this won't matter. These are shoot buds, not flower buds. If they are destroyed, others behind them will develop and take their place. I shall have lost nothing.

I have said that most Group C clematis flower themselves to a standstill, after which nothing more can be expected of them, even though their flowering may be at an end by, say, mid-August. Southern gardeners of an experimental temperament might like to try for a second crop by cutting everything back by half as soon as the first (and generally only) flowering has drawn to a close. If the autumn remains open and warm as autumns so often have, of late years, the clematis will sprout again and have time for a second blossoming before the growing season ends. At least, this worked for me on a *C. viticella* that I so treated and it should be feasible on the earlier Group C performers like Etoile Violette, Hagley Hybrid and Comtesse de Bouchaud.

Another refinement. You were told by Christopher Lloyd that Etoile Violette and *C. flammula* associate prettily together: the froth of white of the one offsetting the substantial violet flowers of the other. On trying this out, however, you found that Etoile Violette flowered so much earlier than flammula that there was no overlap. So you write to C.L. acidly pointing out the error of his recommendation (this actually happened) and he, being pleased rather than distressed at having peeved you, does not reply. But had he liked your tone he could have redressed matters by first apologising and admitting that Gipsy Queen would have been a far more suitable team-mate for *C. flammula* than Etoile Violette, flowering at least a month later. But, as you have already got the first suggested pair growing merrily together, you can manipulate their behaviour. Prune flammula only enough to remove its last year's old flowering panicles, thus encouraging it to flower earlier than normal. Contrariwise, prune Etoile Violette extra hard and extra late, say in April, thereby very considerably delaying the onset of its flowering season. By dint of two opposite pruning treatments Cox shall meet Box at last.

Incidentally, whereas it is so often a good plan to plant two clematis of the same pruning group side by side, it is not so clever to grow a Group C clematis near to one belonging to Group A. I have done just that. *C. viticella* and *C. cirrhosa* var. *balearica*, cheek by jowl. When I prune *C. viticella* in the winter, it is quite easy to pull its shoots out and away from *C. cirrhosa*, but when I want to reduce the latter, following its flowering, which doesn't end till late April, the young shoots of *C. viticella* are already threaded through it and I don't like to spoil them (I could all the same, and I shall one of these days).

There may be occasions when you want to prune Group B clematis at an unconventional season. You remember the example I cited of a Miss Bateman growing under rather starved and parched conditions at the edge of a meadow. She flowers so abundantly in alternate years that she is unable to find the strength to make new shoots on which to flower in the intervening years. Apart from the obvious cure by organising a better diet, you can redress matters to a certain extent in the pruning department by cutting all the flowered wood back immediately following her flowering. This will be sometime in late June and will encourage the production of young shoots rather than the channelling of her energies into ripening seed. Similarly, if you have failed to prune a Group B clematis for several years and it has got out of hand; instead of resigning yourself to drastic treatment in February-March and no flowers in May-June, you can wait till after the May-June flowering and hack back then, including, willy nilly, all the young shoots that have been made that spring.

I must, before leaving this subject, bring up a question to which I don't know the answer. Some clematis, notably Ernest Markham, Huldine and Lady Betty Balfour– in some gardens or in some positions in the same garden but not in others, make masses of growth each year but carry few or no blooms. It is certainly wrong in principle to grow these in a shady position but don't now write and tell me that you have a Huldine in absolute shade that never fails to reward you with cascades of blossom. Such things can be and shade in the south-east of England is very much akin to sun in the north. I know of examples of *C. orientalis* in Ludlow & Sheriff's form (13342) that flower excellently in shade in Sussex and Kent but do nothing more than vegetate in the north, especially when shaded.

In the case of a variety like Lady Betty Balfour, season makes all the difference. I should never dream of planting this clematis north of Trent anyway (but see p. 57) but even in the south and in sunshine she is apt to miss out following a dull summer, but makes a fantastic display after a sunny one.

Sunshine comes into it, then, but is not the whole story and it is frequently suggested that pinching out of young shoots when they are 2m long, will snap them into a flowering condition. Particularly is this suggested of Huldine and Ernest Markham. I can only say that such has not been my experience. If one of these clematis is a recalcitrant non-flowerer in one part of your garden, however, do move it and try it in another. As with the temperamental *Gentiana acaulis*, this may just do the trick and if it does, you won't scratch your head too much in search of a reason. Results speak for themselves.

Young Stock

Finally, the pruning of young, newly acquired clematis. It is standard practice to shorten these back to a pair of buds (which are very likely dormant but will not remain so for even a week after pruning) 15 to 30cm above ground level, in February–March. This is a sound recommendation in most cases. It helps to build up a stout, slug-and-disease-proof stem, in the first place, and it helps build up a strong root system, preventing an overload on its resources. However, I should make an exception in the case of strong plants within Group A: *C. montana, C. alpina, C. macropetala, C. armandii* etc. If these are well grown they should be able to cope with a metre of stem and there'll be flowers to enjoy in the spring.

Should you buy your clematis in spring, they will already have been pruned on the nursery and there will be no need for further shortening back, provided the roots look strong.

CHAPTER 9

Propagation

*

'HOW do you propagate your clematis? It's quite simple, isn't it?' Thus, the visiting public to Lloyd, hard pressed and a trifle brusque, on various occasions between spring and autumn. When you are at the seat of custom and there are others waiting their turn, it is impossible to stop in mid-stream (the current uncomfortably strong) in order to discuss a subject that will occupy quite a long chapter here. By refusing to discuss it, I am not demonstrating a cagey secretiveness in respect of methods that I intend to keep under my hat. Far from it. I immediately refer my questioner to my book (mark 1) and suggest they should borrow a copy from the public library (which won't, unfortunately, put a penny into my pocket). If they are interested enough in the subject, this will not be too great an effort. If they are not all that interested, neither need I be in them.

In the first book to be written on clematis by Moore & Jackman about a century ago, propagation was not so much as mentioned, let alone discussed or described. That a nurseryman should reveal his methods was inconceivable, in those days. Indeed, this particular iceberg has only melted in the 30 years since the last war. But it has melted, almost completely and this says a great deal for human nature. It is the kind of uncelebrated progress that will never make news but that I find marvellously heartening. There is a flourishing and expanding organisation called The International Plant Propagators' Society at whose meetings nurserymen and representatives from research institutes and teaching colleges exchange details of propagation methods with complete lack of reservation and without thought of rivalry. It is true that the press are not invited to these meetings but the proceedings are published in due course and from then on there is no objection to anyone anywhere being informed of what took place.

I find it hard to explain the reason for this changed approach. The younger generation is free of jealousies that were, until very recently, commonplace. They appear to realise that if you are good at your job you have nothing to fear from others knowing how you do it; that shared knowledge both among professionals and with the consumer public is stimulating. I think nurserymen as a body are probably nicer people than they used to be. Whether they are nicer because they have become more communicative or whether being nicer had made them more communicative, I don't know but I can say that as a body, the trade and all those connected professionally with horticulture are lively and pleasing company. I feel sure that two reasons for this are, first, that they known they are doing a worthwhile and interesting job; second, that it is an active industry wherein methods are changing and improving at an incredible rate. Clematis production has not lagged in this respect and the plant's popularity has been met by a greater efficiency in its propagation than could have been dreamed of 30 years ago.

I will start by discussing the subject at the professional level of mass production and then consider what methods are open and most easily accessible to the amateur.

Grafting

Until 25 years ago, the principal method of clematis propagation was by grafting. Only very easily struck groups like the montanas, alpinas and macropetalas were rooted from cuttings.

The most commonly used stock for grafting is *C. vitalba*, with *C. viticella* as a popular runner-up. Seedlings are imported from Holland. They are seldom raised in this country, but from direct sowings in an outside seed bed, are ready in their second year, being ideal for use when 5 to 8mm (¼ to ⅓ in.) thick where the graft is made. January to March is the main season and the stock plants for producing scion wood are brought into early growth under heated structures. Their young trails are ready for use when about a metre long and can then be expected to yield 10 scions (or more) each from five reasonably firm nodes, the tips being discarded. The nodes are split longitudinally and cut with a shield of wood behind each bud. The stock is prepared by cutting across the stem so as to leave 3cm of collar above the roots and a simple whip graft is made. It is tied in from the bottom using wet raffia or, if this rots too quickly, carpet thread is suitable (obtainable from a haberdashery). The grafted seedlings are potted into very small pots, twisting the roots so as to get them in and leaving the scion bud just above the soil surface, where it is less likely to rot than when buried. The pots are stood on a bench (or floor) with bottom heat of 21 degrees C. and covered with clear polythene, this being turned daily so as to obviate undue condensation and, once again, the probable rotting of the eye.

When young growth starts in about a month's time, the temperature is lowered to 15 degrees C. and hardening off is gradually achieved. At 8 weeks the young plants can be given their final potting into 10cm long toms and they will make strong plants for sale in the autumn. It will thus be seen that the whole operation from grafting to the production of a saleable plant is quick: 9 months or less. What may be another advantage is that grafting can be done at a comparatively slack season on the nursery.

The method has been widely criticised on the principal counts that grafted plants are harder to get established in the garden than 'plants on their own roots', that they are more liable to contract wilt disease, that collapse of the scion is seldom followed by regeneration from below ground level and, in sum, that so great is mortality of plants raised in this way that many have given up clematis cultivation in despair. Thus, Ernest Markham ('Clematis' p. 31–32). I agree that many have given up the cultivation of clematis in despair but this has nothing whatever to do with the practice of grafting. The Glasshouse Crops Research Institute's experiments (see their Annual Report 1965, pages 128–131) on the susceptibility of clematis to infection by the fungus causing wilt disease revealed no greater inroads by the disease on grafted plants than on plants raised from cuttings.

Indeed, why should they? You graft on to a seedling whose roots provide the initial boost that enables the scion to get started. The graft union (below the scion bud) is buried beneath the soil surface and the scion quickly begins to make its own roots. In a short time these greatly exceed the stock's roots and by the time sales take place the customer is buying a plant that is virtually (80 per cent, anyway) on its own roots. The graft was a nurse graft. The stock does not provide a root system for the plant's whole life (as is generally the case with roses, for instance) but merely long enough to enable the scion to take over, root and branch. When planted in the garden, a grafted plant should be set low enough for 3cm or so of stem above the highest roots, to be buried below the soil surface and this is a principal safeguard against damage (dogs gnawing) and disease (usually fungal) on the aerial portions. If these collapse or disappear, dormant shoot buds underground will break and off you go again.

These dormant buds, let it be emphasised, will, even on grafted plants, belong to the scion, not to the stock. They will not be undesirable suckers. 'When a grafted plant collapses this is usually its end, and not infrequently the growth of the stock appears in its place.' Markham, again. Now, grafting is done on that piece of seedling stem between its roots and the lowest pair of leaves (seed leaves, known as cotyledons) called the hypocotyl. It is impossible for the stock of a clematis to sucker from here or from its roots. This could only happen if the graft were made high up the stem, above the cotyledons. No doubt that did happen, occasionally, and it is an example of grafting badly practised, but no indictment of the practice of grafting. I have not met a case of a grafted clematis throwing suckers in the past 30 years. (We must not allow ourselves to be confused by the ability of *C. macropetala* and *C. alpina* to sucker on their own roots. These species are never used as stocks for grafting anyway).

Where grafting still persists as a commercial method of clematis propagation it is for one of two reasons. If a nursery has always been geared to this production method and finds it satisfactory, there will be an inbuilt disinclination to change over to another method even if there is a chance or probability that the latter will prove more effective. A considerable disruption in organisation will be entailed, expensive changeover in equipment and a re-deployment of staff duties. This kind of disruption is not lightly embraced.

The other reason for the survival of grafting as a method for raising clematis is that the provision of a ready-made seedling root system enables a great surge of energy to be unleashed on the scion bud. If the scion is habitually weak growing, as is *C. florida* 'Sieboldii' or if there is a difficulty in making the scion bud break dormancy, as in *C. armandii*, then this extra boost may make all the difference between success and failure.

C. armandii being a special case, I will consider the problems it presents to the nurseryman at this point. It is a clematis that he cannot ignore. The public regards it as a highly desirable evergreen, the only clematis combining evergreenery with vigour, reasonable hardiness and a good floral display, so it is astonishingly popular (I am astonished, anyway) and demand unfailingly exceeds supply.

When raised from cuttings, *C. armandii* roots with little difficulty but it can be the devil's own business to make it shoot. This is not to deny that a great many armandii's are raised for sale this way but results are uneven and percentages of success unsatisfactory. I am sure there will be improvements yet. No one has given his mind and attention wholeheartedly to the problem. With so many other varieties to propagate, the nurseryman hasn't much time to offer the odd man out. A tentative experiment by a student at Hadlow College of Agriculture and Horticulture suggests that if the leaf of a rooted cutting is removed, an additional stimulus from the roots is channelled into the dormant bud, which is thereby given a greater chance of shooting.

This could be a line worth following up but pending improvements in the armandii-from-cuttings department, some nurserymen find grafting an excellent method. In this case the stock plant (or plants, but with such vigour, one could well be enough) is generally grown outside on a wall. Its young growth is too coarse and vigorous to be used just like that, so, when about six weeks old, which would be in June (I am citing an actual example) all young trails are shortened by half. The resulting growths are of just the right thickness and they are less likely to carry flower buds. Leaves with axillary flower buds (recognisable by their plumpness) should always be rejected. Each trail or vine should yield 15 to 20 grafts. Grafting can be done from December onwards in the manner already described. I have bought in some of these grafted plants myself and they are of excellent quality. It doesn't matter if they are rather shorter, at planting out time, than most other clematis. As long as an active shoot has been made, it will romp away on finding itself with a free root-run in the garden.

Cuttings

All clematis can be propagated from cuttings (although *C. texensis* is apt to be a bit swinish) and in retrospect it seems odd that this basically simple method should only have gained widespread currency in the last few decades. It is not as though we had to await the discovery and introduction of more sophisticated equipment, even. Propagation under mist is now generally accepted as being less successful, in the case of clematis, than by more traditional and obvious methods. There is too great a tendency for foliage to damp off under mist, especially where there is any leaf overlap. Protective fungicides anyway need to be used regularly from the outset, and I suppose the greater efficacy of modern fungicides compared with what were once available, is the one (not very dramatic) tool in our modern armoury that has contributed to a high measure of success in the propagation of clematis from cuttings today.

Close on a million clematis are propagated annually in the Boskoop region of Holland – most of them for export, of course – but in this country more clematis are being propagated by Treasures of Tenbury than on any other nursery and I shall describe the method as I have seen it used there and as it was expounded to me by Raymond Evison.

They use the floor of a Dutch Light structure in which heating cables are set and covered with 4cm of soil. An initial bottom heat of 24 degrees C in June is reduced to 15 degrees C by the end of September.

Propagation material is taken from one-year-old plants. This is general practice nowadays, and not just with clematis. Young material from young plants gives much the best take. Far better than is obtained from old stock plants kept specially for this purpose. And anyway, old plants take up a lot of permanent space and their growth is far coarser, the leaves inconveniently larger, than in young plants. The latter, after serving as propagation stock, can simply be grown on for sale in the usual way, so there is a complete and constant turn-over of stock (provided you can sell it, of course!)

Cuttings, at Treasures, are taken from 15 June for the next 5 weeks. They could start earlier if work allowed, but what with the Chelsea Flower Show and all the other calls on a nursery's time in spring, it doesn't.

The cuttings are internodal (I will explain about this in a moment) as is normal in this country, and consist of one pair of buds, one leaf (the other is removed) and up to 5cm of inter-node (the stem of the cutting). If the latter is hard, it is wounded, but not otherwise. Wounding consists of the removal with a knife or razor blade of a shaving of rind and soft

Wounding. To help root production, if the stem of the cutting is hard, slice off a shaving about 2 or 3 cm long at the bottom of the internode. *Right*, a sliver removed.

underlying tissue from the side of the bottom 2 or 3cm of the internode. Exposure of this larger area facilitates root production.

If the leaf that remains on the cutting is rather large, the central leaflet can be removed or reduced by half. That this may be necessary will be understood when I go on to say that 100 cuttings per standard seed tray is average, and one wants no overlapping of leaves (otherwise the bottom leaf doesn't get its fair share of light and cannot function properly).

Wooden seed trays (boxes or, as they say in America, flats) are used, the bottom covered with 6mm of gravel, then the cutting compost, which could consist of 2 parts coarse sand and one part peat but every nursery has its own slightly varying recipe and some include a bit of soil. I find the old John Innes recipe satisfactory: 1 part by bulk of sterilised loam, 2 parts peat, 3 parts sand.

The cutting compost is pressed with a board and then topped with fine sand, this being levelled with the hand. The newly made cuttings are put in a colander and dipped in a Captan solution. The base of each cutting is then dipped in Seradix B2 (made by May and Baker but there are a number of equivalent rooting compounds; the main point is that they should be fresh as, after two years, their potency can no longer be depended on). The cuttings are *pushed* into the compost. If so soft that they cannot stand this strain without bending, they are too soft to be of any use anyway. The bud should just rest on the surface of the rooting medium. Cuttings are watered in with a Captan solution (or suspension) and are damped over 4 times a day thereafter using a coarsish rose to the watering can. Alternate waterings include Captan wettable powder in solution. Folosan dusts are also used in the fight against botrytis, the grey mould fungus, since this accounts for one's greatest losses.

Shading has to be heavy at first, using overhead hessian. When shooting begins it may be assumed that rooting has started, in 4 weeks or so. Light can then be increased and watering decreased until, by September, it is necessary only once every 3 or 4 days. Dead leaves must be removed as they appear and all foliage is eventually picked off by the winter when the young plants become dormant and the leaves die naturally but without being naturally shed, alas.

The cuttings root through into the sand beneath their containers. They are left *in situ* till the following February when they are lifted, separated, washed in a Captan solution and then potted into 10cm long tom plastic pots using John Innes No. 2 potting compost. This is the one and only potting and the plants are saleable from the summer onwards. Staking and tying is, of course, another laborious chore.

There are many variants on the production method described. On another Midlands nursery cuttings are taken in April and early May, dipped in Seradix 1 (the weakest) and inserted in pots containing a 2 parts sand, 1 part peat mixture, placed in a close case with bottom heat. When rooted and hardened off they are potted into John Innes seed compost in 6cm (2½in) pots. Particular attention is given to keeping the eyes moist and these then grow freely. If allowed to dry there is a tendency for the buds to remain dormant. The young plants are kept frost-free in their first winter and potted into the usual long toms in December using J.I.P. No.3 (which I should myself prefer to No.2) for the final potting. These same plants are used for cutting material in the following April-May, so, again no stock plants are needed.

There is a continuing tendency for nurseries having no ready supply of loam to use a peat-and-sand potting compost with all nutrients added. I have seen some very starved looking clematis grown in this way but methods are all the time improving and if slow release fertilisers are used and feeding is not neglected, as necessary, excellent results can be obtained.

Internodal cuttings, as I have already remarked, are the type used in this country but in America (the U.S., anyway) nodal cuttings are often preferred. I must explain. A nodal cutting consists of 2 nodes (or joints), each with a pair of opposite buds and leaves. All the leaves except one of the upper pair are removed. The lower node is buried in the rooting medium at such a depth that the upper is just resting on the surface of the cutting compost. However, if the distance between nodes, i.e. the internode, is long, the method is inconvenient, since the top node will be waving about in mid-air. Fortunately clematis

Left, an internodal cutting of the sort commonly used in Britain; *right*, the nodal cutting preferred in America.

are as ready to root from a cut made at any point along the internode as they are from a nodal cut. So the internode is used as an anchor and is tailored to be of any length that suits the propagator – commonly 4 or 5cm. It will also be appreciated that by using only one node to each cutting, twice the number of cuttings can be made from any given quantity of propagating material, as can from nodal cuttings employing 2 nodes. If you are short of material you can double up on it yet again by slicing each internodal cutting longitudinally down its centre with a razor blade. Each cutting will now consist of one leaf, one bud and a length of bisected internode. You will not do this unless you urgently need to increase stock rapidly from a small amount of material, because the fact that each cutting made comprises only one bud instead of two reduces its chances of survival.

And by the same token the American propagators prefer a nodal cutting having 2 pairs of buds because, under their severer climatic conditions (hotter in summer, colder in winter) the upper pair of buds often dies but the cutting is able to regenerate and shoot from the lower, buried buds. The American nurseryman will propagate from very newly rooted

13

1. *C. crispa*
2. *C. texensis*
3. Gravetye Beauty
4. Etoile Rose

5. Sir Trevor Lawrence
6. Duchess of Albany
7. *C. viorna*
8. *C. fusca*

14

1. *C. viticella*
2. *C. viticella* 'Rubra'
3. Purpurea Plena Elegans
4. Minuet
5. Little Nell
6. Alba Luxurians

7. Abundance
8. Etoile Violette
9. Royal Velours
10. Venosa Violacea
11. *C. campaniflora*

material at that stage when it is still packed 100 to the seed tray and before it is potted off. The young growth at this stage has small leaves and short internodes, so there is no problem in handling the material except the business of separating the vines, which will all be clinging one to another. The nurseryman I spoke to assured me that they found this no problem and that his women separated the vines quickly and efficiently and without damaging their foliage.

The Amateur Propagator

Where does or how can the amateur get a look in? He has no stock plants except the one growing in his or a friend's garden. I have said that the material from this will be unsuitably coarse and anyway he probably has no bottom heat, perhaps no frames, no polythene tunnels (also widely used for commercial propagation). Layering will be his best recourse if only the odd extra plant or two are needed, but it is not always convenient to make layers in a friend's garden and return for them when they have rooted. I have done it but the friend needs to be a close one.

Let us look into the possibilities of cuttings without tears first.

If you have no propagating equipment, rather than mess about with a pot covered with a plastic bag, I strongly recommend buying yourself several small propagator units. They are cheap, effective and couldn't be simpler in design. George Ward makes one that consists of a standard plastic seed tray with a clear polystyrene cover that fits snugly over it. The cover is a straight-sided lid that allows plenty of head-room for various types of cuttings and it is fitted, in its covering roof, with adjustable ventilators, so that hardening off is made easy.

Bottom heat speeds up propagation but it is by no means necessary. If you are taking your cuttings in May-June (the best time) when the sun is very hot, the propagator will certainly need pretty heavy shading for a start, but once you see some of your cuttings making new shoots you can admit a little air, and the more air you can admit without the cuttings wilting, the more light you can allow them to have.

Ideally, soft and half-ripe cuttings taken in summer will benefit from all the light available that they can take without wilting and scorching. They need light in order to root and if the humidity of their environment is high enough they can take a good deal and still remain turgid.

High humidity is also ideal for the propagation of fungus spores, and fungal disease is enemy number one in the early stages. So you must spray with a solution of Captan (benomyl is no longer a deterrent to the many strains of botrytis having an inbuilt resistance to it) at frequent intervals. Once a week should be often enough.

An internodal cutting with the terminal leaflet cut off to reduce excess leaf area.

If cutting material is taken from an established plant in the garden, drastic reduction of foliage area will be necessary otherwise the cutting cannot cope with such a large preponderance of leaf and will certainly collapse. So, even though we are talking about only one leaf to each cutting, this will probably need reducing by half or two thirds. Say there were 3 leaflets, you could probably shorten them (a razor blade applied vertically to a hard surface is the easiest method) all by half, or you could remove one completely (especially if, as often happens, it is badly placed and tucked under the others, because of the way the petiole was twisted round its support) and shorten the other two. When you take a young clematis

The easiest way to make clematis cuttings is to place the stem on a hard surface and apply a razor-sharp blade vertically.

trail from the garden you will often find that one of the leaves at each node is clinging by its twisted petiole to a support while the other is unattached and hence undistorted. When you prepare your cutting, remove the awkward, twisted leaf and petiole and leave the straight one. Because, you see, when you have inserted your cutting you don't want any part of the leaf to lie against the compost surface, where it will be permanently wet and inclined to rot; neither do you want any one cutting or part of a cutting to shade another. Both these conditions are met if the leaf and petiole are respectively flat and untwisted.

As I hinted at the start, the most easily rooted clematis are the montanas, alpinas and macropetalas. If you insert these in May, and pot them off into 10cm or larger pots when well rooted, you will have very strong plants by the autumn, a metre or more tall and they will flower in the following spring.

However, if your cuttings are taken rather late and are, furthermore, of large-flowered hybrids that are slower to root, they will, under cold conditions, very probably not root until the end of August or later. Never be tempted to disturb these late rooters, or you will encounter severe winter losses. Leave them in their propagating pots or boxes until the following March and pot them off individually then. This advice applies to most shrubby plants. If they're not well rooted before the end of August, let well alone till the following spring.

I don't see why you shouldn't succeed, in a small way including plenty of failures, with hardwood clematis cuttings, involving no equipment at all. Suppose you were pruning a clematis in October (early autumn is the best moment for taking hardwood cuttings of anything) you could make cuttings of its strong young wood that each consisted of a node supported by 10 or 15cm of internode. Stick them into a plot of light soil in a reasonably shady position (such as the north side of a wall) so that the node and its buds are just visible at the soil surface. Water at droughty times next year and lift in the autumn. I should use a strong rooting compound here: Seradix B3 would be suitable.

A cutting with well-developed roots.

I have even rooted hardwood prunings in a glass of water. The variety was Huldine and the time December. They stood on a windowsill in our dining room and I changed the water occasionally when it turned green, otherwise topping it up. By June, half of them had made roots. More recently I have done the same with Viticella Rubra only in this case I stood the jam jar in a cold frame among pot plants. When the plants were watered the level of the water in the jar was automatically brought up to the rim. There were 8 cuttings and five of them rooted. I potted them individually into John Innes No. 2 on 17 July. These cuttings were internodal and were 15cm long.

For any gardener requiring just the odd extra plant or two, layering offers by far the easiest and in every way most satisfactory method, quickly giving rise to a strong young specimen.

Bury any live piece of clematis stem into moist soil, and it will make roots and shoots. But the piece of stem in question must be firm and mature, not soft and green; current season's wood is seldom suitable, but if you do your layering in winter, which is always a good time because there are no leaves to get in your way and you can see what you are doing; then practically any live wood will make suitable layering material. Even ten-year-old trunks may be layered successfully, though this is not the most convenient material.

You don't need to be at all scientific about layering clematis. Scoop out a hollow, say 10cm deep, in the ground at a convenient point, dip a clematis stem (not a cut off end of stem but a middle portion that goes into the ground and comes out again) into the hollow, hold it in position by pushing in a

Layering clematis. Scoop out a hollow 10 cm deep. Dip a clematis stem into the hollow and hold in position by pushing in a wooden peg. Return the soil and ram home.

wooden peg cut from any branch, into the ground at the bottom of the hollow, return the soil and ram home. It is wise to mark the spot with an upright stick or cane so that the layer doesn't subsequently get dug out before it has rooted.

By the following autumn you will be able to cut the layer lead – that is, the proximal portion of stem where it enters the ground – and shorten the stem to 15 or 20cm beyond its emergence from the ground and then lift what remains, which is your new plant.

You can, as a refinement, plunge a largish pot filled with good soil into the ground and layer into that. Then, at lifting time, there will be no disturbance or damage to the young roots, but these are – at any rate in all the hybrids – almost as tough as boot laces, so not to worry, really. Again, with most layering of shrubs it is important to make a sharp elbow at the layer's lowest point because this checks the sap flow which in turn encourages rooting; furthermore, where the layer makes its exit from the ground you encourage, by staking it, an upright habit so that the young plant is a good shape and not lop-sided. Well, you can't have a lopsided clematis. The plant being flexible can be led in any direction and the elbow isn't necessary to rooting either. You do want to be sure that your layers keep nice and moist throughout the summer, but then that applies equally to the parent plant, whether it has been layered or not. Adequate moisture in the growing season is an axiom in clematis cultivation.

Division

Herbaceous clematis like *C. recta, C. heracleifolia* var. *davidiana* and *C. integrifolia* can be propagated in the dormant season by simple division.

If you have to lift an old specimen of a large-flowered hybrid you will often find that it has a number of stems arising from below ground level. I have known as many as 10 or 12 with Nelly Moser, and this condition is encouraged by deep planting in the first place. All these shoots will have roots on them below the soil and although attached one to another, they are easily cut apart so that a series of ready-made new plants will be the result.

Unless deliberate improvements by hybridisation are being sought (and we can always do with more of them, but it is a fiddling, time-and space-consuming pursuit) the raising of clematis from seed is seldom worthwhile. Never were so many geese born in the guise of swans, as regarded by their proud raisers. I refer to the large-flowered hybrids. Unless you set about a deliberate policy of hybridisation and are extremely critical of the results, you would do best to leave well alone.

These large-flowered hybrids many of them set good seed but it germinates slowly and unevenly over a period of from months to years.

Some of the species come easily and quickly from seed, but you want to be careful. Seedlings from the excellent *C. orientalis* L & S 13342 will be similar but not the same and are unlikely to be as good. *C. texensis* may also give disappointing results. *C. macropetala* is variable and worthless at its worst. So easily is it raised from cuttings, that it is silly not to do so from the good clones that are widely current. The same with *C. alpina* and *C. montana*.

C. flammula is none too easy from cuttings and comes well from seed and these seedlings usually give pretty good results. But if anyone were to take the trouble to raise large batches of flammula and to select only the best for growing on and crossing one with another, I've no doubt the species could be vastly improved by horticultural standards, and we should then be as dissatisfied with any old seedlings as we already are in the case of *C. alpina*, *C. macropetala* and *C. montana*.

Incidentally it was interesting to see at a RHS show in 1974 the results of crosses between *C. macropetala* and *C. montana*. They were worthless, but they did evidence characters from both parents. I find this surprising, considering how different the parents are. I am not sure that there is much to be hoped for by breeding from such dissimilar species but it is nice to know it can be done. I should like to see what happened if one crossed, say, *C. alpina sibirica* 'White Moth' (or one of the blue alpinas) with *C. tangutica*. The former often throw late blooms on young shoots, so the cross would not be a physical impossibility.

My two garden plants of *C. viticella* were both seedlings from Thompson & Morgan seed 25 years ago and, luckily, they are both as fine as any I have seen. One knows how variable this species can be, because it was widely used as a grafting stock in the old days and subsequently sometimes took over from the scion. Its flowers can be very small and insignificant. Also, in the best forms, the flowers stand well out from the foliage on long, thread-like stalks. Colour, too, is variable. I always propagate from mine by cuttings, nowadays, although they seed readily enough.

CHAPTER 10

Clematis Troubles

*

I THINK of this as the wilt chapter. Clematis do have other troubles, which we shall examine in due course, but wilt disease is the most serious by so far and away as to eclipse the rest.

Scenario for Wilt

Let me set the scene. An amateur gardener, new to the game, decides to have a flutter with clematis. Although rather shocked at their price he buys 3 plants, one of them with fat flower buds on it; the others, he is assured will flower later in the season. With conscientious devotion he follows the book's instructions for planting to the letter, and for the next 3 weeks he watches his plants' development with mounting excitement. The one with buds isn't making any fresh growth but the buds are enormous and seem likely to burst open at any moment. The other two are making 5cm of growth every day: he keeps them well watered. Then, one evening, immediately on his return from work when he makes his customary inspection, he finds that all the buds on his joy and pride are hanging limply at the neck. Imagine his horror. He syringes it with water but to no avail. Within less than a week the entire plant has shrivelled and turned black. Then one of the other two goes funny. The tip of its fast-growing shoot hangs disconsolately in the midday sun. The rest of the plant looks all right but not for long. That one shrivels and blackens along with the first. Two gone out of three. He feels ill with chagrin and bitter towards the nurseryman.

One of several things can happen after that but you can see why clematis have earned a reputation for being difficult. They are popular plants but even so I should think twice as many would be grown if it weren't for the wilt deterrent. It is sad that with almost every florist's flower in which, by careful hybrid-isation and selection, increase in flower power has been attained in triumphant celebration of human skill, yet every improvement brings in its train dire pests and diseases of undreamed-of potency that had never attended the unim-proved plant. Roses have to be sprayed every few days to keep them free of blackspot, mildew and rust; lilies develop the most fearful virus diseases and so do dahlias, the plant shrink-ing and losing the whole benefit of its acquired characteristics; irises are rotted by smelly bacterial diseases and disfigured with leaf spotting; rhododendrons get bud blast and evergreen azaleas something else that goes for them just as their long-awaited display is getting into its stride in the spring; the potato famine of 1845 was caused by blight disease and so on. Whereas if we stuck to the unimproved buttercups and daisies as we find them in our lawns, we should never have a moment's worry.

Clematis were all right till the breeders started improving them in the middle of the last century. Wilt was already so serious by the early 1900's, that Morel, the French nursery-man mentioned so often in these pages, gave up breeding clematis in despair. In 1903 he wrote in the Revue Horticole of 'La Maladie Noire des Clématites'. 'A discreet silence has settled on the horticultural press on the subject of this fearful and mysterious disease, but without in any way interrupting its course.' He noticed that it was worst after rain storms and in humid heat and reckoned that it entered the plant by way of small lesions, wounds, twisted stems etc. and he observed that blackened dead areas developed most frequently at or around soil level. All of which is true but the disease is not bacterial, as he hazarded it might be.

There is no reference to pests, diseases or any sort of hindrance to the easy cultivation of clematis in Moore & Jackman (1872, revised 1877) but A. G. Jackman (George Jackman's son), brought the subject of wilt, which he called dying off in those days, into the open. He gave it as one reason for the falling off of clematis breeding after 1880. He, too, thought the trouble was bacterial.

The public, however, ascribed it to the nurseryman's wicked practice of grafting (of which they have ever entertained the deepest suspicions), alleging that the vitalba stock overwhelmed the scion and thus caused its death. A. G. Jackman, in a lecture to the R.H.S. in 1916 made the refutation of this theory his main subject and for the very good reasons that I have discussed in the chapter on propagation. But the public continued to link wilt disease and grafting until very recently indeed. Now that nearly all clematis propagation is done by cuttings and yet wilt continues unabated, that old war-horse has been laid to rest.

Meantime the cause of a stem rot and leaf spot in clematis in the U.S.A. was examined by W. O. Gloyer in 1915 (J.agric.Res., 4, 331–42). The leaf spotting occurred there under glass and we do not find it in this country, but from material showing both symptoms he isolated the fungus *Ascochyta clematidina*. By inoculating it on to healthy plants he was able to reproduce the disease.

That is all that was done on that until our own Glasshouse Crops Research Institute (G.C.R.I.) kindly examined the problem, rather at my instigation, in 1965, just 50 years after Gloyer. It was satisfying to find that they, like him, isolated the same fungus from diseased material, *Ascochyta clematidina*, to wit. The work was done by Miss Marion Ebben and Dr F. T. Last and was written up in the G.C.R.I. Annual Report for 1965. Their pathogenic isolates from the material examined were more or less entirely restricted to *A. clematidina*. This fungus has also been recorded in Holland but their nurserymen seem to be even more afflicted by the wilting caused by another fungus, *Coniothyrium clematidis-rectae*. I shall say no more about this as it has not entered into the picture here.

How the Fungus Works

A. clematidina produces slimy spores and is therefore unlikely to be airborne but the infected leaf blows about and the fungus can be present in the soil around infected plants, so if you get rid of the plant, the fungus is still likely to be there. Where movable stock is plunged in nursery beds, the vacated area can be treated with Formaldehyde diluted at 1 part in 50 and used at 10 litres per square metre. The area must be left vacant for 3 weeks after treatment or, if you are in a hurry, left for a week and then watered hard. Where pots are stood on plastic sheeting under glass, little trouble occurs.

The fungus may attack any part of the growing clematis down to or just below soil level. One of the commonest points of entry is at or just below ground level and this causes the maximum damage. The entire shoot above the point of attack collapses and dies, first symptoms showing themselves by the drooping of the young leaves and shoot tip. Within a week, stems and leaves are black. On the other hand a neighbouring shoot that has not been attacked will continue to grow normally and the affected stem itself will frequently break again from below the point of infection.

When a stem wilts like this you can always find stem discolorations and/or rotting lesions below the lowest pair of wilting leaves. Experiments showed that the fungus gained entry most frequently where the young stem had been damaged, perhaps by wind or by slugs or perhaps by tying. High humidity also seems to help the fungus to penetrate: wilt often occurs most seriously during growing weather in early summer, as Morel noted.

The fungus also attacks leaves on otherwise healthy plants and this primary damage is of no importance and will generally pass unnoticed but infected leaves can act as a source of inoculum spreading the disease to the plant's stems.

When leaves with necrotic (dead) patches on them were collected from 9 different clematis species and cultivars growing in different parts of my garden (these plants being apparently quite healthy apart from the odd leaf), *Ascochyta* was isolated from 7 of the samples. The appearance of infected leaves varies according to the thickness and texture of the leaf itself. On thin-leaved varieties such as Bees Jubilee, Marie Boisselot, Ville de Lyon and Lasurstern the dead areas occur in large amorphous patches, the whole leaf often becoming greyish-brown, dry and wrinkled. *C. armandii*, with its leathery evergreen leaves gets discrete (i.e. separate and distinctly marked off) brown areas with a green halo, either as spots or larger more or less oval areas, often with a raised blacker or darker green edge giving the spot an appliquéd look. On Victoria and Comtesse de Bouchaud buff brown patches are concentrically zoned – this is a very characteristic and easily recognised symptom – the centre of the zonation often being at a leaf edge. So too with the thick-leaved Mrs Hope, which also has spotting like *C. armandii.*

The G.C.R.I.'s investigation concluded that *Ascochyta* is one of the major causes of clematis wilt, affecting grafted and ungrafted plants. They suggested that differences in varietal susceptibility might be attributable to anatomical differences, e.g. in thickness of epidermal tissue, or age at which stems form a protective bark. It had, of course, always been recognised by clematis growers that once a plant was mature enough to have formed a tough stem, the incidence of wilt was much reduced and one can see that the fungus would have much greater difficulty in entering the thick stem of a clematis. It might infect foliage or young stems on the distal portions of the plant, but the damage would be slight and localised, here, and hardly attract the grower's attention.

It is worth noting, by the way, the difference between this wilt disease, where the fungus does not spread within the host plant but causes a localised infection, and other wilt diseases caused by *Fusarium* and *Verticillium* spp., where the fungus spreads systemically through the host plant. Thank heavens we're spared that situation.

Control

To get rid of the disease on a nursery, where large numbers of clematis are grown together and on their own, should not be too difficult by practising routine hygiene (as in the formaldehyde treatment described) and the regular application of fungicides. At least it is possible to keep the disease at a very low incidence – especially in the controlled environment of a glasshouse, but even in outdoor plunge beds.

In the garden, where clematis are grown among mixed plant collections, it's more difficult. Quite apart from everything else, there is the possibility that *Ascochyta* species capable of attacking clematis may be found on entirely different host plants.

But the main difficulty, as I see it, is that you cannot *kill* a fungus without killing the plant. You can spray the plant or treat it with a systemic fungicide as I shall describe, so as to *prevent* the fungus spores from gaining entry. If the fungus is already on the plant the same treatment can prevent its spread but it will still be there and if you let up on your protective treatments it can get on the rampage once more.

I'm afraid it is a sad and inevitable fact of life that the longer you grow clematis and the more you love them, i.e. the more of them you grow in your garden, the greater the build-up you will get of wilt fungus spores in your soil and on your plants. Don't think wilt may never come your way. It will.

However, the situation is not nearly as grim or hopeless as it used to be and we can learn to live with wilt by thwarting its activities with the help of benomyl, the fairly recently syn-thesised systemic fungicide, sometimes sold under the trade name Benlate.

Benlate is expensive, and especially if you buy it in the small sachets put out for the control, by spraying, of various rose diseases. Far better to go bust on a 2lb canister as you can presently buy it from Boots Farm Sales Ltd. at about £10, which will last you for years. Before dilating on its action and use I will draw attention to one possible drawback in benomyl that occurs as a somewhat sinister side-effect: it kills earth-worms. To the nurseryman who plunges his pots in or stands them on beds outside, this will be glad tidings, as worms in pots are a dreadful nuisance, blocking up the drainage and often killing the plant by waterlogging. Also it is difficult or impossible to turn a plant cleanly out of a pot in which worms have been working. But worms in the garden are beneficial and anyway one is always suspicious that if a chemical can kill earthworms its effects on our fauna may not stop there. Still, I shall go on using Benlate until I hear much worse of it.

The advantage of benomyl as a fungicide is that it is trans-located to different parts of the plant from within. Therefore, in its application, you don't have to cover all parts of the plant. In fact, it is better not to use it as a spray at all (it anyway leaves an unsightly deposit). Use it as a drench to the plant's roots. The chemical's potential for movement within the plant is limited and you get it most evenly and thoroughly distributed by allowing the plant to take it into its system through its roots.

There are no officially recommended rates or dosages for the application of benomyl: the G.C.R.I.'s work on wilt stopped short before the new fungicide arrived on the scene. However, I have used the rates suggested by a horticultural adviser to the Ministry of Agriculture, Fisheries and Food, with excellent results. Take 20 grams of Benlate (which is a powder), mix it to a paste in a little water and add to 25 litres of water. (This is approximately ½oz to 4 gallons.) Apply to the ground where the clematis roots are at 10 litres to the square metre (approx. 2 gallons per sq yd.). This should be enough for one average-sized plant growing in the garden but half as much would be enough for a youngster in the first 2 years. Twice as much would be needed for a really large specimen with an extensive root system. The treatment is repeated at monthly intervals from spring (March) to autumn (early October). It has made all the difference to my life and happiness.

The experience of a correspondent who lives near Selkirk is typical of my own and will serve as an example.

'19 March 1973. Dear Mr Lloyd, Some four years ago I was given two Jackmanii Superba Clematis plants. Every year they have suffered from wilt which began just when the flower buds were forming. Last year, from the time of growth beginning, I sprayed them with Captan every 8/9 days but in spite of this they again suffered from wilt. Is there anything I can do for them?'

I gave him the Benlate recommendation and dosage and wrote to him again at the end of the year, asking for news.

'29 Dec. 1973. I just cannot speak too highly of Benlate as a wilt prophylactic for Clematis, and I should have written and thanked you for recommending it. For four consecutive seasons wilt set in just as the Jackmanii Superba were about to come into flower and this was in spite of locally recommended treatments.

'Last season, and as soon as the new shoots started coming away, I watered with a Benlate solution both the vines and the surrounding ground up to 15in to 16in radius and repeated every 12 to 14 days. There was never a trace of wilt to be seen and the plants continued flowering right on until the end of October. I would be pleased to have a copy of the new edition of "Clematis" when available.' I suppose I ought to give him one.

One tiny point of interest. Benlate is reputed to be perfectly harmless to plants and this has indeed proved to be the case with just one exception: my large-flowered strain of *Clematis tangutica* obtained from Jack Drake's nursery years ago. When drenched with Benlate all its foliage shrivels, though the plant is not killed. The same thing happens if it is sprayed with insecticide. It is oddly sensitive.

Apart from the protective use of Benlate against wilt, the other, obvious, step to be taken to counter the disease is the removal and burning of diseased tissue. If a shoot collapses, cut it out *below* the point of attack: this will often be below the soil surface.

Which leads me on to another defensive measure. You should always plant so that the bottom 3 to 5cm of clematis stem is buried. If it subsequently wilts, there will then be a healthy bit of stem left below the lesion and 9 times out of 10 this will, in due course, throw a new shoot or shoots. Keep the plant watered and wait patiently. I have a Nelly Moser that wilted, getting on for 10 years ago and showed no signs life for the next year. It then threw a young shoot and has never looked back since. This story was capped by a visitor's: he had an Ernest Markham wilt case and the plant came to life again after three years. But wait; I've not finished yet. More recently still (1975) John Treasure told me of a Marcel Moser plant on his house that was flowering handsomely, having just returned to life after an absence of *ten* years. Patience is the watchword. It is rather remarkable that clematis roots can keep alive and healthy for such a long time without any help from green leaves above ground.

Gardeners in search of a quiet life without crises and palpitations always want to know which clematis they can grow that

15

1. *C. rehderiana*
2. *C. tangutica*
3. *C. tangutica* (Jack Drake's form)
4. *C. orientalis* (L & S form 13342)
5. *C. songarica*
6. *C. flammula*
7. *C. vitalba*
8. *C. fargesii* var. *souliei*
9. C. × *triternata* 'Rubro-marginata'
10. *C. serratifolia*
11. *C. phlebantha*
12. *C. grata*

16

1. *C. integrifolia*
2. *C. integrifolia* 'Hendersonii'
3. *C. × eriostemon*
4. *C. douglasii* var. *scottii* 'Rosea'
5. *C. integrifolia* 'Olgae'
6. *C. × durandii*
7. *C. jouiniana* 'Praecox'
8. *C. heracleifolia* var. *davidiana* 'Wyevale'
9. *C. × aromatica*
10. *C. douglasii* var. *scottii*
11. *C. heracleifolia* 'Campanile'
12. *C. recta*
13. Edward Prichard

are immune to wilt. None can positively be said to be immune but in practice there are some that rarely if ever contract the disease. *C. alpina, C. macropetala* and their cultivars, for instance. The montana group are pretty safe, too, though young plants of *C. chrysocoma* and some of the more special cv's of *C. montana* like Tetrarose and Picton's Variety, can die in their first winter but never while growing and I doubt if the cause is wilt.

The viticellas can certainly get it but seldom do. All the large-flowered hybrids, which are the ones to which the new gardener is first attracted, are susceptible.

When a 10-year-old Perle d'Azur or *C. flammula*, for instance, takes and dies, probably in the winter, it will be found that its thick trunk has become quite hollow and has rotted through from the inside. This condition is common to clematis making thick trunks (seldom the montanas) but cannot be ascribed to wilt. Indeed, the thick trunk protects it against the wilt fungus.

Mildew

Powdery mildew can be a very tiresome and disfiguring disease of some clematis in some situations. Especially where they are sheltered, as on a wall or in an enclosed garden or greenhouse, the fungus attacks flowers, foliage and young stems. Growth is crippled, flowers are much reduced in size and their characteristic colour is so overlaid with grey and white as to be utterly travestied. The fungus does not get into its stride until late June, so early flowers are unaffected. Varieties that flower twice, like Lady Northcliffe, may have a normal first crop and a crippled second. Those that are entirely later-flowering are the worst sufferers, if that way inclined – I have never seen mildew on Lady Betty Balfour or Mme Baron Veillard. As special martyrs I would single out Ville de Lyon, Durandii, Jackmanii and its close relative Superba, Comtesse de Bouchaud and Star of India; also Etoile Rose, Gravetye Beauty and Sir Trevor Lawrence in the Texensis orbit.

Fortunately the Benlate drench treatment works miracles

against mildew, so I need only refer the reader back to Control of Wilt. For control of botrytis on cuttings, please turn to the section on propagation.

Viruses

The incidence and identification of viruses in clematis have never been investigated. Our plants are therefore not officially subject to virus diseases. The evidence of one's eyes neverthe-less suggests that they do occur, but as the nurseryman will naturally be inclined to choose healthy-looking material for propagation, any virus or viruses present cannot be giving serious and evident trouble. But they may, without our notic-ing, be reducing the vigour of a plant.

For many years I owned a plant of Mrs Cholmondeley whose young foliage was invariably mottled with a pale and darker green mosaic, while the outline of the leaves was notably distorted. As the growth matured, the symptoms became masked and the plant grew and flowered reasonably well. Another plant, this time Comtesse de Bouchaud, used to develop a green and yellow mosaic pattern on its expanded foliage, following the outline of the veins. I currently have a young plant of *C. rehderiana* showing the same pretty pattern-ing and without its vigour being noticeably impaired. One is somewhat disturbed and I have little doubt that these are expressions of virus disease. Certain old cultivars that used to be noted for their vigour and easy cultivation have mysteri-ously become difficult with the passing of the years, or if not actually difficult at least they can no longer, in most situations, be called vigorous. One suspects virus as the cause of this weakening.

It doesn't do to worry too much about these things. If a plant or variety becomes weak, we automatically discard it and another, stronger, takes its place. The situation takes care of itself.

Pests

The trouble about any chewing pest is that there is not merely the primary damage to weep over but the fact of the damage letting in *Ascochyta clematidina*, the wilt fungus. Still, if it's around, I suppose it'll get in somehow even if the entire plant is strung with burglar alarms.

Slugs and snails can be very troublesome on newly planted clematis, destroying young shoots at ground level as soon as they appear. If allowed to continue, this can kill the plant altogether. On this subject I shall quote from a letter Hugh Thompson wrote me in 1971. Apropos of wilt: 'My impression is that the most important thing is to stop slug-gnawing at ground level. This damaged area nearly always gets infected by the fungus. I suffer badly from friends and relatives with out of control dogs so in protection put a sunk collar 6-9 inches high round the base of each clematis. The collar is made of claritex, and I find very few slugs overcome this obstacle, and with very intermittent addition of slug pellets I can stop this ground level damage.'

It is no use thinking you will gain permanent control of slugs with pellets alone. The slugs are there, with the one thought in their minds of eating your clematis, for 365 days in the year, sometimes 366. Your mind is on them only now and then. They'll always have the last chew on you.

Snails are great climbers and if the clematis is against a wall they may enjoy it at a considerable height. But it is the ground level meals that really matter. Snails do at least hibernate in the cold weather.

Rabbits have been very troublesome on my nursery stock, of late. They are fondest of young leaves and prevented newly potted cuttings of Jouiniana Praecox from making any headway for several months in spring and early summer. (Subsequently we had a merciful recrudescence of myxomatosis.) Other young clematis managed to grow above rabbit range and only had their lower leaves removed, the stems being left intact. Doubtless hares and deer would cause similar trouble only worse. Squirrels have the playful habit of eating off the swelling flower bud just before it is ready to burst open.

Mice are keen. Here is Hugh Thompson again. 'The local very handsome mouse, *Sylvaemus flavicollis*, abounds in my neighbourhood [he lived at Churt in Surrey], and as it has about twice the volume of an ordinary fieldmouse, eats twice as many clematis shoots. Flavicollis even killed a long established tangutica by shredding the inch-thick woody stem for nesting material.'

Man himself must be considered a pest within this category and again I have Mr Thompson to thank for this information. 'I note in a French Encyclopaedia that clematis.shoots are greatly esteemed for eating particularly by Italians and Russians! It does not go so far as to suggest that some difficult large flowered hybrids are the most favoured. The moral appears to be not to have an Italian gardener; nor do I much fancy the prospect of some bulky commissar in a disputed territory sitting down to a meal of macropetala.'

All the same, I do find the young shoots of *C. recta* tempting, and they are so very numerous and strong . . . but there, I need further encouragement and information before daring and especially as Mrs M. Grieve in 'A Modern Herbal' writes in particular of the bruised leaves and flowers of *C. recta* as irritating 'the eyes and throat, giving rise to a flow of tears and coughing; applied to the skin they produce inflammation and vesication, hence the name Flammula Jovis. They are diuretic and diaphoretic, and are used locally and internally in syphilitic, cancerous and other foul ulcers.' Good Lord deliver us. She continues: '*C. flammula* is said to contain an alkaloid, Clematine, a violent poison.' Clematine might be a good name for a poisonous child.

Birds have lately taken to pecking out the swelling buds of the early flowering alpinas, macropetalas and montanas in my neighbourhood. At Sissinghurst Castle they have to net their plants in order to obtain any blooms. For the first time ever I had virtually no bloom at all on any of my montanas in 1975. I cannot see myself netting them. If the trouble persists I shall give up growing them. 'Curb' and the latest follow-up to 'Curb' (? 'Curb Improved'?) were of no avail at Sissinghurst in 1975, their head gardeners told me, but the early part of the year was unusually wet, admittedly.

Among the small fry, earwigs are the most serious clematis pest. Their populations build up throughout the summer – more in some years than in others – and from July onwards they are liable to eat all young clematis shoots so that nothing remains except the stalks and midribs, while the flowers are gashed into tatters.

All this at night. Gardeners are mainly diurnal in their habits; if they go into their gardens after dark it is to saunter and to sniff at their tobacco plants, not to search for pests. They often fail, in consequence, to identify the real cause of the trouble. Yet it is only necessary, by day, to pull aside any folded or overlapping sepals to find the culprits snugly roosting, while torchlight will reveal them dangling in hordes as they revel in their midnight feasts.

DDT, when we were allowed to use it, was the most effective spray control for earwigs. Nowadays any BHC preparation is likely to be as (in)effective as any other. Just follow the maker's instructions and blame yourself if the results are nil.

Aphids (greenfly) can be a nuisance on the softest extension growth of young clematis shoots, especially in May-June, before the aphids' parasites have built up in numbers. When this has happened, aphid populations will suddenly drop like the temperature in a thunderstorm (and a sudden thunderstorm can be highly deleterious to aphids, also). I have never found that aphid damage was so serious in the garden as to demand action on my part, but on nursery stock you do have to spray at irregular intervals during the growing season.

Discoloured Flowers

In May, when the first blooms expand on your large-flowered hybrids, you may be amazed to find that they are not at all the colour you expected, not even white when they should have been white, but green. According to your temperament and upbringing you will find this intriguing, dull or repulsive. Hugh Thompson wrote me in August 1972: 'I have found this a very mixed year for clematis, the sunless cool early summer affected some but not all. Ville de Lyon and The President have been very deficient in flowers and I am sure the same will prove true of Lady Betty Balfour. The cv's that are liable to green have never been greener. Double green Countess of Lovelace in great quantity was very odd – just the thing for a zany flower arranger. Barbara Dibley passed direct from green to your "dust and ashes" stage without any development of the petunia pigment. Quite hideous at all stages.'

The next year, 1973, in mid-June I received a letter from a customer in Surrey. 'Dear Mr Lloyd, The Barbara Dibley clematis which I bought from you last year has flowers which are very far removed from the one I saw at your place and the description in your catalogue. Instead of being petunia red they are a sort of greeny white with faint purple bars. Rather a boring colour, in fact . . . Could the strange colour be due to the soil, the position or might the plant have been wrongly labelled? I'd be grateful for your comment as it's disappointing as it is.'

I wrote her that deprived plants were liable to this condition in their *early* blooms, especially when the spring had been cold and if they were short of water. But I assured her that matters would right themselves. She replied a few days later that the subsequent blooms were getting progressively nearer the colour she had expected.

The double white Duchess of Edinburgh is also very liable to this greenness and one must, I think, bear in mind the fact that the division, in clematis, between leaves, bracts and sepals is often not hard and fast. The trouble is sometimes ascribed to potash deficiency, on the same principle, I take it, as greenback in tomatoes being known to have lack of potash as its cause. No experimental work has been done on clematis to determine whether this theory is correct, nor is it ever likely to be. It could do no harm to give them an extra dose of sulphate of potash and it might help.

Spring Frosts

Damage by spring frosts can be especially regular and depressing to the gardener (especially as he frequently fails to understand what has happened) when the montanas, alpinas and macropetalas have been grown in an exposed position. These are such hardy clematis that they are frequently not coddled by allocating them a cosy wall. On the contrary, they are expected to cover garage roofs, which are open to the skies, and to deck trees and shrubs which are often pretty exposed themselves. If early warmth unfolds the protective leaves in which the flower buds were nestling, a subsequent sharp radiation frost can polish off the lot. But as the buds were small and colourless, the gardener doesn't notice that they've been blackened, at the time. Later on, when no flowers appear, he ascribes their absence to a bad strain of clematis or to his incorrect pruning. But I don't think you can really be expected to fend off all these acts of God (except by touching wood, of course). Next year is sure to be better.

Descriptions of Clematis in Cultivation

*

IN Chapters 5 and 6 I discussed and compared a large number of clematis. This chapter should be used in conjunction with what I wrote there but it also includes brief notes on many more species and cultivars, not mentioned elsewhere. Either they are new to me or unfamiliar to me or they strike me as of minor horticultural importance. I am therefore recording rather than passing judgement. Even so, I have not included by any means all cultivars to be found in nursery catalogues. Were I to do so, without having seen the cv's in question, I could only transcribe the catalogue descriptions and as these are sometimes more optimistic than accurate, I prefer to stand aside.

On the clematis that I do know well I have written notes in some detail, having stood or sat in front of examples of each of these, armed with pen and paper and a ruler. I hope these efforts may help readers who are trying to sort out questions of identification. There is, after all, a great deal of confusion in naming and not much can or should be taken for granted.

No doubt I shall be adding, unwittingly, to the confusion myself, at times (and Marjorie Blamey also). Some of my descriptions are derived from clematis grown in pots or under glass. Their performance and appearance will not then be characteristic of their behaviour in the garden. This is especially true of leaf and flower size; also of flower colour. Some of the material Mrs Blamey worked on was pot-grown under glass.

I have not, in most cases, attempted to give times of flowering as these can vary wildly according to where you live, how you pruned (or didn't prune) your plant and the nature of the season from one year to the next. In this year that I am writing, *Clematis armandii* was flowering in many gardens in

January and February, whereas March-April might be considered normal and May in a cold year.

You can get the relative times of flowering from the letters A, B or C appearing in brackets after the name of each clematis: (A) early, (B) mid-season, (C) late. These letters also refer to pruning methods as given in Chapter 8. Where (B or C) is given as an alternative pruning method it also means that, adopting the B method you will get an early crop of blossom followed later by more flowers on the young growth whereas using the C method of hard pruning, the entire concentration of blossom will come late.

Abundance (C). Vigorous. Leaflets, five, and further subdivided. Flowers semi-nodding, 5cm across. Sepals 4 or 5, pink red with darker veins. Stamens creamy.

C. addisonii (C). Viorna group from S.E. United States. I have only seen a flower of this, which is characteristically urn-shaped. Sepals 4, their tips slightly recurved. Rosy purple outside, cream within with an edge of cream extending to the outside margin. Anthers cream.

C. afoliata (syn. *C. aphylla*) (A). New Zealand, North and South. Introduced 1908. Climber to 8ft or more. Evergreen in a special sense; no true foliage, the leaf being reduced to a tendril. Stems rush-like, green, becoming yellowish in winter. Flowers in clusters of 2, 3 or 4, nodding, 2 to 2·5cm across at mouth. Sepals normally 4, 3·5cm long, obliquely spreading, pale-straw-coloured with green undertone. Dioecious. Untidy grower, but pleasing in flower.

Alba Luxurians (C). Vigorous. Leaflets 7, further subdivided. Flowers 9cm across. Sepals 4, white, with green, recurved tips. Pronounced eye of dark stamens.

Alice Fisk (B). The only time I saw this clematis it was suffering from cold and had greenish tints but it is really lavender with purple anthers.

C. alpina (syn. *Atragene alpina*) (A). Europe to N.E. Asia. 1792. Deciduous climber to 3m. Flowers nodding. Sepals 4, 3 to 4cm long. Whitish petaloid stamens. Var. *sibirica,* introduced from Siberia 1753, has yellowish-white flowers. For named cultivars of these two see under Columbine, Frances Rivis, Pamela Jackman, Ruby and White Moth.

Annabel (B). A new cv from Pennell with Beauty of Worcester as the seed parent (always a good bet) pollinated by Marie Boisselot. A well presented flower. Six sepals of a lightish blue with cream stamens. Not very different from other, established blue's.

C. armandii (A). China. 1900. Vigorous evergreen climber to 6m but requiring wall protection. Leaves ternate, large and tough; coppery when young. Flowers 5cm wide in dense axillary clusters. Delightful scent. Sepals, 5 or 6, white. Stamens creamy. Several clones shelter under the pleasing names of Snowdrift and Apple Blossom.

C. × aromatica (syn. *C. coerulea-odorata*) (C). (*C. flammula* × *C. integrifolia*). circa 1845. Semi-herbaceous, non-clinging, to 2m. Leaves sometimes simple, ovate or irregularly lobed; sometimes compound, with 3 or 5 leaflets. Panicles of 4cm-wide, violet-blue flowers with white stamens. Scented.

Ascotiensis (C). Vigorous. Leaves simple or ternate. Flowers 13cm across. Sepals 4, 5 or 6, ovate, 5cm wide. Bright lavender-blue. Stamens greenish.

Barbara Dibley (B). Moderately vigorous. Leaves ternate. Flowers 15 to 18cm across. Sepals 8, long, narrow and fine pointed. Sumptuous petunia red throughout. Fades badly. Anthers reddish-purple.

Barbara Jackman (B). Moderately vigorous. Leaves ternate. Flowers up to 15cm across. Sepals 8, broad, overlapping, tapering briskly to sharp points. Bluish-purple with vivid magenta bar, at first; fades to pale mauve but central bar remains crimson. Contrasting eye of creamy stamens.

Beauty of Richmond (B or C). Vigorous. Leaves simple or ternate. Flowers 15cm or more across. Sepals 6, rosy-blue. Anthers creamy.

Beauty of Worcester (B or C). Compact grower. Leaves simple or ternate. Double flowers on old wood; single on young. Sepals 6 on single blooms, straight edged, overlapping, tapering to sharp points. Well formed, solid flower of rich, deep blue with slight reddish flush at centre base of sepals. Distinct creamy stamens, with tinge of green.

Bees Jubilee (B). Weakish. Leaves trifoliate. Flowers 15 to 18cm across. Sepals usually 8. Colouring as for Nelly Moser but more intense and vivid.

Belle Nantaise (C). Moderate vigour. Leaves simple or ternate. Flowers 20cm across. Sepals 6 or 7, tapering to acute points. Pale lavender with whitish stamens.

Belle of Woking (B). Moderately vigorous. Leaves simple, broad and rounded. Flowers very double, 10cm across, silvery-mauve.

Blue Gem (B or C). Leaves simple (usually) or ternate, cordate or ace-of-spades-shaped, *not* drawn to fine points. Buds slender, woolly. Flowers up to 15cm across. Sepals 7 or 8, overlapping with blunt, wide-angled points. Light lavender blue, somewhat darker at centre-base of each sepal; veins throughout darker than background. Stamens fairly conspicuous; filaments white, anthers purple. Not much character.

Blue Giant. *See* Frances Rivis.

Bracebridge Star (B). Weakish. Leaflets 3, widely separated on long sub-petioles. Flowers 13cm across. Sepals 8, narrowish, inclined to be gappy. Mauve with deeper rosy-mauve bar. Anthers rosy-mauve.

C. brachiata (C). South Africa. Vigorous climber, more or less evergreen. Leaves pinnate. Leaflets usually 5 with large, coarse teeth. Flowers in axillary panicles (with up to 30 in each leaf axil) throughout the terminal 0·8m of every current season's shoot. Flowers 4cm across, sepals 4, occasionally 5, ovate lanceolate, spreading or slightly recurved, green-tinted white. Stamens prominent, greenish yellow. Scent very slight, of a pleasing vegetable quality. Hardiness not properly tested, yet.

C. calycina. See *C. cirrhosa* var. *calycina.*

C. campaniflora (C). Portugal, 1820. Vigorous, climbing to 4·5m. Leaves pinnate with 5, 7 or 9 leaflets, subdivided into threes. Small, 3cm-wide bell-flowers. Sepals 4, bluish-white.

Campanile. See *C. heracleifolia* 'Campanile'.

Capitan Thuilleaux (B). A Nelly Moser-type clematis from France with 8 rounded sepals. Broad vivid carmine bar against narrow pale margins.

Charissima (B). A new clematis from Pennell's with Nelly Moser as the seed parent pollinated by Kathleen Wheeler. A large flowers with 8 sepals. Pink with dark central rib and dark red stamens.

C. chrysocoma (A). Yunnan 1884. As we know and grow it in this country, a vigorous climber to 9m. Leaves trifoliate, purplish when young, both surfaces covered with down as also are leaf and flower stalks. Leaflets often as wide as long, giving entire leaf a broad look quite distinct from *C. montana* in which the leaflets are lanceolate. Leaflets in *C. chrysocoma* usually 3-lobed, merely toothed in *C. montana*. The 2 side-leaflets are about half the size of the central one. Flowers in axillary clusters of 3 to 5, 6cm across on extra-long, 8 to 10cm stalks. Sepals 4, broad and rounded, soft pinkish mauve. (Others call them pink, but this is a question of how you see and define colours.) No scent.

C. chrysocoma var. **sericea** (syn. *C. spooneri*) (A). Vigorous climber to 8m. Leaves ternate, leaflets only a little less broad than long, downy on both surfaces, markedly serrate. Flowers bold, 8cm across. Sepals 4, broad, obovate (4cm long by 3·5cm across), white but slight pinkish mauve flush along sepal midribs. No scent.

C. cirrhosa (A). Southern Europe, Asia Minor, 1596. Evergreen climber to 4m. Leaves simple, ovate or three-lobed with serrated margins. Flowers nodding, 4cm across, each subtended by a pair of green perfoliate bracts. Sepals 4, greenish white. Mainly winter-flowering. Bean describes the seed vessels terminated by plumose styles, forming large, beautifully silky heads. I had never seen these until recently in a Dorset-shire garden. Seen in mid-February, the seed heads were just reaching the silky stage, having flowered well before Christmas.

C. cirrhosa var. **balearica** (syn. *C. balearica, C. calycina*) (A). Mediterranean islands etc. Introduced 1783. Besides what I have already written on this clematis (see pages 66–67) it is worth remarking that with *C. cirrhosa* itself there are many confusing variations. It is known as the fern-leaves clematis but the *C. cirrhosa* var. *balearica* that received an A.M. in 1974 and that is in most general cultivation, is not nearly as cut-leaved or ferny as other clones I have seen. A form of *C. cirrhosa* sent me by Mr Fisk has greeny-cream bells without freckles and is apt to flower in summer as well as in winter.

C. colensoi. See *C. hookeriana*.

C. columbiana. See *C. verticillaris* var. *columbiana*.

Columbine (A). A selection of *C. alpina* (q.v.). Flowers 8cm across when wide open, but sepals usually obliquely spreading. Light blue. Staminodes white.

Comtesse de Bouchaud (C). Vigorous but not tall, 3m. Leaflets usually 5. Flowers 13 to 15cm diameter at start of season, smaller later. Sepals 6, markedly channelled along midribs, margins and tips recurved on opening but becoming incurved with age. Bright pinky-mauve. Stamens cream. An abundant flowerer.

Corona (B or C). Bred by Tag Lundell of Sweden and introduced by Treasures 1972. They describe it as 'purple suffused pink with an orange highlight' which sounds theatrical. My own note from seeing it at Chelsea is: sepals 8 typically. Coloured petunia red like Barbara Dibley on opening but sepals blunt-ended. Filaments pale, anthers dark reddish. Not unlike Crimson King. Vigour said to be moderate.

Côte d'Azur. See *C. heracleifolia* 'Côte d'Azur'.

Countess of Lovelace (B). Tricky to start but can be vigorous enough when established. Leaves ternate. Flowers 15cm across packed with approximately 70 narrow, pointed sepals. Lilac-blue, fading. Stamens whitish. Carpels form a greenish eye. Light crop of single blooms on new wood.

Countess of Onslow (C). Probably no longer in cultivation.

Crimson King (B). Rather weak grower. Leaves simple or ternate. Flowers up to 13cm across. Sepals 5, 6 or 7, rather gappy and recurving along margins with age. Fairly uniform but tired crimson lake. Filaments white, anthers markedly brown.

C. crispa (C). South-eastern United States, 1726. Semi-woody climber to 1·5m. Leaflets 3, 5 or more. Flowers solitary, bell-shaped, 4 to 5cm long, scented. Sepals 4, pale blue, not unlike *C. heracleifolia davidiana* with recurved points but more solid. Related to *C. texensis* with which it has been crossed.

C. W. Dowman (B). Moderate vigour. Leaves ternate with rather long narrow segments, distinctly boat-shaped. Sepals 8, ovate, sharp-pointed, narrow at base with gaps. A lively pink at first but soon bleaching. Anthers beige.

Daniel Deronda (B or C). Moderate vigour. Leaves simple or ternate, bronzed. Flowers semi-double, flattish, 18cm across, bluish purple. May miss out on these and go straight to single flowers later, with paler centre to sepals. Cream stamens.

C. davidiana. See *C. heracleifolia* var. *davidiana.*

Dawn (B). Habit compact though free flowering. Leaves ternate (occasionally simple) on long petioles. Leaflets broadly cordate with purple margins. Sepals 8, rounded, bluish white, pinkest near tips, fading to white throughout but contrasting purple anthers. Slight scent. Introduced by Treasures (originally as Aurora) 1969.

C. douglasii var. ***scottii*** (C). Herbaceous, non-clinging, 1m tall. Leaves glaucous, bipinnate, the leaflets narrow, lanceolate. Petioles and underside of leaves downy. Flowers urn-shaped, 3·5cm across, 4cm long; sepals 4, recurved at tips. Outer surface downy, lavender-coloured, a pinker tinge

within. Masses of creamy stamens, slightly protruding. cv
Rosea is a good shade of pink.

Duchess of Albany (C). Vigorous semi-woody climber to 3m.
Leaflets 5. 4cm-long bell flowers. Sepals 4, nearly pink.

Duchess of Edinburgh (B). Moderate vigour. Leaves ternate,
a yellowish green. Flowers double, white rosettes, 13cm
across, often misshapen and green. Stamens creamy.

Duchess of Sutherland (B or C). Sometimes difficult to start
but vigorous when happy and established. Leaves ternate.
Light pruning allows small crop of flattish double flowers,
15cm across. Main crop on young wood later. Sepals 6, very
broad and widely overlapping, tapering to sharp right-angular
points. Soft rosy-red. Filaments creamy, anthers reddish
purple.

C. × durandii (*C. × jackmanii* × *C. integrifolia*) (C). Sub-
shrub to 2·5m. Leaves simple, ovate, non-clinging. Flowers
10cm across, rich indigo blue. Sepals 4, 5 or 6, with deeply
furrowed midribs. Stamens off-white.

Edith (B or C). Brought out by Treasures 1974. A seedling of
Mrs Cholmondeley and much the same shape. Flowers 15 to
20cm across, white with faint marginal bluing. Dark stamens.
Said to be a good performer over a long season.

Edouard Desfossé (B). Only moderate vigour. Leaves simple
or ternate. Flowers 15cm across. Sepals 8, long, rather gappy;
deep mauve-purple, fading. Reddish purple central bar. Conspicuous reddish purple anthers.

Edward Prichard (C). Herbaceous, 1 to 1·5m, non-clinging.
Leaflets 5, deeply toothed. Flowers in terminal and axillary
panicles, cruciform, 4cm across. Sepals narrow, wedge
shaped, pale mauve, deepest near their blunt tips. Picks well,
its pleasant scent filling a room. From a cross between *C. recta*
and *C. heracleifolia* var. *davidiana*.

Elsa Späth (B or C). Moderate vigour. Leaflets 3 or 5. Very
large, floppy flowers, 20cm across. Smaller blooms of better
form, later. Sepals 6, 7 or 8, broad and overlapping, rich

lavender-blue. Anthers reddish purple. Sometimes sold a Xerxes; in Australia as Blue Boy.

C. × *eriostemon* (syn. *C. bergeronii, C. chandleri, C. intermedia, C. hendersonii*) (C). Introduced 1835. A cross b tween *C. viticella* and *C. integrifolia* made at different times different places. Herbaceous, non-clinging to 2·5cm. Leafle up to 7. Nodding lantern flowers up to 5cm across, very lik *C. integrifolia*. Sepals 4, dusky purple.

Ernest Markham (B or C). Vigorous to 2·5m. Leaflets, 3 (usually) 5. Light pruning (B) allows preliminary small crop large flowers, 15cm across. Main crop always on young shoot flowers 13cm across. Sepals 6, broad, overlapping, rough te tured, magenta. Stamens beige, inconspicuous.

Etoile de Paris (B). Fairly vigorous but compact. Leav trifoliate, small, dark and leathery. Flowers 15cm across. Se als 8, fine pointed, gappy, strong mauve-blue with reddi central bar. Anthers dusty, greyish-purple.

Etoile Rose (C). Herbaceous or sub-shrubby climber 3·5m. Nodding bell flowers, 5cm long to 5cm wide at mout Sepals 4, silvery-pink at margins, cherry-purple-centred.

Etoile Violette (C). Vigorous. Leaflets 5. Deep purpl cream-eyed, 10cm-wide flowers. Sepals 6 (sometimes 4 or 5 recurved at tips.

Fair Rosamond (B). Vigour only moderate. Leaflets 3 or Fat globular buds opening to full, well-formed flower, 13 15 cm across. Prominent cushion of bright purple anther Sweet scent.

Fairy Queen (B). Rather weak growing. Leaflets 3. Flowe 18cm or more across. Sepals 8, 4cm across, a little gappy. Fles coloured with rosy-mauve bar. Anthers dusty purple.

C. fargesii var. *souliei* (B or C). China 1911. Vigorous to 4r Young stems purple where exposed to light. Leaves pinna up to 0·3m long with 5 to 6cm between pinnae. Pinnae usual ternate, each pinnule tri-lobed and with jagged, uneven teet Both surfaces slightly hairy, especially when young. Peduncl

7 to 9cm. Flowers typically in 3's arising from one point at which are 2 subtending foliar bracts, 2cm long. Centre flower opens some 10 days before subtending buds and one or both of the latter frequently abort. Buds rounded coming to a short sharp point. Stamens greenish to cream. Sepals 6, white with tinge of green, recurved at margins, which are crimped. No scent.

C. finetiana (syn. *C. pavoliniana*) (B). China, 1908. Evergreen. Leaves simple or ternate, cordate at base, tapering to fine points, 8cm long. Flowers 3 to 7 in axils, 4cm across, strongly hawthorn scented. Sepals 4, narrow, white. Stamens and styles white. June. Needs a warm wall. Inferior to the related *C. armandii.*

C. flammula (C). Southern Europe, 1590. Vigorous, to 4m. Foliage rich, dark green. Leaves biternate. Flowers 3cm across in great quantities, powerfully scented. Sepals 4, pure white.

C. florida 'Plena' (syn. *C. florida* 'Alba Plena') (B). Probably the clone introduced by Thunberg from Japan 1776. Fully double without distinction between sepals and staminodes in colour or form. Greenish-white throughout.

C. florida 'Sieboldii' (syn. *C. florida bicolor, C. sieboldii*) (B). Weak but capable of reaching 2·5m. Hardy, though early spring growth often cut. Leaflets 5. Flowers borne singly in leaf axils of terminal metre of young growth. Peduncle 20cm long with conspicuous foliar bracts. Flowers up to 10cm across. Sepals 6, ovate, 4cm across; pale green, slowly expanding and maturing to white. Anthers petal-like, massed in a domed boss, eventually 5cm across, changing from green to rich purple and persisting for some time after the sepals have fallen.

C. forsteri (A). A dioecious species from New Zealand where it is a common ingredient of lowland scrub on the North Island. Evergreen. Leaflets with crenate margins. Flowers greeny yellow, 2·5 to 4cm across with 6 sepals. Fluffy seed heads. Lemon-scented. I have only seen this under glass at Treasures but it might do on a sunny wall outside.

Descriptions

Frances Rivis (A). The largest-flowered cultivar of *C. alpina* and deep blue in colouring.

C. fusca (B). North-east Asia, 1860. Herbaceous or semi-woody climber to 4m. Leaves pinnate, the terminal leaflet often absent. Flowers solitary, urn-shaped. Sepals 4, 2cm long with recurved tips, dusky dark red. A collector's piece, interesting as an Asiatic relative of the mainly North American Viorna group.

Gillian Blades (B). From Fisk. White with a faint mauve edge. Sepals 8, pointed. Pale stamens. Looked nice at the Chelsea Flower Show 1975.

Gipsy Queen (C). Vigorous. Leaves ternate. Flowers 13cm across. Sepals 6, broad and rounded, purple fading to violet. Anthers reddish-purple.

Gladys Picard (B). From Fisk. A large very pale mauve flower with 8 broad, overlapping sepals and white stamens. Pretty as shown at Chelsea Flower Show.

C. grata var. **grandidentata.** C. grata is typically a Himalayan species not in cultivation. This variety was introduced by E. H. Wilson at Veitch's Nursery 1904 and is of Chinese origin. Vigorous climber to 9m. Closely akin and very similar to *C. vitalba,* but said to flower May-June so don't ask the author how it should be pruned. Flowers in terminal panicles, suggesting (C) pruning, but a later flowering season.

Gravetye Beauty (C). Vigorous herbaceous climber. Leaflets 5, often cordate. 7cm-long bell flowers open out into 9cm-wide stars. Sepals 4, 5 or 6, with incurved margins but recurved tips. Cherry-red, ageing pinker. Filaments cream, anthers red as sepals.

Guiding Star (B). Leaves ternate, bronzed when young. Flowers 11cm across, dished. Sepals 6, sometimes 8, very sharp-pointed, bluish purple but not dark. Centre of sepal fades to paler colour than rest, in which there are reddish undertones. Filaments white, anthers brown.

Hagley Hybrid (C). So abundant in flower production for

three solid months that growth tends to be limited. Seldom taller than 2·5m. Leaves usually ternate. Flowers 13 to 15cm across. Sepals 6 (or 5), cupped, tapering to fine points. A delightful rosy-mauve at first but fading. Handsome purplish anthers.

Henryi (syn. Bangholme Belle) (B). Vigour moderate once established but young plants often fail. Young foliage characteristically bronzed. Leaves simple or ternate. Flowers 15 to 18cm across. Sepals 6, scarcely overlapping, pure white. Contrasting eye of brown-tipped stamens. Two crops.

C. heracleifolia (C). Eastern China, 1837. Coarse, non-clinging sub-shrub to 1·5m. Large ternate leaves, the central leaflet twice the size of the other two. Flowers hyacinth-like in size and shape, borne in axillary clusters and whorls. Sepals 4 (5 or 6), blue. Best known in gardens in 3 named cultivars and one natural variety, but see also Mrs Robert Brydon. *C.h.* var. *davidiana,* Northern China 1864, is entirely herbaceous and clump-forming. Flowers dioecious (usually male in cultivation), pale blue, larger and opening wider (4cm) than in the type-plant. Very fragrant. Wyevale is a slightly deeper shaded cultivar with markedly larger flowers and as strong a scent. *C.h.* cv 'Campanile' is a sub-shrub to 1·5m. Hermaphrodite. Numerous, densely clustered, 2cm-long, mid-blue bell-flowers. Côte d'Azur, similar; perhaps, nowadays, the same.

H. F. Young (B). Mid-blue, nicely shaped flower. Sepals 8, widely overlapping. Stamens white.

Hidcote Purple (B). Sepals 7 or 8, rather pointed, reflexed in mature flowers. Light rosy purple. Dark anthers.

C. hookeriana (syn. *C. colensoi*) (A). Leaves pinnate, described as being somewhat fern-like, the pinnae up to 8cm long. Flowers in axillary clusters, star-like, up to 4cm across, scented. Sepals usually 6, green or yellow-green; stamens likewise. A New Zealand species from north and south shores of Cork Strait, ascending to 900m inland. Introduced by Collingwood Ingram 1937 and grown in his Kentish garden whence he exhibited it 15 May 1961 and it received an A.M. as *C. colensoi.* Should be grown on a sheltered wall.

Horn of Plenty (B). Leaves ternate with purplish margin Flowers large, somewhat cupped. Sepals usually 8, symmetrcally elliptic, overlapping, rather blunt-tipped. Rich ro: purple fading to a good blue-mauve. Stamens numerou and a prominent feature with reddish-purple anthers.

Huldine (C). Vigorous. Leaflets 5. Flowers 10cm across. Se als usually 6, not overlapping, with slightly incurved margir but recurved tips. Upper surface white; under surface pa mauve, with darker central bar. Stamens greenish-white.

Hybrida Sieboldii. *See* Ramona (B).

C. integrifolia (C). Southern Europe, 1573. Herbaceous 1m. Leaves simple, ovate with 3 grooved longitudinal vein non-clinging. Flowers borne singly, nodding, 5cm across. Se als 4, obliquely spreading, mid-blue on both surfaces, the margins recurved and somewhat twisted. Stamens whit forming a tube. cv Hendersonii is larger, while cv Olgae h: very waved sepal margins and is scented.

C. × *jackmanii* (C). Leaves simple (at base of young shoots ternate (along middle of young shoots) or in fives (towar extremities of young shoots). Flowers 13cm across. Sepals (5 or 6), gappy, rough-textured with channelled mid-rib Bluish-purple. Stamens greenish-beige. cv Superba differs : its broader sepals composing a fuller flower and the reddi: tinge in its purple colouring, especially noticeable in new opened blooms.

Jackmanii Alba (B or C). Very vigorous with pale gree foliage. Leaflets 3. First crop of flowers, 13cm across, sem double, of ragged outline with sepals of unequal lengths ar often undecided whether to be leaves, on the outside of tl flower; or stamens, in the flower's centre. White with pale bl veins. Second crop, single. Sepals 5 or 6, white. Anthe brown. Not very free flowering.

Jackmanii Rubra (B or C). Fairly vigorous. Leaves ternat Flowers semi-double from year-old wood, slightly lopside single blooms soon develop and take over for the remainder its long season. Sepals 4, 5 or 6, velvety crimson-lake. Crea stamens.

Joan Wilcox (B). A large pale mauve-pink flower with 8 grooved sepals and crimped margins. Dark purple anthers make a good feature.

John Warren (B or C). Habit, compact. Leaves simple or ternate. Large flowers up to 25cm across. Sepals 6 (or 7) tapering to acute points. Pinkish lilac but richer on opening and poorer on fading, darkest along margins and mid-rib. Reddish stamens.

C. × jouiniana (*C. heracleifolia* var. *davidiana* × *C. vitalba*) (C). Non-clinging sub-shrub to 4m. Leaves dark green, glabrous; leaflets 5 (or 3). Huge, compound, leafy panicles of wide-opening flowers 3 to 5cm across. Sepals 4, 5 or 6, off-white shading to grey-blue at tips. Stamens cream. September-October, but cv Praecox starts flowering 6 weeks earlier.

Kathleen Dunford (B). Large, semi-double, with two symmetrical rows of fairly narrow sepals. A rather dim magenta. Anthers brown. Some single flowers, with 6 sepals, later.

Kathleen Wheeler (B). Flowers terminal on longish young shoots. Leaves simple or, more usually, ternate with narrow, lanceolate leaflets. Flowers large, 16cm across; sepals 6, elliptical, rather gappy. A strong shade of rosy mauve or 'plummy mauve' but the 3 sunken veins in centre of each sepal are darker and pinker. Stamens creamy with a touch of lavender in the outer ones.

Kermesina (C). Of medium vigour with small, wine-red flowers like those of Viticella Rubra. See p. 88.

King Edward VII (B or C). Leaves large, often simple and cordate; also ternate. Tends to carry solitary, terminal blooms on 60cm-long shoots of current season. Early blooms can be very green/grey and weird. Flowers 17cm across. Sepals 8, overlapping, obovate but with fine points; strong lilac-mauve with rosy flush in central area. Cream filaments, brownish anthers. A bold bloom but not prolific.

King George V (C). Vigour moderate. Leaves ternate.

Flowers 15cm across. Sepals 6 or 7, flesh pink with bright pink bar. Shy flowering.

Lady Betty Balfour (C). Vigorous to 4m or more. Leaves usually ternate, shiny, coppery when young. Flowers 13cm across. Sepals 6, rather cupped, fine-pointed. Rich purple fading to bluer shade. White central bar on underside. Stamens creamy, conspicuous. September. Needs full sun.

Lady Caroline Nevill (B or C). Fairly vigorous. Leaves simple or ternate. Flowers 15 to 18cm across. Sepals 8, fairly pale lavender with very faintly darker midrib. Filaments white, anthers beige. Sometimes semi-double in first flush.

Lady Londesborough (B). Growth moderate. Leaves ternate. Flowers 13 to 15cm across, beautifully formed. Sepals 7, broad, round-tipped with wide overlap of margins. Pale mauve, fading to silvery mauve and finally palest grey. Prominent dark stamens.

Lady Northcliffe (B or C). Fairly vigorous once established. Slight coppery tinge in young leaves; simple, ternate or in fives. Flowers 15cm across. Sepals usually 6, broadly overlapping, wavy and never lying flat, much blunter than Lasurstern. Deep, slightly richer blue than Lasurstern. Stamens greenish-white, less prominent than those of Lasurstern.

Lasurstern (B or C). Fairly vigorous to 3m. Leaves sometimes simple, usually ternate. Flowers 15 to 18cm wide, opening perfectly flat. Sepals 7 or 8 with wavy margins (cf. Lady Northcliffe in which entire sepal is twisted), tapering to fine points. Rich, deep blue fading to campanula blue. Greenish-white bar on under-surface. Stamens pale creamy. Second crop flowers only 13cm across.

Lawsoniana (B). Leaves simple or ternate. Flowers up to 24cm across, rosy lavender becoming lavender blue. Tends to flower out of sight unless deliberately planted to be seen from above.

Lincoln Star (B). Frequently little vigour but can make a good plant. Leaves ternate. Flowers 13cm across, shapely with 8 narrow, pointed sepals. Brilliant raspberry pink almost to margins, though sometimes this colour is confined to a central bar and autumn blooms may be quite washy and uncharacteristic. Anthers crimson, showy.

Little Nell (C). Vigorous to 6m. Leaflets 5 or 7 and further subdivided. Flowers 5cm across on 15cm pedicels. Sepals 4 or 6, recurved at margins. Broad outer band of pale mauve; white central bar. Stamens greenish.

Lord Nevill (B or C). Vigorous. Leaves simple or ternate, deeply bronzed when young. Flowers 15 to 18cm across. Sepals 8 (sometimes 6), broad and overlapping, very wavy edged, tapering broadly to sharp points. Purplish-blue, especially purple towards centre-base. Veins conspicuously darker throughout the sepal and especially as the flower bleaches. Purple anthers form no contrast.

C. macropetala (syn. *Atragene macropetala*) (A). Northern China, Siberia, 1910. Vigorous to 4m. Leaves biternate, serrate. Flowers nodding 8cm across, conspicuously and fully double. Sepals 4, 4cm long by 2cm wide, lavender with blue margins. Numerous slender staminodes, 2·5cm long; the outer 10 to 14 blue, the inner ones whitish. Cultivars include Maidwell Hall and Markham's Pink (syn. Markhamii).

Mme Baron Veillard (C). Vigorous, to 4m in a season. Leaves ternate, each leaflet on a long stalk. Flowers rather cupped at centre but with slightly reflexed tips, 13cm across. Sepals 6, obovate, slightly gappy, a nice rosy-lilac shade. Stamens greenish-white.

Mme Edouard André (C). Not vigorous but a good doer, to 2·5m. Leaves simple or ternate. Buds narrow, pointed, Flowers up to 13cm across, rather cupped. Sepals 6, very pointed; margins incurved (cf. Ville de Lyon). Uniformly deep wine red, matt surfaced. Stamens creamy.

Mme Grangé (C). Vigorous. Leaflets 5. Flowers 13cm across, freely borne. Sepals 4, 5 or (usually) 6; inrolled margins most pronounced on young plants. Upper surface deep purplish-red, velvety. Lower surface pubescent, dusky. Stamens grubby, nondescript.

Mme Julia Correvon (C). Vigorous. Leaflets 5, further subdivided. Flowers 13cm across. Sepals 4, 5 or 6, narrow and gappy with recurved tips, the upper surface deeply channelled. Clear rosy red. Stamens greenish-cream. Very free.

Mme Le Coultre. *See* Marie Boisselot.

Maidwell Hall (A). A bluer form of *C. macropetala.*

Marcel Moser (B). Rather weak growing, tending to flower at the expense of young growth. Leaves ternate, pubescent when young, longer and more narrowly tapering than those of Nelly Moser. Flowers 20cm across. Sepals 8, tapering to fine points. Rosy-mauve with carmine central bar. Bleaches badly. Handsome reddish-purple stamens.

Margaret Hunt (C). No more to record on this clematis than is given on page 60.

Margot Koster (C). Robust and prolific. Leaflets 5. Flowers 8cm across. Sepals 4, 5 or 6, obovate, gappy with reflexed margins and tips. Rosy-red. Stamens whitish.

Marie Boisselot (syn. Mme Le Coultre) (B or C). Vigorous. Leaves simple or ternate, very broad. Flowers 15 cm across, beautifully formed, opening flat. Sepals 8, very broad, overlapping so widely as sometimes to give semi-double impression. Faint pink flush at unfolding; soon pure white. Stamens white.

Markham's Pink (syn. *C. macropetala* 'Markhamii') (A). Similar to *C. macropetala* apart from its colour. Outer surface of sepals bright reddish-purple with narrow pale lilac margin. Inner, concealed staminodes, greenish-cream.

Maureen (B). Bushy, neither tall nor vigorous but free. Sepals 6, reddish purple (bluer than Mme Grangé). A good colour and a nice clematis.

C. maximowicziana (syn. *C. paniculata*) (C). Japan 1860. Better known by its synonym, though *C. paniculata* is correctly the New Zealand species long known as *C. indivisa*. *C. maximowicziana* is a vigorous (more vigorous than the related *C. flammula*) climber to 10m. Leaves smooth, dark green on both sides with 3 or (more usually) 5 leaflets, edentulate, not even lobed and resembling, as Bean describes it, 'in form and colour the leaves of the common lilac.' Flowers cruciform, 3cm across, white, scented. Late season.

C. meyeniana (A). Far East. Introduced circa 1821. Vigorous evergreen related to *C. armandii*. Leaves trifoliate up to 10cm long, leathery. Flowers white, 2·5cm across in large, loose axillary panicles. Sepals usually 4, narrowly oblong. A.M. 1920. Generally requires cool greenhouse treatment.

Minuet (C). Vigorous. Leaflets up to 7, and further subdivided. Flowers 5cm across on long pedicels, each with two foliar bracts. Sepals 4, margined in deep mauve, the inner area off-white with mauve veins. Stamens green.

Miriam Markham (C). Moderate vigour. Large, loosely built, double flowers, shaded lavender. Shy flowering.

Miss Bateman (B). Fairly vigorous. Leaves ternate. Flowers 15cm across, opening flat and well formed. Sepals 8, broad, overlapping, creamy-white. Reddish-purple anthers make a striking eye.

Mrs Bush (B). Fairly vigorous. Leaves simple or ternate. Flowers 15 to 18cm across or more. Sepals 6 to 8, of soft, silky texture, fairly narrow. Uniformly pale bluish-mauve. Anthers pale brown.

Miss Crawshay (B). Vigour moderate. Leaves ternate. Buds very fat, opening into (usually) semi-double blooms, 15cm across. Single blooms have 8 sepals, round-tipped, narrow at base. Pale rosy-mauve. Anthers pale fawn.

Mrs Cholmondeley (B or C). Vigorous. Leaflets 3 or 5. Flowers 20cm across, prolific. Sepals usually 6, obovate, narrow at base and with gaps between sepals. Lavender-blue with darker reticulations in veins. Fades pleasantly. Stamens brownish. Long season. The blowsy old girl makes a splendid show.

Mrs George Jackman (B or C). Reasonably vigorous. Leaves simple or (more often) ternate. Flowers 15 to 18cm across with (usually) eight broad overlapping sepals and sometimes an extra 2 or 3, giving slightly doubled effect. White. Anthers pale beige forming a more conspicuous eye than Marie Boisselot but less so than Henryi and Miss Bateman.

Mrs Hope (B or C). Vigorous. Leaves nearly all simple, up to 20cm long and 10cm broad in mature plants. Flowers 18cm across at first flowering, 13cm at second. Sepals 8, very broad (6cm across) and thus overlapping to give semi-double effect. Light blue with slightly darker central bar. Anthers rich purple. A different clematis is frequently sold as Mrs Hope.

Mrs N. Thompson (B). Like a very dark Barbara Jackman. Sepals 6, overlapping. Petunia central bar with bluish-purple margins. Stamens reddish. Slow to get started.

Mrs Oud (B). Weak grower. Leaves ternate. Large white flowers, well shaped. Sepals broad and overlapping though pinched and upturned near base, leaving a gap here. Dark anthers.

Mrs P. B. Truax (B). Fairly vigorous. Leaves ternate. Flowers 14cm wide. Sepals usually 8, not much overlapping, very narrow and gappy at base. Mid to light blue, fading. Stamens creamy. Short season. Has been sold as Xerxes.

Mrs Robert Brydon (C). Either a cv of *C. heracleifolia* or a clone of *C.* × *jouiniana* (*C. heracleifolia* var. *davidiana* × *C. vitalba*). Sub-shrubby to 2m, requiring good support. Leaves coarse, though not specially obtrusive. Flowers very pale off-white with faint bluish tinge, looking dirty. Sepals 4 or 5, entirely separate and gappy, rolled right back. Prominent white stamens.

Mrs Spencer Castle (B). Vigour moderate. Leaves ternate. Large, pale mauve-pink flowers with cream anthers. Sepals usually 6, but extra ones at first flowering, giving semi-double effect.

C. montana (A). Himalaya, 1831. Exceptionally vigorous, to 12m. Leaves ternate with serrated margins. Flowers in axillary clusters up to five, 5 to 8cm across, vanilla scented. Sepals usually 4, white.

C. montana var. **rubens** (A). China, 1900. Leaves purplish, especially when young. Flowers rosy-mauve, 5 to 8cm across, vanilla scented.

C. montana var. **wilsonii** (A). Central China, circa 1900. Flowers a month later than other montanas. Flowers 9cm across. Sepals 4, each 2cm across, white, rolling back along margins in older blooms. Prominent brush of stamens. Strong hot chocolate scent. Often sold untrue to name; Wilson himself introduced at least 2 clones.

The following cultivars of *C. montana* are some of those in commerce, but there are many more:

Elizabeth. Large, light pinkish flowers, sometimes white if grown in shade. Scented.
Grandiflora. Flowers up to 8cm across with very wide white sepals. No scent.
Picton's Variety. Less vigorous than average. Sepals 4, 5 or 6, of varying widths. Opens deep rosy-mauve (most intense in sunlight), fading only a little. Anthers whitish. Scent negligible.
Pink Perfection. Very like Elizabeth.
Tetrarose. Large rosy-mauve tetraploid cultivar.

C. napaulensis (syn. *C. forrestii*) (A). Northern India, China. Introduced by Forrest, 1912. Vigorous evergreen, winter flowering and somewhat tender species. Leaves ternate, untoothed or a few large teeth. Flowers in axillary clusters of up to 10, each subtended by a perfoliate bract (similar to that found in the related *C. cirrhosa*). Sepals 4, greenish white, 1·5cm long, somewhat recurved at tips. Stamens 3cm long, protruding and conspicuous because purple throughout. No scent.

Nelly Moser (B). Vigorous to 3·5m. Leaves ternate, smooth (cf. Marcel Moser). Flowers 17cm across, opening flat. Sepals 8, fairly blunt tipped, rosy-mauve with carmine bar. Brilliance of this bar varies greatly from one season to another. Bleaches badly. Anthers reddish-purple.

Niobe (C). For once an attractively and appropriately named new clematis. The one thing everyone remembers about Niobe is that she was 'all tears'. Sepals 6. Lovely, very deep, velvety red. Lighter, greenish stamens.

C. orientalis (syn. *C. graveolens*) (C). Asia, 1731. Vigorous to 5m. Size and bright yellow colouring of flowers similar to *C. tangutica,* but the 4 sepals often opening wide to 5cm, though sometimes campanulate. The L. & S. form No. 13342 outclasses all others. Introduced by Messrs Ludlow and Sherriff, 1947. Leaflets up to 9 and further finely subdivided. Flowers broadly campanulate with very thick, fleshy sepals. Stamens conspicuous, with reddish-purple filaments and white anthers.

Pamela Jackman (A). A selection of *C. alpina.* Flowers 8cm across at mouth. Sepals 4·5cm long, 2cm wide; of generous proportions for this species. Rich, deep azure. Staminodes in a tight cluster, the outer ring bluish, the inner ones creamy.

C. paniculata (syn. *C. indivisa,* by which name it is still more familiar in this country) (A). New Zealand, abundant in both islands and their showiest species. 1840. Evergreen, dioecious, the males being showier than females. Leaves ternate, the leaflets entire or lobed as is said to be the case in the cv Lobata, though my specimen had no lobes. Flowers 8cm across, borne in axillary panicles. Sepals 6 to 8, spathulate, pure white. Stamens yellow.

C. parviflora (A). Vigorous evergreen New Zealander with a wide distribution along lowland forest margins as far south as Nelson. Small, delicately divided leaves, usually with 5 pinnae, which are themselves subdivided. Flowers in axillary clusters of 2, 3 or 4 making dense ropes of blossom. Each flower 4cm across. Sepals 6, lanceolate making a star shape. Colour throughout, including stamens, a slightly yellow shade of green. Pretty but not eye-catching. Strong lemon scent.

Percy Lake (B). Large flowers. Sepals 7 or 8, washed-out mauve-white; stamens the same.

Percy Picton (B). Fairly weak growing. Leaves ternate. Flowers 18cm across. Sepals usually 8 (sometimes only 6 or 7), perfectly ovate, a rich intense mauve. Anthers purple.

Perle d'Azur (C). Vigorous to 4m. Leaflets 3 or 5. Flowers up to 15cm across, but, with recurved tips, appearing less. Sepals 6 (occasionally fewer), broadly obovate, 7cm across at broadest. Deeply channelled mid-ribs. Light blue with pinkish-mauve flush towards centre-base. Stamens pale greenish. Very free.

C. phlebantha (A) is as fully described as I intend, p. 68. Also written up in the RHS Journal 1968.

C. pitcheri (syn. *C. simsii*) (C). U.S.A., 1878. Climber to 3m. Leaflets 3, 5 or 7 and further subdivided. Flowers solitary, urn-shaped. Sepals 4, violet outside, purple within, 3cm-long with recurved tips. Related to *C. texensis* with which it has been confused by French hybridisers.

Prins Hendrik (syn. Prince Henry) (B). Weak growing but enormous flowered. Leaves usually simple. Sepals 7, broad, with crimped, wavy margins and fine points; lavender-blue. Anthers purple. Best under glass.

Proteus (B). Moderate vigour. Leaves trifoliate. Buds globular. Flowers fully double in first crop; pompon rosettes 15cm across. Sepals about 100, rosy-lilac. Second crop flowers, single; sepals 6, darkest at margins. Stamens cream.

Ramona (syn. Hybrida Sieboldii) (B). A large, lavender-blue clematis, very close to Blue Gem, Mrs Bush and Mrs Hope. Lady Caroline Nevill has also been seen as this!

C. recta (syn. *C. erecta*). Europe and Asia. 1597. Herbaceous climber. Height variable; 1 to 2m. Deep green pinnate foliage; leaflets 5. Flowers in panicles, white, 2cm wide, cruciform, sometimes scented, midsummer-flowering. Conspicuous seed heads. The cv Purpurea, with purple young foliage maturing green, is not a fixed clone.

C. rehderiana (syn. *C. nutans; C. nutans thyrsoidea*) (C). Western China, 1898. Vigorous to 6m. Leaves and shoots very downy; leaflets 7 or 9, coarsely toothed. Flowers in axillary panicles, bell shaped, 1·5 to 2cm long. Sepals 4, recurved at tips, straw yellow. Strongly cowslip scented.

Richard Pennell (B or C). A new clematis of Walter Pennell's raising, Richard being his son. The seed parent is Vyvyan Pennell (in human terms also), pollinated by Daniel Deronda (ahem). Sepals 8 with strongly waved margins. Lavender with whitish intimations. Very prominent whirling stamens with red filaments which curve over at the tips; cream anthers. A pretty flower at all stages and, as far as I can judge from having only seen it, not yet grown it, an outstanding clematis.

Royal Velours (C). Vigour moderate, considering its viticella blood. Leaflets 5 and further subdivided. Flowers 8cm across. Sepals usually 4, dark rich purple, of velvety texture.

Rubro-marginata. *See C. × triternata* 'Rubro-marginata'.

Ruby (A). A selection of *C. alpina.* Flowers up to 8cm across. Sepals 4cm long, of a dim lilac colouring. Staminodes off-white with mauve tinge.

Scartho Gem (B or C). A Nelly Moser-type clematis from Pennell. The seed parent is Lincoln Star pollinated by Mrs N. Thompson. Bright, rosy carmine with narrow, paler sepal margins. Beige stamens. Eye-catching.

Sealand Gem (B or C). Fairly vigorous. Leaves simple or trifoliate. Flowers 13 to 15cm across. Sepals 6, perfectly ovate, 4cm across. Pale rosy-mauve with carmine bar quickly fading to give uniform colouring. Anthers mauvish, not standing out. Main flowering on young shoots.

Serenata (B or C). Introduced by Treasures 1970. Sepals usually 6 (often 4 on young wood), purple. Stamens cream-white. Most truly purple clematis flower late, so the early blooms of this one make an original contribution.

C. serratifolia (C). Korea c. 1918. Vigorous woody climber to 4m. Leaves biternate, smooth though surface often puckered. Coarse, uneven teeth. Flowers usually in 3's, the centre one opening earliest, nodding open-bell-shaped with somewhat spreading segments, 4cm across at mouth. Sepals 4, up to

1·5cm wide, gappy, pale yellow with tinge of green. Stamens very distinctive being purple throughout. Notable lemon scent.

Silver Moon (B or C). Rather unkindly noticed on pp. 45–46 but vigorous and bushy to 3m and has a long season. Excellent on a north or other sunless exposure which is, indeed, the only position where its colouring is acceptable.

Sir Garnet Wolseley (B). Moderate vigour. Leaves nearly all ternate (occasionally entire); leaflets up to 7cm across, 9cm long tapering to fine points. Flowers 13cm across. Sepals 7 or 8, obovate, tapering at base to leave gaps. Colour good at all ages, velvety purple with reddish flush at first, fading to blue-mauve. Anthers reddish purple.

Sir Trevor Lawrence (C). Vigorous semi-herbaceous climber. Leaflets 3, 5 or 7. Flowers shaped like upright bells, 5cm long. Sepals up to 6, very much the same cherry-red as Gravetye Beauty but slightly more luminous. Fades to bluer shade. Stamens cream throughout (cf. Gravetye Beauty's red anthers).

C. songarica (C). Non-climbing sub-shrub to 2m. Leaves simple, toothed, up to 11cm long, 3·5cm across, very smooth, shiny and green. Stems ribbed and grooved. Inflorescence terminal, consisting of about 30 blooms. Flowers 3·5cm across but tips of sepals rolled back. Sepals 5 (or 4), pure white, hawthorn- or meadow sweet-scented. Introduced 1880 from S. Siberia, Mongolia etc and the region of the river Sungari, from which it takes its name.

C. spooneri. See *C. chrysocoma sericea.*

C. stans. Herbaceous. Ht. 1m, non-clinging, flopping. Leaves up to 18cm long, ternate. Central leaflet 3-lobed, about same size as lateral leaflets. Flowers monoecious, 2cm long, tube slender, not swollen at base, opening into 4 segments which curl back at tips. Blue-tinged white.

Star of India (C). Vigour moderate. Leaflets 3 or 5, broad and bold. Flowers 14 to 16cm diameter, of excellent shape with 4, 5 or 6 broadly ovate sepals, up to 9cm wide. Purple with broad reddish-purple central bar which gradually fades out. Stamens grubby, nondescript. Handsome and dashing.

C. tangutica (C). China, 1898. Vigorous to 5m. Leaflets up to 7, unevenly toothed. Flowers campanulate, 2·5 to 4cm long. Sepals 4, butter yellow inside and out. Conspicuous seed heads with feathery styles. The variety *obtusiuscula*, introduced by Wilson from W. Szechwan, China, in 1908; also a selection from it, Gravetye Variety, have smaller, deeper yellow flowers.

The President (B or C). Vigorous. Leaves simple or ternate; young foliage bronzed. Flowers up to 18cm across, somewhat cupped and readily showing undersurface. Sepals 8, overlapping with tapered points. Upper surface uniform light purple; lower surface pale with silvery-white central bar. Anthers reddish-purple.

C. × triternata 'Rubro-marginata' (syn. *C. × rubro-marginata, C. flammula* var. *rubro-marginata*) (C). A cross between *C. flammula* and *C. viticella*. Vigorous to 4m. Flowers 2·5cm across. Sepals 4 to 6, white centred, shading to purple margins. Scented like *C. flammula*.

Twilight (C), but flowering rather early on its young wood like Comtesse de Bouchaud. Plenty of vigour. Leaves simple or ternate. Flowers 11cm across, almost carmine at first with greeny-yellow stamens in marked contrast. Colour soon fades pleasantly to rosy mauve with stronger rosy colouring maintained in central bar for some time. Stamens yellow. Sepals 6, broad, blunt (no points) and overlapping. A good flower, inappropriately named.

C. uncinata (syn. *C. leiocarpa*) (C). China. Evergreen with pinnate or biternate foliage. Flowers in axillary panicles from current season's growth. About 4cm across with 4 narrow, white sepals. Slight but not agreeable scent. Requires wall protection. Easily raised from seed. Introduced by Wilson, 1901. A.M. 1922.

C. × vedrariensis (*C. chrysocoma* × *C. montana rubens*) (A). Vigorous once established, to 6m. Leaves trifoliate, downy, deeply serrated. Flowers rosy-mauve, 7 to 8cm across on 10cm, downy stalks. Sepals 4, 5 or 6. cv Rosea (syn. *C. spooneri rosea*) is very similar. Highdown is a selection of *C.* × *vedrariensis.*

C. *veitchiana* (C). Very close to *C. rehderiana* but the leaves are bipinnate, not pinnate. Leaflets 20 or more. More numerous but smaller than in *C. rehderiana.* Bracts on the inflorescence small and awl-shaped (larger and ovate or oval in *C. rehderiana*). Introduced by Wilson from W. China 1904.

Venosa Violacea (C). Vigorous. Leaflets 5, subdivided into threes or fives. Viticella-type, but with 10cm-wide, upward facing flowers. Sepals 5 or 6 with purple incurved margins and white, purple-veined centres. Stamens abortive.

Venus Victrix (B or C). Although not at present on offer, as far as I know, there are still a few plants around claiming to be this old cv for which Cripps, the raisers, obtained a F.C.C. in 1876. The specimen I saw was under glass at Carolside, Berwickshire. Growth coarse. Leaves usually simple, sometimes ternate, cordate. Flowers terminal, not freely borne, large, semi-double with 2 rows of sepals, approximately 8 sepals in each row. Clear lavender mauve. Filaments white, anthers purplish. Moore & Jackman give this as a double clematis with 6 or 8 rows of sepals. This could well be so on an outdoor specimen. Their description otherwise tallies with the notes I made on the spot. Not unlike Miriam Markham.

Veronica's Choice (B). A new Pennell clematis named after his daughter. The seed parent is Vyvyan Pennell pollinated by Percy Lake. Fully double, the centre of the flower pale mauve or even French grey; the outer, guard sepals a little more intense. I like this.

C. *verticillaris* (syn. *Atragene americana*) (A). North America: Hudson Bay to Utah but now rare. 1797. Woody climber to 3m. Leaves ternate. Flowers solitary, nodding, 5 to 8cm wide. Sepals 4, 4cm long purplish-blue as also outer staminodes. This it e North American counterpart of *C. macropetala* and *C. alpina* from the old world. *C.v.* var. *columbiana* is commoner in cultivation but not easy.

Victoria (C). Vigorous. Leaflets 5. Flowers 15cm across, opening flat, without recurving. Sepals 6 (sometimes 4 or 5), with deep central veins and minutely puckered surface, broadly ovate, 5cm across. Light rosy-purple with more intensely flushed central bar. Fades pleasantly. Buff stamens.

Ville de Lyon (B or C). Vigorous to 4m. Leaflets 3 or 5. Flowers in 2 big crops. Maximum diameter 14cm; 8 to 10cm later. Sepals 6, obovate, broad and blunt tipped with margins and apex curved back. Deep carmine on opening, fading in centre to mauve while margins remain dark. Stamens creamy.

C. viorna (C). Eastern U.S.A., 1730. Herbaceous climber to 2m. Leaflets 3, 5 or 7, their tips acting as tendrils. Flowers solitary, almost globular but for recurved sepal tips which give overall urn-shape. Sepals 4, very thick and succulent, 2cm long, dusky reddish. Seed heads green and conspicuous.

C. vitalba, Traveller's Joy, Old Man's Beard (C). Europe, including Britain; North Africa, Caucasus. Rampant climber to 10m. Leaflets 5, coarsely toothed. Flowers 3cm across in panicles. Stamens more prominent than the 4 sepals, all being dingy creamy-white with greenish undertones. Little or no scent. Seed heads woolly and conspicuous, persisting in winter.

C. viticella (C). Southern Europe. Vigorous climber to 3 or 4m. Leaflets 7, further subdivided. Nodding purple flowers 4 to 9cm across. Sepals 4, often recurved at margins. Pedicels 15cm-long, thread-fine (with foliar bracts) giving graceful appearance to the shrub in bloom. cv 'Purpurea Plena Elegans' (syn. 'Elegans Plena') is a strong-growing hybrid with flowers 5cm across, packed with sepals in a dense rosette. Soft 'old rose' purple. The vigorous cv 'Rubra' is also of hybrid origin. Leaflets 7. Flowers outward-facing. Sepals 4 (or 5), 3cm wide, deep velvety crimson, white at base. Styles very dark red, almost black. Anthers brownish. Often misnamed Kermesina.

Vyvyan Pennell (B). The most vigorous large-flowered double clematis. Leaves ternate. Flowers form neat rosettes, 15cm across. Frame of large lilac guard sepals. Cushion of smaller lavender-blue inner sepals. A few single flowers on young wood. Mr Pennell made this cross between Daniel Deronda and Beauty of Worcester.

Wada's Primrose (B). Similar to Yellow Queen (alias Moonlight) and similarly prone to wilt. Does not have the long leaflet stalks of the above. Flowers even paler. Possibly another clone of the same Patens sub-species or hybrid.

Walter Pennell (B). Mr Pennell describes this as a companion to Vyvyan Pennell, which is the seed parent pollinated by Daniel Deronda. The overall colouring is deep lilac, redder than Vyvyan in the outer row of guard sepals which have a deep carmine bar. Centre of flower greyish showing pale stamens when fully open but looking better before this stage is reached. One does not name a flower after oneself unless one thinks highly of it, but my own reaction is that we have here a clematis inviting comparison with Vyvyan Pennell yet without striking a new chord. Time will tell.

W. E. Gladstone (B or C). Not vigorous though with very long internodes and capable of reaching 3m. Leaves simple or ternate. Leaflets large, up to 9cm across and 15cm long. Upper surface very shiny when young. Flowers up to 25cm across. Sepals 6 or 7 (though Moore & Jackman give 8), obovate, uniformly lavender. Stamens prominent; anthers purple.

White Moth (A). A selection of *C. alpina* var. *sibirica*. Light, yellowish-green, biternate foliage. Flowers 6cm across, white throughout with hint of green. Sepals 3·5cm long, 1·5cm wide. First row of 4 staminodes 3cm long, projecting beyond sepals but very narrow; inner staminodes conspicuous and numerous. Hence a fat, fully double flower resembling *C. macropetala* but smaller. Latest flowering of its group.

Will Goodwin (B). Pale lavender, with 6 to 10 broad, 7cm-wide sepals, overlapping, corrugated, wavy margined. Cream stamens. Not unlike a smaller version of Prins Hendrik.

William Kennett (B or C). Vigorous. Leaves nearly all simple. Flowers 15 to 18cm across. Sepals 8, broad and overlapping, rough textured with crimped margins. Strong lavender-blue with reddish-purple central stripe on opening (far more marked than in Mrs Hope), gradually fading out. Dark purple anthers.

Xerxes. The true plant is no longer in cultivation. Of recent years Elsa Späth and Mrs P. B. Truax have both been erroneously listed as Xerxes in this country while in Australia a white cv has for years been sold under this magnetic name.

Yellow Queen (syn. Moonlight) (B). A bit tricky and not too vigorous in cultivation, being liable more than most to wilt disease. Leaves ternate, each leaflet with a long petiole (especially the centre one). Leaf margins apt to be paler than central area. Flowers cream-white, retaining colour best in shade. Sepals 8, obovate, gappy. Stamens cream. A pretty thing.

CHAPTER 12

Names: their Spelling and Pronunciation

*

Ascotiensis was received by Wyevale Nurseries without a name. A plant without a name is no use to a nurseryman so they called it Wyevale Blue. Only subsequently did they discover . . . but by then it was too late to go back, as any nurseryman will appreciate. (The general public may not.)

Bees Jubilee. There is no apostrophe anywhere in Bees. If there ever was one it has long since atrophied. I am always forgetting this and may have slipped one in here and there in the text.

Bouchaud. Comtesse de Bouchaud is correct but you as often see Bouchard. I asked Hugh Thompson which was correct and he originally inclined to Bouchard, since this was an old family and 'royal or aristocratic patronage played such a part in naming Clematis in the past. My earliest reference agrees with yours, a reference to Bouchaud in some notes Morel wrote for an early edition of Robinson's famous book. I observe though that Markham who clearly knew Morel and many other French growers used Bouchard. The first Comte de Bouchard lived in the 10th century, and was variously known as 'le Vénerable', 'le vieux' and 'Chauve Souris'. His daughter burned herself to death in public apparently without making it quite clear why she took this somewhat drastic action. Later the Bouchards secured the Vendome title before being appointed Comtes Royal de Paris. In 1371 the 7th Comte married Isabella de Bourbon, and from then appeared to be absorbed by the Bourbons. I have not checked whether the Bouchard title has been used by minor Bourbons, or the offspring of those that had committed indiscretions, the usual fate of secondary titles in continental Europe. It would be interesting today to flush a de Bouchard from the inner recesses of the French Jockey Club.'

That was on 28 March 1969 but a little later that spring he wrote in a p.c. 'Evidence for BOUCHAUD almost clinched in my opinion. I was re-examining the evidence for Morel's claim that Ville de Lyon was a texensis hybrid (you will recollect that he claimed it was produced by crossing coccinea with Viviand Morel) and I found he sent Ville de Lyon to Monsieur le Comte de Bouchaud 'l'amateur passioné d'horticulture' who grew it and flowered it in his garden at Chasselay (Rhône) for several years before it was made available to commerce. Both Edouard André and de Bouchaud added their support for Morel's claims to its ancestry, for seemingly inconclusive reasons. This unexpected light on the subject makes me suspect that when he produced this pink clematis he named it after de Bouchaud's wife between 1900 and 1906. I am still baffled at the complete lack of recognition of any Bouchaud Title in books that specialise in such matters.' This reference to M. le comte de Bouchaud is in Revue Horticole 1899, p. 274.

Campanile. Pronounced Campaneely.

Cholmondeley. Pronounced Chumley. I remember overhearing the musings of a woman visiting my garden when she contemplated a defunct but still labelled specimen. 'Mrs Chol-mon-deley. Mrs Chol-mon-deley is dead. Poor Mrs Chol-mon-deley.'

Clematis. The correct pronunciation is, unequivocally, clĕm'atis, with a short e and the accent on the first syllable. All the dictionaries are agreed on this and even Fowler's 'Modern English Usage', in a (to me) impenetrable article on False Quantity, comes down in favour.
    But 'This climber's common fate is
        To be pronounced clemā'tis',
with the accent on the second syllable and ā long a. In America clemå'ttis is common, rhyming with lattice.
    Most nurserymen in this country use clĕm'atis correctly: Pennell, Fisk, Picton, Treasure, Jackman, to wit, though the Saunders family of Knight's Nurseries prefer clemä'tis. So did Margery Fish while Percy Thrower, as another sinner, must

have a considerable influence on box viewers. When he brought his programme to my garden he kindly tied in with my pronunciation. In return, I referred with him to the grey foliage plant as *Cineraria maritima* instead of *Senecio cineraria* as I normally should have. What's known as being flexible.

For the plural of clematis I (and many others) use the same word. I cannot say this is correct but if enough of us go on doing so for long enough, it will become correct. The English language is overburdened with sibillants, especially in the final syllable or syllables. Crocuses and irises are tolerable but clematises leaves the tongue congealed and torpid. Imagine 'she possesses 66 clematises'. Most unpleasant.

The word clematis has both Latin and Greek origins though the O.E.D. tells us that it referred to some climbing or trailing plant unspecified but probably periwinkle.

Correvon. G. S. Thomas used to refer to the plant at Hidcote Manor, of which he had a good colour transparency, as Mme Jules Correvon. Through his great influence and the trust we all place in him, this gained currency, following the cultivar's emergence from long eclipse. Unfortunately, when some of us had delved into early records, it transpired that the much less easily spoken Mme Julia Correvon is correct.

Elsa Späth. We can all pronounce Elsa but Späth is the devil if you've no teutonic foundations. It's something like Shpāte, with a long ā. If English printers cannot rise to the German umlaut (the ¨ over the a) which makes it a long vowel, they should write it Spaeth (as they do for the lilac, Souvenir de Louis Spaeth), never Spath, which is inevitably pronounced with a short ă.

Eva Maria. I know nothing about this clematis but cannot help wondering if it didn't start as Ave Maria and undergo a sea change.

Fair Rosamond not Rosamund.

Gipsy Queen not Gypsy.

Huldine. A French name, roughly Hooldeen.

Jackmanii. When English names are Latinised it is best for the English to pronounce the surname as near as possible to the way you would in ordinary speech and then tack on the necessary suffix. Thus, having discovered that *Halesia* is named in honour of a person of the name of Stephen Hales, you can never again say Haleesia. It's different with foreign names like Fuchs giving rise to *Fuchsia.* Foreigners (including Scots like Menzies) must look after themselves. Hell! I've done my best for them in this book, haven't I? There are limits.

In this case the house of Jackman is being celebrated. Just say Jackman and then tack on a long i. So simple. If you must hiccough, I allow you Jackmannyi. But what we so often hear is Jackmarny. 'I'm so tired of it', I told Mr Jackman, once. 'So am I', he agreed, emphatically.

King Edward VII is the name, not Edward VII (Treasures please note) or it'll be Teddy VII or King Tum-Tum before we know where we are. King Edward the Seventh.

Lasurstern. A German name. My Dutch gardener pronounces it with ease and grace – so naturally. I do envy him; I'm always being asked how it should be said and invariably succumb to hoarseness and spluttering. Stern is German for a star and Lasur presumably means azure. Azure Star. Not a bad name. How about it?

Macropetala. Say the word so that it means what it is trying to say. Macro = big. Petal = petal. Then *say* petal and not Macropetarla.

Nelly Moser not Nellie. It was always Nelly from the first report in the Revue Horticole in 1897.

Nevill as in Lord Nevill, Lady Caroline Nevill, the family that lives at Eridge near Tunbridge Wells. They doubtless patronised Cripps (later Wallace of the Old Gardens) at Tunbridge Wells and were honoured by having new clematis named after them. There is no e terminating the name as in Lord Rupert Neville.

Niobe. Pronounce the final e as you would in Hebe, Phoebe, Nerine and Irene (let's hope).

Lady Northcliffe *not* Northcliff (the sort of cliff that faces north).

Mrs Oud is pronounced Owd. A Dutch word meaning old and a common surname. We seem to prefer Young in this usage.

Pennell, Vyvyan, Walter, Richard and descendants to the last trump. Pronounce with the accent on the first syllable as in Fennel (the herb).

Perle d'Azur, not Perle D'Azure. If we're going to stick to the French (and we do) then it is no use semi-anglicising. The only possible alternative is to go the whole hog with Azure Pearl, as also

Prins Hendrik, which can be translated into Prince Henry and very welcome too. But don't try to be authentic and get it wrong, e.g. Prins Hendrick.

Royal Velours not Velour. Velours derives from the old French velous, which in turn is supposed to derive from Villosus (hairy). The English word, of course, is velvet.

Sepal. Pronounce with a short ĕ as you do petal. Not seeple.

The President is correct though often shortened to President *tout court.* I have been guilty of this myself as you never know, where the definite article is included, whether to look the word up, alphabetically, under President, The or The President. However, as Mr Rowland Jackman rightly observed, The President was the name that Charles Noble gave to the plant and The President it is, like it or not.

Mrs P. B. Truax. A dreadful name, admittedly but not improved by being misspelt Traux.

Ville de Lyon. Lyon has to be spelt the French way, without a terminal s, otherwise the only alternative would be City of Lyons.

William Kennett has and always had two t's. Not to be confused with Lord Kennet, whose name having made news has probably caused the confusion.

Wolseley. Sir Garnet Wolseley was the gentleman's name; no relation of Cardinal Wolsey.

Xerxes. Don't try and pronounce the first letter as a separate syllable: Exerxes. Pronounce it as a Z, Zerxes. In any case there is no such clematis but Pennell's have applied this good selling name to Elsa Späth and Fisk has fallen from grace and followed suit.

Glossary of Botanical Terms Used

*

ANTHER. The part of the stamen containing the pollen grains.

AXIL. The junction of leaf and stem. AXILLARY. Arising therefrom.

BIPINNATE. Of a leaf in which the primary divisions are themselves pinnate.

BITERNATE. Of a leaf divided into three parts which are themselves divided into three.

BRACT. A modified leaf growing near the flower.

CARPEL. One of the units of the female part of the flower.

CORDATE. Heart shaped.

CULTIVAR. A plant which has originated in cultivation. Abbreviated to cv.

DIOECIOUS. Having the sexes on different plants.

FILAMENT. The stalk of the anther, the two together forming the stamen.

FOLIAR. Leaf-like.

GENUS. A group of species with common structural characters. The name of the genus is, in designating a plant, placed first and has a capital initial letter.

GLABROUS. Without hairs.

GLAUCOUS. Bluish.

HERMAPHRODITE. Containing both stamens (male) and ovary (female) in the same flower.

LANCEOLATE. Narrowly elliptical, tapering at both ends.

MONOECIOUS. Having unisexual flowers, but both sexes on the same plant.

NODE. A point on the stem where one or more leaves arise. Adjective NODAL.

OBOVATE. Broadest above the middle (of a leaf).

OVATE. Broadest below the middle (of a leaf).

PANICLE. An axial flower stem along which the flowers are arranged on branching stalks.

PEDICEL. The stalk of a single flower.

PEDUNCLE. The stalk common to a branch of flowers.

PERFOLIATE. Having the stem apparently growing through the leaf where 2 opposite leaves are united at the base.

PERIANTH. The floral leaves as a whole, including petals and sepals if both are present.

PETALOID STAMENS. Stamens which are petal-like in colour and texture.

PETIOLE. The stalk of a leaf.

PHOTOSYNTHESIS. The synthesis, made by the green plant parts, of sugar and starch from carbon dioxide and water, in the presence of daylight.

PINNATE. Of a leaf composed of more than 3 leaflets arranged in 2 rows along a common stalk.

PUBESCENT. Shortly and softly hairy.

SEPAL. One of the parts forming the outermost whorl of the flower.

SERRATE. Toothed like a saw.

SPATHULATE. Paddle-shaped.

SPECIES. A group of individuals which have the same constant and distinctive characters. The name of the species is, in designating a plant, placed second, and has a small initial letter.

STAMEN. One of the male reproductive organs of the plant.

STAMINODE. An infertile stamen.

SYNONYM (SYN.). A superseded or alternative name.

TERNATE. Of a compound leaf divided into 3 parts.

VARIETY (VAR.). A natural group within a species, occurring in the wild; normally given a name of Latin form.

WHORL. More than 2 organs of the same kind arising at the same level.

× The sign for hybridisation.

Index

*

Plate references are in *italic* type

Abundance 21, 86, 89, 169, *Pl. 14*
C. *addisonii* 80, 81, 169
Admiration 83
C. *afoliata* 66, 71–2, 169, *Pl. 11*
Alba Luxurians 86, 87, 169, *Pl. 14*
Alice Fisk 169
C. *alpina* 15, 16, 73–4, 118, 123, 133, 138,
    151, 161, 169–70, 173, 188, 190, 193
    Blue Giant 73, 171
    Columbine 73, 74, 123, 170, 173, *Pl. 11*
    Frances Rivis 73–4, 170, 178, *Pl. 11*
    Pamela Jackman 73, 74, 170, 188, *Pl. 11*
    Ruby 73, 74, 170, 190, *Pl. 11*
C. *alpina* var. *sibirica* 73, 74, 169–70, 195
    White Moth 73, 74, 151, 170, 195, *Pl. 11*
Annabel 170
C. *aphylla* 169
Apple Blossom 70–1, 170
C. *armandii* 66, 69–71, 107, 108, 118,
    121–3, 133, 139, 156, 157, 168–9,
    170, 177, 185, *Pl. 11*
    Apple Blossom 70–1, 170
    Snowdrift 70–1, 170
C. × *aromatica* 98–9, 170, *Pl. 16*
Ascotiensis 39, 42, 170, 197, *Pl. 5*
Atragene genus 16
Atragene alpina 169
    americana 193
    macropetala 183
Aurora 39, 46, 49, 174

C. *balearica* 173
Bangholme Belle 179
Barbara Dibley 36, 62, 64, 166, 170, 173,
    Pl. 10
Barbara Jackman 62, 64, 170, 186, *Pl. 10*
Beauty of Richmond 44, 170, *Pl. 12*
Beauty of Worcester 39, 40, 42, 46, 57, 59,
    107, 170–1, 195, *Pl. 9*
Bees Jubilee 62, 63, 156, 171, 197, *Pl. 10*
Belle Nantaise 44–5, 171
Belle of Woking 18, 47, 48–9, 171
C. *bergeronii* 19, 176

Blue Boy 176
Blue Gem 39, 41, 171, 189
Blue Giant 73, 171
Bracebridge Star 62, 65, 171
C. *brachiata* 90, 97–8, 171
C. *buchananiana* 94

C. *calycina* 66–7, 119, 122, 172, 173
C. *campaniflora* 86, 90, 172, *Pl. 14*
Campanile 98, 100, 172, 179, 198
Capitan Thuilleaux 62, 64, 172
C. *chandleri* 19, 176
Charissima 172
C. *chrysocoma* 26, 75, 76, 79, 118, 161, 172,
    192, *Pl. 12*
C. *chrysocoma* var. *sericea* 75, 76, 79, 80,
    172, 191, *Pl. 12*
C. *cirrhosa* 69, 172–3, 187
    var. *balearica* 66–7, 119, 132, 173, *Pl. 11*
    var. *calycina* 172
C. *coccinea* 52, 63, 82, 85
C. *coccinea major* 82
C. *coerulea odorata* 98, 170
C. *colensoi* 173, 179
C. *columbiana* 173
Columbine 73, 74, 123, 170, 173, *Pl. 11*
Comtesse de Bouchaud 36, 59, 61, 85, 120,
    131, 157, 161, 162, 173, 192, 197, *Pl. 5*
Corona 46, 173
Côte d'Azur 98, 100, 173, 179
Countess of Lovelace 39, 41–2, 107, 165,
    173–4, *Pls. 8, 9*
Countess of Onslow 83, 174
Crimson King 52, 54, 173, 174, *Pl. 4*
C. *crispa* 80, 81, 174, *Pl. 13*
C. W. Dowman 62, 65, 174, *Pl. 10*

Daniel Deronda 46, 55, 58, 127, 174, 190,
    195, *Pls. 8, 9*
C. *davidiana* 174
Dawn 47, 49, 174
C. *douglasii* var. *scottii* 85, 98, 104, 174–5,
    Pl. 16

Index

Rosea 98, 104, 175, *Pl. 16*
Duchess of Albany 80, 81, 83–4, 107, 119, 175, *Pl. 13*
Duchess of Edinburgh 47–8, 49, 118, 127, 166, 175, *Pl. 8*
Duchess of Sutherland 21, 52, 54, 119, 175, *Pl. 4*
Duchess of York 83
C. × *durandii* 39, 43–4, 107, 161, *Pl. 16*
    form Pallida 44

Edith 175
Edouard Desfossé 55, 58, 175
Edward Prichard 98, 102, 175, *Pl. 16*
Elegans Plena 88, 194
Elsa Späth 20, 39, 42, 175–6, 196, 199, 202, *Pl. 1*
C. erecta 103, 189
C. × *eriostemon* 19, 98, 99–100, 176, *Pl. 16*
    Hendersonii 19
Ernest Markham 21, 36, 52, 54, 119, 132, 133, 160, 176, *Pl. 4*
Etoile de Paris 39, 42, 176, *Pl. 6*
Etoile Rose 23, 80, 81, 84–5, 107, 161, 176, *Pl. 13*
Etoile Violette 35, 86, 90, 131, 176, *Pl. 14*
Eva Maria 199

Fair Rosamond 47, 49–50, 59, 176, 199, *Pl. 3*
Fairy Queen 62, 63, 176
C. fargesii 68, 94
    var. *souliei* 90, 94, 176–7, *Pl. 15*
C. finetiana 177
C. flammula 14, 50, 56, 90, 95–6, 98, 119, 131, 151, 161, 164, 170, 177, 184, 192, *Pl. 3*
    var. *rubro-marginata* 192
C. flammula roseo-purpurea 96
C. florida 17, 18, 66, 72
    Alba Plena 72, 177
    bicolor 17, 44, 72, 177
    Plena 17, 72, 177
    Sieboldii 17, 44, 72, 107, 139, *Pl. 8*
C. forrestii 187
C. forsteri 177
Fortunei 17–18, 20, 47
Frances Rivis 73–4, 170, 171, 178, *Pl. 11*
C. fusca 178, *Pl. 13*

Gillian Blades 178
Gipsy Queen 39, 55, 56, 57, 85, 96, 120, 131, 178, 199, *Pl. 5*
Gladys Picard 178
C. × *globulosa* 85
Grace Darling 83
C. grata 101, 178, *Pl. 15*
    var. *grandidentata* 178
C. graveolens 91, 188
Gravetye Beauty 80, 85, 107, 161, 178, 191, *Pl. 13*

Gravetye Variety 192
Guiding Star 55, 58, 178, *Pl. 6*

Hagley Hybrid 22, 59, 60, 119, 131, 178–9, *Pl. 5*
C. hendersonii 19, 99, 176
Henryi 20, 35, 47, 50–1, 179, 186, *Pl. 3*
C. heracleifolia 98, 100–101, 179, 186
    Campanile 98, 100, 172, 179, 198, *Pl. 16*
    Côte d'Azur 98, 100, 173, 179
    Crépuscule 96, 98, 101
C. heracleifolia var. *davidiana* 98, 100–101, 102, 150, 174, 175, 179, 181, 186
    Wyevale 98, 101, 179, *Pl. 16*
H. F. Young 39, 41, 179, *Pl. 1*
Hidcote 80
Hidcote Purple 179
Highdown 80, 193
C. hookeriana 173, 179
Horn of Plenty 55, 59, 180, *Pl. 6*
Huldine 23, 36, 47, 50, 51, 86, 89, 132, 133, 148, 180, 199, *Pl. 5*
Hybrida Sieboldii 44, 180, 189

C. indivisa 184, 188
C. indivisa lobata 69
C. integrifolia 16, 17, 19, 43, 57, 98, 99, 150, 170, 175, 176, 180, *Pl. 16*
    Hendersonii 19, 98, 99, 180, *Pl. 16*
    Olgae 98, 99, 180, *Pl. 16*
C. × *intermedia* 19, 176

C. × *jackmanii* 19, 20, 28, 34, 43, 47, 53, 55, 56, 57, 58, 61, 62, 90, 109, 119, 161, 175, 180, 200
    Superba 55, 56, 161, *Pl. 5*
Jackmanii Alba 23, 47, 127, 180
Jackmanii Rubra 52, 54–5, 127, 180, *Pls. 3, 4, 9*
Joan Wilcox 181
John Warren 59–60, 181, *Pl. 5*
C. × *jouiniana* 98, 101–2, 181, 186
    Praecox 98, 102, 163, 181, *Pl. 16*

Kathleen Dunford 181
Kathleen Wheeler 59, 172, 181
Kermesina 86, 88–9, 181, 194
King Edward VII 62, 63, 181, 200
King George V 21, 62, 63, 181–2, *Pl. 7*

Lady Betty Balfour 21, 35, 36, 54, 55, 57, 61, 119, 120, 132, 133, 161, 165, 182, *Pl. 7*
Lady Caroline Nevill 44, 45, 60, 182, 189, 200, *Pl. 7*
Lady Londesborough 47, 49, 182
Lady Northcliffe 39, 40, 41, 161, 182, 201, *Pl. 1*
C. lanuginosa 17, 18–19, 20, 44, 57, 58
Lasurstern 35, 39–40, 118, 123, 126, 156, 182, 200, *Pl. 1*

Index

Lawsoniana 20, 44, 182, *Pl. 2*
C. *leiocarpa* 192
Lincoln Star 62, 64, 182-3, 190, *Pl. 10*
Little Nell 86, 89, 183, *Pl. 14*
Lord Nevill 39, 40, 183, 200, *Pl. 1*
Lucie Lemoine 20, 47-8

C. *macropetala* 15, 16, 73, 74, 118, 123,
  133, 138, 151, 161, 183, 184, 193,
  195, 200, *Pl. 11*
  Lagoon 74
  Maidwell Hall 73, 74, 183, 184
  Markhamii 183, 184
  Markham's Pink 73, 74, 183, 184, *Pl. 11*
  Ruby 74
Mme Baron Veillard 59, 61, 161, 183, *Pl. 7*
Mme Edouard André 52, 53-4, 183, *Pl. 4*
Mme Grangé 20, 52, 55, 56-7, 183, 184,
  Pl. 4
Mme Jules Correvon 199
Mme Julia Correvon 20, 52, 53, 131, 184,
  199, *Pl. 4*
Mme Le Coultre 51, 184
Maidwell Hall 73, 74, 183, 184
Marcel Moser 34, 62-3, 64, 119, 125-6,
  160, 184, 187, *Pl. 10*
Margaret Hunt 59, 60, 184
Margot Koster 59, 61, 86, 184
Marie Boisselot 18, 35, 47, 51, 119, 156,
  170, 184, 186, *Pl. 3*
Markham's Pink 73, 74, 183, 184, Pl. 11
Maureen 55, 59, 184
C. *maximowicziana* 69, 90, 96-7, 184-5
C. *meyeniana* 185
Minuet 86, 89, 90, 185, *Pl. 14*
Miriam Markham 44, 45, 127, 185, 193,
  Pl. 8
Miss Bateman 34, 35, 47, 49-50, 118, 126,
  132, 185, 186, *Pl. 3*
Miss Crawshay 59, 60, 185, *Pl. 8*
Mrs Bush 44, 185, 189
Mrs Cholmondeley 39, 41, 118, 119,
  126-7, 162, 175, 185, 198, *Pl. 1*
Mrs George Jackman 35, 47, 51, 185-6,
  Pl. 3
Mrs Hope 38, 39, 40-1, 157, 186, 189,
  196, *Pl. 2*
Mrs N. Thompson 62, 65, 186, 190, *Pl. 10*
Mrs Oud 47, 51, 64, 186, 201, *Pl. 3*
Mrs P. B. Truax 39, 41, 64, 186, 196, 201,
  Pl. 1
Mrs Robert Brydon 98, 101, 179, 186
Mrs Spencer Castle 59, 60, 186, *Pl. 9*
C. *montana* 14, 26, 50, 75-7, 79, 105, 115,
  118, 120-1, 129, 133, 151, 172, 186,
  Pl. 12
  Elizabeth 75, 76, 187, *Pl. 12*
  Grandiflora 75, 76, 77, 187
  Picton's Variety 75, 76-7, 161, 187, *Pl. 12*
  Pink Perfection 75, 187
  Tetrarose 75, 76, 77, 161, 187, *Pl. 12*

C. *montana* var. *rubens* 75-7, 187, 192,
  Pl. 12
C. *montana* var. *wilsonii* 75, 77-9, 187,
  Pl. 12
Moonlight 39, 46, 50, 195, 196
C. *napaulensis* 66, 67-8, 187, *Pl. 11*
Nelly Moser 13, 34, 36, 49, 62, 118, 119,
  124, 125-6, 129, 150, 160, 171, 172,
  184, 187, 200, *Pl. 10*
Niobe 187-8, 200
C. *nutans* 189
  var. *thyrsoidea* 94, 189

Old Man's Beard 94-5, 194
Orange Peel 91, 92
C. *orientalis* 35, 36, 90, 91-2, 93, 94, 115,
  129, 133, 151, 188, *Pl. 15*
  Burford Variety 92

Pamela Jackman 73, 74, 170, 188, *Pl. 11*
C. *paniculata* 66, 69, 96, 184, 188, *Pl. 11*
  Lobata 69, 188
C. *parviflora* 188
C. *patens* 17, 18, 20, 50, 53, 58
C. *pavoliniana* 177
Percy Lake 39, 188, 193
Percy Picton 39, 55, 59, 188-9, *Pl. 6*
Percy Robinson 39
Perle d'Azur 23, 36, 39, 40, 42-3, 61, 119,
  120, 131, 161, 189, 201, *Pl. 5*
C. *phlebantha* 66, 68, 189, *Pl. 15*
C. *pitcheri* 80, 82, 189
Pourpre Mat 86, 89-90
Prince Henry 189
Prins Hendrik 44, 45, 189, 195, 201, *Pl. 2*
Proteus 59, 60-1, 127, 189, *Pls. 8, 9*
Purpurea Plena 86, 87-8
Purpurea Plena Elegans 86, 87-8, 194,
  Pl. 14

Ramona 44, 180, 189
C. *recta* 98, 102, 103, 150, 164, 175, 189,
  Pl. 16
  Purpurea 98, 103, 189
  form Flore Pleno 103
  form Plena 103
C. *rehderiana* 50, 90, 93-4, 107, 119, 162,
  189-90, 193, *Pl. 15*
Richard Pennell 22, 190, 201
Rouge Cardinal 22, 52, 55
Royal Velours 36, 86, 89, 107, 119, 190,
  201, *Pl. 14*
C. × *rubro-marginata* 190, 192
Ruby (C. *alpina*) 73, 74, 170, 190, *Pl. 11*
Ruby (C. *macropetala*) 74
Rush-stemmed clematis 71

Scartho Gem 190
Sealand Gem 62, 63-4, 190
Serenata 55, 59, 190
C. *serratifolia* 90, 92, 93, 190, *Pl. 15*

Index

C. sieboldii 17, 72, 177
Silver Moon 44, 45–6, 191
C. simsii 189
Sir Garnet Wolseley 55, 58, 191, 202, *Pl. 6*
Sir Trevor Lawrence 63, 80, 83, 84, 107,
   161, 191, *Pl. 13*
Snowdrift 70–1, 170
C. songarica 98, 103–4, 191, *Pl. 15*
C. spooneri 79–80, 172, 191
C. spooneri rosea 80, 193
Standishii 17, 18, 20
C. stans 98, 100, 101, 191
Star of India 36, 55–6, 63, 131, 161,
   191–2, *Pl. 5*
Stead's Variety 69
Superba 55, 56, 161, *Pl. 5*

C. tangutica 22, 35, 50, 90, 91–3, 96, 105,
   119, 129, 151, 160, 188, 192, *Pl. 15*
Gravetye Variety 192
C. tangutica var. *obtusiuscula* 92–3, 192
C. texensis 16, 20, 23, 52, 53, 63, 80–2, 85,
   107, 140, 151, 174, 189, *Pl. 13*
The Czar 57
The Kelpie 57
The Kelpie's Bride 57
The Premier 57
The President 34, 35, 55, 57–8, 165, 192,
   201, *Pl. 6*
Traveller's Joy 194
C. × *triternata* Rubro-marginata 90, 96,
   190, 192, *Pl. 15*
C. tubulosa 100
Twilight 46, 59, 60, 192

C. uncinata 192

C. × *vedrariensis* 26, 76, 80, 192–3, *Pl. 12*
Hidcote 80
Highdown 80, 193
Rosea 193
C. veitchiana 94, 193
Venosa Violacea 86, 90, 193, *Pl. 14*

Venus Victrix 46, 193
Veronica's Choice 22, 193
C. verticillaris 16, 73, 193
   var. *columbiana* 173, 193
Victoria 39, 55, 56, 157, 194, *Pl. 5*
Ville de Lyon 22, 52–3, 85, 119, 120, 127,
   156, 161, 165, 183, 194, 198, 201,
   Pl. 4
Viorna genus 16
C. viorna 16, 80, 81, 82, 194, *Pl. 13*
C. vitalba 15, 90, 94–5, 101, 108, 136, 178,
   181, 186, 194, *Pl. 15*
C. viticella 16, 17, 19, 53, 55, 57, 85, 87–7,
   96, 119, 131, 132, 136, 152, 176, 192,
   Pl. 14
Atrorubens 19, 23, 80, 81
Elegans Plena 87–8, 194
Etoile Rose 84–5, 107, 161, 176
Purpurea Plena 86, 87–8
Purpurea Plena Elegans 86, 87–8, 194,
   Pl. 14
Rubra 36, 86, 88–9, 131, 148, 181, 194,
   Pl. 14
C. viticella elegans plena 87–8
Viticella Rubra 86, 88–9, 131, 148, 181,
   194
Viticella Venosa 90
Viviand Morel 52
Vyvyan Pennell 22, 40, 44, 46, 118, 127,
   190, 193, 194–5, 201, *Pls. 8, 9*

Wada's Primrose 47, 50, 195
Walter Pennell 195, 201
W. E. Gladstone 18, 44, 45, 195, *Pl. 7*
White Moth 73, 74, 151, 170, 195, *Pl. 11*
Will Goodwin 44, 46, 195, *Pl. 2*
William Kennett 34, 39, 41, 195–6, 201,
   Pl. 2
Wyevale Blue 197

Xerxes 42, 176, 186, 196, 202

Yellow Queen 47, 49, 50, 195, 196, *Pl. 3*